NYSTCE
065

CST
Literacy
Teacher Certification Exam

By: Sharon Wynne, M.S.

XAMonline, INC.
Boston

To obtain permission(s) to use the material from this work for any purpose including workshops or seminars, please submit a written request to:

XAMonline, Inc.
25 First Street, Suite 106
Cambridge, MA 02141
Toll Free 1-800-509-4128
Email: info@xamonline.com
Web: www.xamonline.com
Fax: 1-617-583-5552

Library of Congress Cataloging-in-Publication Data

Wynne, Sharon A.
    CST Literacy 065: Teacher Certification / Sharon A. Wynne. -3rd ed.
    ISBN 978-1-60787-057-9
        1. CST Literacy 065.   2. Study Guides.   3. NYSTCE
        4. Teachers' Certification & Licensure.   5. Careers

Disclaimer:
The opinions expressed in this publication are the sole works of XAMonline and were created independently from the National Education Association, Educational Testing Service, or any State Department of Education, National Evaluation Systems or other testing affiliates.

Between the time of publication and printing, state specific standards as well as testing formats and Web site information may change that is not included in part or in whole within this product. Sample test questions are developed by XAMonline and reflect similar content as on real tests; however, they are not former tests. XAMonline assembles content that aligns with state standards but makes no claims nor guarantees teacher candidates a passing score. Numerical scores are determined by testing companies such as NES or ETS and then are compared with individual state standards. A passing score varies from state to state.

Printed in the United States of America   œ-1

NYSTCE: CST Literacy 065
ISBN: 978-1-60787-057-9

Table of Contents

SUBAREA I.   FOUNDATIONS OF LITERACY

Competency 1.0   Understand theories of literacy acquisition and development
.... 1

Competency 2.0   Understand the relationships among reading, writing,
listening, and speaking 6

Competency 3.0   Understand individual differences in literacy development ... 7

Competency 4.0   Understand formal and informal techniques for assessing
literacy skills... 10

Competency 5.0   Understand how to use and communicate the results of
literacy assessments 22

SUBAREA II.   READING INSTRUCTION AND ASSESSMENT

Competency 6.0   Understand phonological and phonemic awareness 25

Competency 7.0   Understand the development of concepts of print.............. 32

Competency 8.0   Understand the development and application of phonics
skills... 42

Competency 9.0   Understand a variety of word identification strategies
.... 53

Competency 10.0   Understand the development of vocabulary knowledge and
skills... 61

Competency 11.0   Understand reading comprehension skills and strategies... 76

Competency 12.0   Understand reading skills associated with content-area
literacy 91

Competency 13.0   Understand the development of effective study
skills... 105

Competency 14.0   Understand the role of oral and written language in the
development of reading proficiency 106

Competency 15.0   Understand strategies for promoting the reading development of students with reading difficulties............. 106

SUBAREA III.   THE ROLE OF THE LITERACY PROFESSIONAL

Competency 16.0   Understand how to organize effective literacy environments and to manage literacy programs 107

Competency 17.0   Understand curriculum development and instructional planning for literacy programs... 113

Competency 18.0   Understand how to select and use diverse instructional materials to promote literacy development 115

Competency 19.0   Understand how to collaborate and communicate with colleagues, parents, caregivers, and members of the educational community to promote students' literacy development 118

Competency 20.0   Understand professional responsibilities of literacy professionals... 120

SUBAREA IV.   READING INSTRUCTION AND
ASSESSMENT:

CONSTRUCTED-RESPONSE ASSIGNMENT

Page 124

Glossary 131

Directory of Theorists and Researchers...................................... 142

Bibliography of Print Resources 149

Webliography 163

Tools for teaching and testing... 165

Sample Test... 169

Answer Key 203

Rationales for Sample Questions.. 204

Additional Citations 267

Great Study and Testing Tips!

What to study in order to prepare for the subject assessments is the focus of this study guide, but equally important is *how* you study.

You can increase your chances of truly mastering the information by taking some simple, but effective steps.

Study Tips:

1. Some foods aid the learning process. Foods such as milk, nuts, seeds, rice, and oats help your study efforts by releasing natural memory enhancers called CCKs (*cholecystokinin*) composed of *tryptophan*, *choline*, and *phenylalanine*. All of these chemicals enhance the neurotransmitters associated with memory. Before studying, try a light, protein-rich meal of eggs, turkey, and fish. All of these foods release the memory-enhancing chemicals. The better the connections, the more you comprehend.

Likewise, before you take a test, stick to a light snack of energy boosting and relaxing foods. A glass of milk, a piece of fruit, or some peanuts all release various memory-boosting chemicals and help you to relax and focus on the subject at hand.

2. Learn to take great notes. A by-product of our modern culture is that we have grown accustomed to getting our information in short doses (i.e. television news sound bites or *USA Today*–style newspaper articles).

Consequently, we've subconsciously trained ourselves to assimilate information better in neat little packages. If your notes are scrawled all over the paper, it fragments the flow of the information. Strive for clarity. Newspapers use a standard format to achieve clarity. Your notes can be much clearer through use of proper formatting. A very effective format is called the "Cornell Method."

Take a sheet of loose-leaf lined notebook paper and draw a line all the way down the paper about 1–2 inches from the left-hand edge.

Draw another line across the width of the paper about 1–2 inches up from the bottom. Repeat this process on the reverse side of the page.

Look at the highly effective result. You have ample room for notes, a left-hand margin for special emphasis items or inserting supplementary data from the textbook, a large area at the bottom for a brief summary, and a little rectangular space for just about anything you want.

3. Get the concept then the details. Too often we focus on the details and don't gather an understanding of the concept. However, if you simply memorize only dates, places, or names, you may well miss the whole point of the subject.

A key way to understand things is to put them in your own words. If you are working from a textbook, automatically summarize each paragraph in your mind.

If you are outlining text, don't simply copy the author's words. *Rephrase* them in your own words. You remember your own thoughts and words much better than someone else's and subconsciously tend to associate the important details to the core concepts.

4. Ask why? Pull apart written material paragraph by paragraph and don't forget the captions under the illustrations.

Example: If the heading is "Stream Erosion," flip it around to read, "Why do streams erode?" Then answer the questions.

If you train your mind to think in a series of questions and answers, not only will you learn more, but it also helps to lessen the test anxiety because you are used to answering questions.

5. Read for reinforcement and future needs. Even if you only have 10 minutes, put your notes or a book in your hand. Your mind is similar to a computer; you have to input data in order to have it processed. *By reading, you are creating the neural connections for future retrieval.* The more times you read something, the more you reinforce the learning of ideas.

Even if you don't fully understand something on the first pass, *your mind stores much of the material for later recall.*

6. Relax to learn, so go into exile. Our bodies respond to an inner clock called biorhythms. Burning the midnight oil works well for some people but not everyone.

If possible, set aside a particular place to study that is free of distractions. Shut off the television, cell phone, and pager, and exile your friends and family during your study period.

If you really are bothered by silence, try background music. Light classical music at a low volume has been shown to aid in concentration over other types. Music that evokes pleasant emotions without lyrics is highly suggested. Try just about anything by Mozart. It relaxes you.

7. Use arrows not highlighters. At best, it's difficult to read a page full of yellow, pink, blue, and green streaks. Try staring at a neon sign for a while and you'll soon see that the horde of colors obscures the message.

A quick note, a brief dash of color, an underline, and an arrow pointing to a particular passage is much clearer than a horde of highlighted words.

8. Budget your study time. Although you shouldn't ignore any of the material, *allocate your available study time in the same ratio that topics may appear on the test.*

Testing Tips:

1. Get smart, play dumb. *Don't read anything into the question.* Don't make an assumption that the test writer is looking for something else than what is asked. Stick to the question as written and don't read extra things into it.

2. Read the question and all the choices *twice* before answering the question. You may miss something by not carefully reading, and then rereading both the question and the answers.

If you really don't have a clue as to the right answer, leave it blank on the first time through. Go on to the other questions, as they may provide a clue as to how to answer the skipped questions.

If later on you still can't answer the skipped ones . . . *guess.* The only penalty for guessing is that you *might* get it wrong. Only one thing is certain; if you don't put anything down, you will get it wrong!

3. Turn the question into a statement. Look at the way the questions are worded. The syntax of the question usually provides a clue. Does it seem more familiar as a statement rather than as a question? Does it sound strange?

By turning a question into a statement, you may be able to spot if an answer sounds right, and it may also trigger memories of material you have read.

4. Look for hidden clues. It's actually very difficult to compose multiple-foil (choice) questions without giving away part of the answer in the options presented.

In most multiple-choice questions you can often readily eliminate one or two of the potential answers. This leaves you with only two real possibilities, and automatically your odds go to fifty-fifty for very little work.

5. Trust your instincts. For every fact that you have read, you subconsciously retain something of that knowledge. On questions that you aren't really certain about, go with your basic instincts. *Your first impression on how to answer a question is usually correct.*

6. Mark your answers directly on the test booklet. Don't bother trying to fill in the optical scan sheet on the first pass through the test.

Just be very careful not to miss-mark your answers when you eventually transcribe them to the scan sheet.

7. Watch the clock! You have a set amount of time to answer the questions. Don't get bogged down trying to answer a single question at the expense of 10 questions you can more readily answer.

COMPETENCY 1.0   UNDERSTAND THEORIES OF LITERACY
                               ACQUISITION AND DEVELOPMENT

KNOWLEDGE OF THE SIGNIFICANT THEORIES, APPROACHES, PRACTICES, AND PROGRAMS FOR DEVELOPING READING SKILLS AND READING COMPREHENSION[tac91]

Decoding

In the late l960s and the l970s, many reading specialists, most prominently Fries[TAR2] (l962), believed that successful decoding resulted in reading comprehension. This meant that if children could sound out the words, they would then automatically be able to comprehend them. Many teachers of reading and many reading texts still subscribe to this theory.

Asking Questions

Another theory or approach to the teaching of reading that gained currency in the late 1960s and the early 1970s was the importance of asking inferential and critical thinking questions of the reader, which would challenge and engage the children in the text. This approach to reading went beyond the literal level of what was stated in the text to an inferential level of using text clues to make predictions and to a critical level of involving the child in evaluating the text. While asking engaging and thought-provoking questions is still viewed as part of the teaching of reading, it is only viewed currently as a component of the teaching of reading.

Comprehension "Skills"

As various reading theories, practices, and approaches percolated during the 1970s and l980s, many educators and researchers in the field came to believe that the teacher of reading had to teach a set of discrete "Comprehension Skills" (Otto et al. l977[TAR3]). Therefore the reading teacher became the teacher of each individual comprehension skill. Children in such classrooms came away with the main idea, sequence, cause and effect, and other concepts that were supposed to make them better able to comprehend. However, did it make them lifelong readers?

Transactional Approach

During the late 1970s and early 1980s, researchers in the field of education, psychology, and linguistics began to examine how the reader comprehends. Among them was Louise Rosenblatt, who posited that reading is a transaction between the reader and the text. It is Rosenblatt (1978) who explained successful reading as the reader constructing a meaning from the text that reflected both the reader and the text. She described two general purposes for reading: *efferent* and *aesthetic*. Efferent reading is looking for and remembering information to use functionally. Examples would be filling out a job application, reading a story in preparation for a test, or reading a newspaper article to find out who won the state basketball championship. Aesthetic reading is done to connect one's own life to the text, to be swept away by the beauty of a poem, or to respond emotionally to a book such as *Bridge to Terabithia*.

These differing purposes call for somewhat different reading strategies: one might skim the newspaper article for basketball information but read a poem closely 10 times and create mental images of different passages. Lastly, when children are asked to read all fiction efferently (What's the setting? What's the main conflict in the plot? There will be a test on this on Thursday!), it can thwart a child's joy in the written word and work against the student's desire to be a lifelong reader.

BOTTOM-UP, TOP-DOWN, INTERACTIONAL THEORIES OF READING

Bottom-up theories of reading assume that children learn from part to whole, starting with the smallest segments possible. Instruction begins with a strong phonics approach, learning letter-sound relationships, and often using basal readers or *decodable books*. Decodable books are vocabulary-controlled using language from word families with high predictability. Thus we get sentences like "Nan has a tan fan." Reading is seen as skills-based, and the skills are taught one at a time.

Top-down theories of reading suggest that reading begins with the reader's knowledge, not the print. Children are seen as having a drive to construct meaning. This stance views reading as moving from the whole to the parts. An early top-down theory was the *whole word* approach. Children memorized high-frequency words to assist them in reading the Dick and Jane books of the 1930s. Then teachers helped children discover letter-sound correspondences in what they read. A more recent top-down theory is the *whole language* approach. This approach was influenced by research on how young children learned language. It was thought that children could learn to read as naturally as they learned to talk. Children were surrounded by print in their classrooms, using quality literature often printed in Big Books, and were viewed as writers from the start. For example, kindergarten children were asked to keep journals. Advocates of whole language viewed the "skill'em-drill'em-and kill'em" approach based on bottom-up theories as a deadly dull introduction to the world of reading.

Interactive theories of reading combine the strengths of both bottom-up and top-down approaches. Teachers need to be able to teach decoding, vocabulary, and comprehension skills to support children's drive for meaning and desire for a stimulating exchange with high-quality literary texts from their earliest days in school. Strategies include shared, guided, and independent reading, Big Books, reading and writing workshops, and the like. Today this approach is called the *balanced literacy approach.* It is considered to be a synthesis of the best from bottom-up and top-down methods.

LITERACY AND LITERACY LEARNING

To be literate in the 21st century means more than being able to read and write. To live well and happily in today's society, an individual has to be able to read, not only newspapers and books, but also e-mails, blogs, directions for how to use one's cell phone, and the like. There has evolved a disconnect between the isolated reading comprehension skills the schools were teaching and the literacy skills, including listening and speaking, that are crucial for employment and personal and academic success. Thornburg[TAR4] (1992, 2003) has also noted that technology capacities and the ability to communicate online are now integral parts of our sense of literacy.

J. David Cooper (2004) views literacy as reading, writing, thinking, listening, viewing, and discussing. These are not viewed as separate activities or components of instruction, but rather as developing and being nurtured simultaneously and interactively. Children learn these abilities by engaging in authentic explorations, readings, projects, and experiences.

Just as in learning how to ride a bike, where one goes through various approximations before learning how to actually ride the bike, so too does the reader, with the scaffold (support) of the teacher, go through various approximations before developing his/her own independent literacy skills and capacities.

Emergent literacy is the concept that young children are emerging into reading and writing with no real beginning or ending point. Children are introduced into the word of print as soon as their parents read board books to them at the age of 1 or 2. When children scribble write or use invented spelling during the preschool years, they reveal themselves as detectives of the written word, having watched parents and teachers make lists, write thank-you notes, or leave messages. This view of the reader assumes that all children have a drive to make meaning in print and will begin doing it almost on their own if surrounded by a print-rich environment.

Reading readiness is an approach that is antithetical to emergent literacy in that it assumes all children must have mastered a sequence of reading skills *before* they can begin to read. This approach stands in contrast to emergent literacy.

Language acquisition is continuous and never-ending. From the perspective of this theory and research, all children come to school with a language base that the school must build on. As a consequence of the connection between oral language and reading, it is important that schools build literacy experiences around the language the child brings to the school.

PRIOR KNOWLEDGE, SCHEMATA, BACKGROUND, AND COMPREHENSION

Schemata are structures that represent generic concepts stored in our memory (Rumelhart 1980[TAR5]). Young children develop their schemata through experiences. Prior knowledge and the lack of experiences in some cases influence comprehension. The more closely the reader's experiences and schemata approximate those of the writer, the more likely the reader is to comprehend the text. It is obvious that for many children from non-native English language speaking backgrounds and perhaps for those from struggling socioeconomic family structures, schemata deficits indicate the need for intense teacher support as these children become emergent and early readers.

Often the teacher will have to model and scaffold for the child the steps to form a schemata from the information provided in a text.

Comprehension

Cooper defines comprehension as "a strategic process by which readers construct or assign meaning to a text by using the clues in the text and their own prior knowledge." We view comprehension as a process where the reader transacts with the text to construct or assign meaning. Reading and writing are both interconnected and mutually supportive. Comprehension is a strategic process in which readers adjust their reading to suit their purpose and the type or genre of text they are reading. Narrative and expository texts require different reading approaches because of their different text structures.

Strategic readers also call into play their metacognitive capacities as they analyze texts so that they are self-aware of the skills needed to construct meaning from the text structure.

THE ROLE OF LITERATURE IN DEVELOPING LITERACY

The balanced literacy approach advocates the use of "real literature"— recognized works of the best of children's fiction and nonfiction trade books and winners of such awards as the Newbery and Caldecott medals for helping children develop literacy. Balanced literacy advocates argue the following:

- Real literature engages young readers and assures that they will become lifelong readers.
- Real literature also offers readers a language base that can help them expand their expressiveness as readers and as writers.
- Real literature is easier to read and understand than grade-level texts

There are districts in the United States where the phonics-only approach is heavily embedded. However, the majority of school districts would describe their approach to reading as the balanced literacy approach, which includes phonics work as well as the use of real literature texts. To contrast the phonics and balanced literacy approaches as opposite is inaccurate, since a balanced approach includes both.

It is important to go online and to visit the key resources of the NCTE (National Council of Teachers of English) and the IRA (International Reading Association) to keep abreast of the latest research in the field.

COMPETENCY 2.0   **UNDERSTAND THE RELATIONSHIPS AMONG READING, WRITING, LISTENING, AND SPEAKING**

Reading, writing, listening, and speaking are the four main components of language arts at any grade level. They are interrelated and complement each other. By ensuring that all four of these strands are woven into your language arts classes, you can ensure that you provide a balance of experiences to give students the instruction and support that they need. With such a balance, the students are able to integrate all of the English language processes and build on their prior knowledge and experiences.

Speaking and listening may be viewed as separate from reading and writing, but all four form the main communication system of the English language. They are interdependent and all other forms of communication depend on the ability to speak and listen. They are also the foundation for many other language skills, which is why teachers should provide ample opportunities for students to speak and listen in class as part of the daily routine. Classrooms are places where talk flows freely, and by taking advantage of this talk to find out where students are in their thinking about topics, themes, and responses to literature, teachers can easily assess this component of language arts. When students can express ideas in their own words, it helps them to make meaning of their experiences with reading.

Although students don't have particular problems with speaking in class, listening is something that has to be nurtured and taught. Good listeners will respond emotionally, imaginatively, and intellectually to what they hear. Students need to be taught how to respond to presentations by their classmates in ways that are not harmful or derogatory in any way. There are also different types of listening that the teacher can develop in the students:

- Appreciative listening to enjoy an experience;
- Attentive listening to gain knowledge; and
- Critical listening to evaluate arguments and ideas.

COMPETENCY 3.0   **UNDERSTAND INDIVIDUAL DIFFERENCES IN LITERACY DEVELOPMENT**

Sociologically, schools have faced many unique challenges. As schools are charged with educating all students within the neighborhood, changes in demographics and economics have impacted schools. While laws have been set up to eliminate segregation in schools, many inner-city children attend highly segregated schools based on the demographic compositions of their neighborhoods. For some time, districts instituted bussing policies to combat this. This is where a student in one neighborhood might be put on a bus and sent to a school in another neighborhood with a different ethnic or racial mixture. Many districts did find that this was impractical, as it caused some students to have to spend hours per day on busses when they could have been doing other more productive things.

Many districts around the country are just learning how to deal with larger immigrant populations, as more immigrants leave the historically popular entry points such as Texas and California. Those districts must learn how to develop appropriate English language programs to assist their children in learning English; they must also learn to work with parents who may be scared about involvement with schools.

In reading, this is a particular challenge. Diversity increases the difficulty in teaching vocabulary and contextual information. It is important for teachers to keep cultural differences in mind so they can help provide additional background knowledge if necessary. Also, they can include a variety of texts, which different cultures may better relate to, encouraging greater comprehension.

Some of the most prominent learning theories in education today include brain-based learning and multiple intelligence theory. Supported by recent brain research, brain-based learning suggests that knowledge about the way the brain retains information enables educators to design the most effective learning environments. As a result, researchers have developed the following 12 principles that relate knowledge about the brain to teaching practices:

- The brain is a complex adaptive system.
- The brain is social.
- The search for meaning is innate.
- We use patterns to learn more effectively.
- Emotions are crucial to developing patterns.
- Each brain perceives and creates parts and the whole simultaneously.
- Learning involves focused and peripheral attention.
- Learning involves conscious and unconscious processes.
- We have at least two ways of organizing memory.
- Learning is developmental.
- Complex learning is enhanced by challenge (and inhibited by threat).

- Every brain is unique.

Educators can use these principles to help design methods and environments in their classrooms to maximize student learning in the area of reading.

Multiple intelligence theory, developed by Howard Gardner, suggests that students learn in (at least) eight different ways. These include visually/spatially, musically, verbally, logically/mathematically, interpersonally, intrapersonally, bodily/kinesthetically, and naturalistically.

The most current learning theory of constructivist learning promotes allowing students to build their own understanding of concepts through interactions with materials, ideas, and one another. For constructivist teachers, the belief is that students create their own knowledge through processing, observing, and reflecting on the world around them. Students are constantly constructing new ideas or schema, which serve as frameworks for learning and teaching. Researchers have shown that the constructivist model is comprised of the following four components:

1. The learner creates knowledge.
2. The learner constructs and makes meaningful new knowledge into existing knowledge.
3. The learner shapes and constructs knowledge by life experiences and social interactions.
4. In constructivist learning communities, the student, teacher, and classmates establish knowledge cooperatively on a daily basis.

Constructivist learning for students is dynamic and ongoing. For constructivist teachers, the classroom becomes a place where students are encouraged to interact with the instructional process by asking questions and posing new answers to old theories. The use of cooperative learning, which encourages students to work in supportive learning environments using their own ideas to stimulate questions and propose outcomes, is a major aspect of a constructivist classroom.

Metacognitive learning theory deals with "the study of how to help the learner gain understanding about how knowledge is constructed and about the conscious tools for constructing that knowledge" (Joyce and Weil 1996[TAR6]). The cognitive approach to learning involves the teacher's understanding that teaching the student to process his/her own learning and mastery of skill provides the greatest learning and retention opportunities in the classroom. Students are taught to develop concepts and teach themselves skills in problem solving and critical thinking. The student becomes an active participant in the learning process, and the teacher facilitates that conceptual and cognitive learning process.

Social and behavioral theories look at the social interactions of students in the classroom that instruct or impact learning opportunities. The psychological approaches behind both theories are subject to individual variables that are learned and applied either proactively or negatively in the classroom. The stimulus of the classroom can promote situations conducive to learning or evoke behavior that is counterproductive for both students and teachers. Students are social beings that normally gravitate toward action in the classroom, so teachers must be cognizant in planning classroom environments that provide both focus and engagement in maximizing learning opportunities.

Designing classrooms that provide optimal academic and behavioral support for a diversity of students in the classroom can be challenging for teachers. The ultimate goal for both students and teachers is creating a safe and productive learning environment.

COMPETENCY 4.0   **UNDERSTAND FORMAL AND INFORMAL TECHNIQUES FOR ASSESSING LITERACY SKILLS**

Assessment is the practice of collecting information about children's progress, and evaluation is the process of judging the children's responses to determine how well they are achieving particular goals or demonstrating reading skills.

Assessment and evaluation are intricately connected in the literacy classroom. Assessment is necessary because teachers need ways to determine what students are learning and how they are progressing. In addition, assessment can be a tool that can also help students take ownership of their own learning and become partners in their ongoing development as readers and writers. In this day of public accountability, clear, definite, and reliable assessment creates confidence in public education.

There are two broad categories of assessment: *Informal* assessment utilizes observations and other non-standardized procedures to compile anecdotal and observational data/evidence of children's progress. It includes but is not limited to checklists, observations, and performance tasks. *Formal* assessment is composed of standardized tests and procedures carried out under circumscribed conditions. Formal assessments include state tests, standardized achievement tests, NAEP (National Assessment of Educational Progress) tests, and the like.

To be effective, assessment should have the following characteristics:

1. It should be an ongoing process with the teacher making informal or formal assessments on an ongoing basis. The assessment should be a natural part of the instruction and not intrusive.
2. The most effective assessment is integrated into ongoing instruction. Throughout the teaching and learning day, the child's written, spoken, and reading contributions to the class can be continually noted.
3. Assessment should reflect the child's actual reading and writing experiences. The child should be able to show that he or she can read and explain or react to a similar literary or expository work.
4. Assessment needs to be a collaborative and reflective process. Teachers can learn from what the children reveal about their own individual assessments. Children, even as early as grade 2, should be supported by their teacher to continually and routinely ask themselves questions assessing their reading. They might ask, "Am I understanding what the author wanted to say?" "What can I do to improve my reading?" and "How can I use what I have read to learn more about this topic?" Teachers need to be informed by their own professional observation *and* by children's comments as they assess and customize instruction for children.

5. Quality assessment is multidimensional and may include but not be limited to samples of writings, student retellings, running records, anecdotal teacher observations, self-evaluations, and records of independent reading. From this multidimensional data, the teacher can derive a consistent level of performance and design additional instruction that will enhance the child's reading performance.

6. Assessment must take into account children's age and ethnic/cultural patterns of learning.

7. Assessment should lead to teaching children from their strengths, not their weaknesses. Find out what reading behaviors children demonstrate well and then design instruction to support those behaviors.

8. Assessment should be part of children's learning process and not done *to* them, but rather done *with* them.

CHARACTERISTICS AND USES OF CRITERION-REFERENCED AND NORM-REFERENCED TESTS TO ASSESS READING DEVELOPMENT AND IDENTIFY READING DIFFICULTIES

Criterion-referenced are tests where the children are measured against criteria or guidelines that are uniform for all the test takers. Therefore, by definition, no special questions, formats, or considerations are made for the test taker who is either from a different linguistic/cultural background or is already identified as a struggling reader/writer. On a criterion-referenced test, it is possible that a child test taker can score 100% because the child may have actually been exposed to all of the concepts taught and mastered them. A child's score on such a test would indicate which of the concepts have already been taught and what he or she needs additional review or support to master.

Two criterion-referenced tests that are commonly used to assess children's reading achievement are the Diagnostic Indicators of Basic Early Literacy Skills (DIBELS) and the Stanford Achievement Test. DIBELS measures progress in literacy from kindergarten to grade 3. It can be downloaded from the Internet free at dibels.uoregon.edu. The Stanford is designed to measure individual children's achievement in key school subjects, including reading skills. Both DIBELS and the Stanford are group-administered.

Degrees of Reading Power (DRP)

This test is targeted to assess how well children understand the meaning of written text in real-life situations. It is supposed to measure the process of children's reading, not the products of reading, such as identifying the main idea and author's purpose.

CTPIII

This is a criterion-referenced test that measures verbal and quantitative ability in grades 3–12. It is targeted to help differentiate among the most capable students (those who rank above the 80th percentile on other standardized tests). This is a test that emphasizes higher-order thinking skills and process-related reading comprehension questions.

Norm-Referenced

This is a test in which the children are measured against one another. Scores on this test are reported in percentiles. Each percentile indicates the percent of the testing population whose scores were the same as or lower than a particular child's score. A percentile is defined as a score on a scale of 100 showing the percentage of a distribution that is equal to or below it. This type of state standardized norm-referenced test is being used in most districts today in response to the No Child Left Behind Act. While this type of test does not help track the individual reader's progress in his/her ongoing reading development, it does permit comparisons across groups.

There are many more standardized norm-referenced tests to assess children's reading than there are criterion-referenced. In the norm-referenced tests, scores are based on how well a child does compared to others, usually on the local, state, and national level. *If* the norming groups on the tests are reflective of the children being tested (for example, the same spread of minority, low income, and gifted students), the results are more trustworthy.

One of the best known norm-referenced test is the Iowa Test of Basic Skills. It assesses student achievement in various school subjects and has several subtests in reading. Other examples of norm-referenced tests used around the country are the Metropolitan Achievement Tests, the Terra Nova-2, and the Stanford Diagnostic Reading Test-4. These are all group tests. An individual test reading specialists use with students is the Woodcock Reading Mastery Test.

CONCEPTS OF VALIDITY, RELIABILITY, AND BIAS IN TESTING

Validity is how well a test measures what it is supposed to measure. Teacher-made tests are therefore not generally extremely valid, although they may be an appropriate measure for the validity of the concept the teacher wants to assess for his/her own children's achievement.

Reliability is the consistency of the test. This is measured by whether the test will indicate the same score for the child who takes it more than once.

Bias in testing occurs when the information within the test or the information required to respond to a multiple choice question or constructed response (essay question on the test) is information that is not available to some test takers who come from a different cultural, ethnic, linguistic, or socioeconomic background than do the majority of the test takers. Since they have not had the same prior linguistic, social, or cultural experiences that the majority of test takers have had, these test takers are at a disadvantage in taking the test, and no matter what their actual mastery of the material taught by the teacher, they cannot address the biased questions. Generally, other non-biased questions are given to them and eventually the biased questions are removed from the examination.

To solidify what might be abstract to the reader, on a recent reading test in one school system, the grade 4 reading comprehension multiple choice had questions about the well-known fairy tale of the gingerbread boy. These questions were simple and accessible for most of the children in the class, but two children who recently arrived from the Dominican Republic did not learn English in the United States. They were reading on a grade 4 level, but in their Dominican grade school, the story of the gingerbread boy was not a major one. Therefore, a question about this story on the standardized reading test did demonstrate examiner bias and was not fair to these test takers.

THE CHARACTERISTICS AND USES OF FORMAL[tac97] AND INFORMAL ASSESSMENTS

Informal Assessments

A running record of children's oral reading progress in the early grades (kindergarten through third) is a pivotal informal assessment. It supports the teacher in deciding whether a book a child is reading is matched to his/her stage of reading development. In addition, this assessment allows the teacher to analyze a child's miscues to see which cueing systems and strategies the child uses and to determine which other systems the child might use more effectively. Finally, the running record offers a graphic account of a child's oral reading.

Generally, a teacher should maintain an annotated class notebook with pages set aside for all the children, or individual notebooks for each child. One of the benefits of using running records as an informal assessment is that they can be used with any text and can serve as a tool for teaching, rather than an instrument to report on children's status in class.

Another point about using running records is that they can be taken repeatedly and frequently by the teacher, so that patterns of error can be truly observed. This in turn provides the educator with sufficient information to analyze the child's reading over time. As any mathematician or scientist knows, the more samples of a process you gather over time, the more likely the teacher is to get an accurate picture of the child's reading needs.

Using the notations that Marie Clay developed and shared in her *An Observation Study of Early Literacy Achievement*, Sharon Taberski offers in her book *On Solid Ground* a lengthy walk-through keeping a running record of children's reading. She writes in the child's miscue on the top line of her running record above the text word. Taberski advises the teacher to make all the miscue notations as the child reads, since this allows the teacher to get additional information about how and why the child makes miscue choices. Additionally, the teacher should note self-corrections (coded SC) when the child is monitoring his/her own reading, crosschecks information, and uses additional information.

As part of the informal assessment of primary grade reading, it is important to record the child's word insertions, omissions, requests for help, and attempts to get the word. In informal assessment, the rate of accuracy can be estimated by dividing the child's errors by the total words read.

Results of a running record assessment can be used to select the best setting for the child's reading. If a child reads from 95% to 100% correct, he or she is ready for independent reading. If the child reads from 92% to 97% right, he or she is ready for guided reading. Below 92%, the child needs a read-aloud or shared reading activity. Note that these percentages are slightly different from those one would use to match books to readers

One of the increasingly popular and meaningful forms of informal assessment is the compilation of the literacy portfolio. What is particularly compelling about this type of informal portfolio is that artists, television directors, authors, architects, and photographers use portfolios in their careers and jobs. This is a most authentic format for documenting children's literacy growth over time. The portfolio is not only a significant professional informal assessment tool for the teacher, but a vehicle and format for the child reader to take ownership of his or her progress over time. It models a way of compiling one's reading and writing products as a lifelong learner, which is the ultimate goal of reading instruction.

Portfolios can include the following four categories of materials:

1. Work samples: These can include children's story maps, webs, K-W-L charts, pictures, illustrations, storyboards, and writings about the stories that they have read.
2. Records of independent reading and writing: These can include the children's journals, notebooks, or logs of books read with the names of the authors, titles of the books, date completed, and pieces related to books completed or in progress.
3. Checklists and surveys: These include checklists designed by the teacher for reading development, writing development, ownership checklists, and general interest surveys.
4. Self-evaluation forms: These are the children's own evaluations of their reading and writing process framed in their own words. They can be simple templates with starting sentences such as the following:

    a. I am really proud of the way I . . .
    b. I feel one of my strengths as a reader is . . .
    c. To improve the way I read aloud I need to . . .
    d. To improve my reading I should . . .

Generally at the beginning of a child's portfolio in grade 3 or above there is a letter to the reader explaining the work that will be found in the portfolio, and from the fourth-grade level up, children write a brief reflection detailing their feelings and judgments about their growth as readers and writers.

When teachers are maintaining the portfolios for mandated school administrative review, district review, or even for their own research, they often prepare summary sheets. These provide identifying data on the children, a timeline of the teacher's review of the portfolio, plus professional comments on the extent to which the portfolio documents satisfactory and ongoing growth in reading.

Portfolios can be used beneficially for child/teacher and, of course, parent/teacher conversations to review the child's progress, discuss areas of strength, set future goals, make plans for future learning activities, and evaluate what should remain in the portfolio and what needs to be cleared out for new materials.

Rubrics

Holistic scoring involves assessing a child's ability to construct meaning through writing. It uses a scale called a rubric, which can range from 0 to 4.

- 0– This indicates the piece cannot be scored because it does not respond to the topic or is illegible.
- 1– The writing does respond to the topic but does not cover it accurately.
- 2- This piece of writing does respond to the topic but lacks sufficient details or elaboration.
- 3– This piece fulfills the purpose of the writing assignment and has sufficient development (which refers to details, examples, and elaboration of ideas).
- 4– This response has the most details, best organization, and presents a well-expressed reaction to the original writer's piece.

Miscue analysis

This is a procedure that allows the teacher a look at the reading process. By definition, the miscue is an oral response different from the text being read. Sometimes miscues are also called unexpected responses or errors. By studying a student's miscues from an oral reading sample, the teacher can determine which cues and strategies the student is correctly using or not using in constructing meaning. Of course, the teacher can customize instruction to meet the needs of this particular student.

Informal reading inventories (IRI)

These are a series of samples of texts prearranged in stages of increasing difficulty. Listening to children read through these inventories, the teacher can pinpoint their skill level and the additional concepts they need to work on.

CHARACTERISTICS AND USES OF GROUP VERSUS INDIVIDUAL READING ASSESSMENTS

In assessment, tests are used for different purposes. They have different dimensions or characteristics whether they are given individually or in a group and whether they are standardized or teacher-made. The chart below shows the relationships of these elements.

	Standardized	Teacher-made
Individual	*Characteristics* • is uniformly administered *Uses* • is best for younger children • helps with placement for special services	*Characteristics* • has more flexibility *Uses* • assists teaching decisions • used for diagnostic purposes
Group	*Characteristics* • is uniformly administered • is time efficient *Uses* • permits comparisons across groups • used for policy decisions by administrators	*Characteristics* • has high face validity • is time efficient *Uses* • informs teach-reteach and enrichment decisions • documents students' learning

TECHNIQUES FOR ASSESSING PARTICULAR READING SKILLS

Taberski recommends that the teacher build in one-on-one time for supporting individual children as needed in considering what makes sense, sounds right, and matches the letters.

She has noted that emergent and early readers tend to focus on meaning without adequate attention to graphophonic cues. She suggests using the following prompts for children who are having problems with graphophonic cues:

- Does what you said match the letters?
- If the word were what you said ___, what would it have to start with?
- Look carefully at the first letters, then look at the middle letters, and then look at the last letters. What could it be?
- If it were ____, what would it end with?

Oral retellings can be used to test children's comprehension. Children who are retelling a story to be tested for comprehension should be told that that is the purpose when they sit down with the teacher.

It is a good idea to let the child start the retelling on his or her own because then the teacher can see whether he or she needs prompts to retell the story. Many times more experienced readers summarize what they have read. This summary usually flows along with the characters, the problem of the story, and other details.

Other signs that children understand what they are reading when they give an oral retelling include their use of illustrations to support the retelling, references to the exact text in the retelling, emotional reaction to the text, making connections between the text and other stories or experiences they have had, and giving information about the text without the teacher asking for it.

AWARENESS OF TEXT LEVELING

In the context of the balanced literacy approach to reading instruction, the classroom library is focused on leveled books. These are books that have been leveled with the support of Fountas and Pinnell's *Guided Reading: Good First Teaching for All Children* and *Matching Books to Readers: Using Leveled Reading in Guided Reading,* K-3.

The books that are leveled according to the designations laid out by Fountas and Pinnell need to be stored in bins or crates with front covers facing out. This makes them much easier for the children to identify. In that way, the children can go through the appropriate levels and find books that they are particularly interested in that are also at the right level for them to read, allowing them the right degree of reading accuracy. When young children can see the cover of a book, they are more likely to flip through the book until they can independently identify an appealing book. Then they will read a little bit of the book to see if it's "just right."

"Just right" leveled books that children can read on their own need to be available for them during independent reading times. The goal is for the more fluent readers to select books on their own. Ultimately the use of leveled books helps the children, in addition to the teacher, decide which books are "good" or "just right" for them.

Levels are indicated by means of blue, yellow, red, and green dot stickers at their right-upper corners, which parallel emergent, early, transitional, and fluent reading stages. They are then kept in containers with other books labeled with the same colors.

Other lists and resources that can be used to match children with "just right" books include the Reading Recovery level list. Ultimately, the teacher has to individualize whatever leveling is used in the library to address the individual child learners' needs.

AWARENESS OF THE CHALLENGES AND SUPPORTS IN A TEXT

Illustrations can be key supports for emergent and early readers. Teachers should not only use wordless stories (books that tell their narratives through pictures alone) but can also make targeted use of Big Books for read-aloud time so that young children become habituated to the use of illustrations as an important component for constructing meaning. The teacher should model for the child how to reference an illustration for help in identifying a word in the text the child does not recognize. Of course, children can also go on a picture walk with the teacher as part of a mini-lesson or guided reading and anticipate the story (narrative) using the pictures alone to construct meaning.

Decodability is the use of literature that contains examples of letter-sound correspondences the teacher wishes to teach. First, read the literature with the children or read it aloud to them. Then take a specific example from the text and have the children reread it as the teacher points out the letter-sound correspondence to the children. Next, ask the children to go through the now-familiar literature to find other letter-sound correspondences. Once the children have correctly made the letter-sound correspondences, have them share similar correspondences they find in other works of literature.

Cooper (2004) suggests that children can become word detectives so that they can independently and fluently decode on their own. The child should learn the following word detective routines so that he or she can function as an independent fluent reader who can decode words on his/her own.

- The child should read to the end of a sentence.
- The child should search for word parts that he or she knows and also try to decode the word from the letter sounds.
- As a last resort, the child should ask someone for help or look up the word in the dictionary.

TECHNIQUES FOR DETERMINING STUDENTS' INDEPENDENT, INSTRUCTIONAL AND FRUSTRATION READING LEVELS

Independent reading is generally judged to be at the 95% to 100% accuracy level, although Taberski places it between 92% and 97%. Taberski tries to enhance the independent reading levels by making sure that students on the instructional reading levels read a variety of genres and have a range of available and interesting books within a particular genre. The instructional reading level is from 90% to 95%, and the frustration level is any score under 90%.

Taberski's availability for reading conferences helps her to both assess first hand her children's frustration levels and to model ongoing teacher/reader book conversations by scheduling child-initiated reading conferences when she personally replenishes their book bags.

In order to allay children's frustration levels and to foster their independent reading, it is important to some children that the teacher personally take time out to hear them read aloud and to check for fluency and expression. Children's frustration level can be immeasurably lessened if they are explicitly told by the teacher after they have read aloud that they need to read without pointing and that they should try chunking words into phrases that mimic their natural speech.

ASSESSMENT OF THE READING DEVELOPMENT OF INDIVIDUAL STUDENTS

For young readers who are from ELL backgrounds, even if they were born in the United States, the use of pictures validates their story authoring and storytelling skills and provides them with equity and access to the literary discussion and book talk of their native English-speaking peers. These children can also demonstrate their storytelling abilities by drawing sequels or prequels to the story detailed in the illustrations alone. They might even be given the opportunity to share the story aloud in their native language or to comment on the illustrations in their native language.

Since many stories today are recorded in two or even three languages at once, discussing story events or analyzing pictures in a different native language is a beneficial practice that can be accomplished.

Use of pictures and illustrations can also help the kindergarten through third-grade educator assess the capabilities of children who are struggling readers if their learning strength is spatial. Through targeted questions about how the pictures would change if different plot twists occurred or how the child might transform the story through changing the illustrations, the teacher can begin to assess struggling reader's deficits and strengths.

Children from ELL backgrounds can benefit from listening to a recorded version of a particular story that they can read along with the tape. This gives them another opportunity to hear the story correctly pronounced and presented and to begin to internalize its language structures. In the absence of taped versions of some key stories or texts, the teacher may want to make sound recordings her or himself.

Highly proficient readers can also be involved in creating these literature recordings for use with ELL peers or younger peers. This, of course, develops oral language proficiency and also introduces these skilled readers into the intricacies of supporting ELL reading instruction. When they actually see their tapes being used by children, they will be tremendously gratified.

COMPETENCY 5.0   **UNDERSTAND HOW TO USE AND COMMUNICATE THE RESULTS OF LITERACY ASSESSMENTS**

See Competency 4.0.

IN THE DIAGNOSIS OF READING DIFFICULTIES, THE SPECIALIST SHOULD USE TOOLS THAT MEASURE THE CHILD'S LISTENING COMPREHENSION, ORAL READING SKILLS, SILENT READING SKILLS, AND HIS ABILITY TO RESPOND TO READING IN WRITTEN FORM.

Listening Comprehension: In the case of listening comprehension, teachers will learn if the student has developed complex comprehension skills when reading is removed from the process. This can later weed out comprehension issues that are solely related to the reading process.

Oral Reading: Listening to a child read orally provides insight into the skills that are developed and those that are missing. Teachers can hear fluency, phonetic errors, and vocabulary deficits and even pick up on phonemic awareness issues. They can also watch the student attack the text and see whether she or he is relying on visual, semantic, or structural cues to solve problems in unknown words. Comprehension skills can also be assessed by asking oral questions of varying difficulty and comparing the answers to the results of listening comprehension skills.

Silent Reading: It is important to assess silent reading in addition to oral reading. This is important because when taking an assessment, reading for homework, or completing independent activities, children will need to read silently. In fact, as adults we rarely read out loud, it is through silent reading that all comprehension occurs.

Written Responses: As with silent reading, written responses to reading are the end skill required throughout life. We need to assess their skills from the earliest age. This not only provides insight into reading skills and reading comprehension, but it also can also show insight into written language difficulties.

The ideal screening will include assessments in all of the above areas. It is the comprehensive picture that provides enough information to determine an appropriate course of action for the student.

Sometimes it is overwhelming to examine all of the available assessment data on students and understand what the next steps to take should involve. New teachers can be seen referring to textbooks used in the methods courses and the case studies provided for guidance.

Throughout their careers, it would be beneficial for reading specialists to track certain students and develop their own case studies. The information will not only be beneficial for themselves but can also be shared with colleagues as necessary.

It is important for the teacher to keep identifiable information confidential and change it to be somewhat generic. Keeping all of the assessment data and reporting it in detail is critical. Things that the specialist knows about the child need to be documented clearly.

Once the history and diagnostic areas are discussed and documented, the next stage is to completely describe the intervention plan the teacher will be implementing with the child. Details are critical when compiling a case study for others; they will not have the same information as the teacher unless it is provided for them.

Throughout the intervention plan, it is important to make notes of lessons taught, as well as the responses of the student. It is not necessary to log every single word used, but it is important to share concepts and situations that arise. If the case study is to be of value to the teacher later and available to others, the more details provided, the better. If adjustments are made to the intervention plan, this should be documented as well.

Post-evaluation results should also be included in the case study report. Including this information will allow for later reflection on the success of the intervention. Also, the readers will be able to reproduce and/or understand the situation if provided all of the information.

Keeping case study information can be quite time consuming, but it provides for reflection and learning at future times. Sometimes the act of writing down the steps of intervention helps the recorder see things they might not have otherwise noted. In this way, information can be brought out that might otherwise be overlooked. Reading and writing case studies is helpful for the person keeping them and anyone reading them.

As part of gathering the necessary screening data, it is important to filter out of all of the information for the students' reading strengths and needs. The strengths are important to document because they can be used to help address some of the deficits. Tapping into strengths is a strategy used frequently across disciplines to address other areas of weakness. Looking closely at the strengths of a student in reading can provide insight into learning styles and preferences.

Students who are strong in the more auditory skills may benefit from having their information presented orally. The same can be said with visual or other information. Working through strengths is an excellent strategy and important diagnostic tool.

Also, when documenting the needs of the student, it is important to examine those needs very closely. In this way, the specialist can use the needs to develop an intervention plan. The intervention plan should be specifically designed for that student. The materials and methodologies to be used should be clearly explained in detail. They should focus on student strengths as well as researched information to ensure student success.

Selecting methods and materials is a complex set of procedures. Keeping in mind the areas of deficits, the student strengths, the knowledge of reading instruction and even available materials can seem overwhelming but are all key pieces of information to consider.

First, knowing the specific deficits to address with the specialist can begin to narrow down a large variety of materials and methods into a more manageable list. Ruling out can continue by examining strengths as discussed previously. At this point, it is time for the specialist to trust her/his training and experience to match materials and methods to the student.

Sometimes this is a trial and error approach to find the one that will be the most beneficial for the student. Periodic progress monitoring will help the reading teacher to understand when to change either materials or methods. When a student's progress is flat or not growing at an adequate rate, something needs to change.

It is no longer acceptable to try a strategy for an entire year, waiting for end-of-the-year test results. Keeping up to date with the progress the student is making on a weekly or biweekly basis can help to determine when changes should be incorporated.

SUBAREA II.   READING INSTRUCTION AND ASSESSMENT

COMPETENCY 6.0   UNDERSTAND PHONOLOGICAL AND PHONEMIC
                      AWARENESS

Phonological awareness means the ability of the reader to recognize the sounds or phonemes of spoken language. This recognition includes how these sounds can be blended together, segmented (divided up), and manipulated (switched around). This awareness eventually leads to phonics, a method for decoding language by unlocking letter-sound or grapheme-phoneme relationships.

Development of phonological skills for most children begins during the prekindergarten years. Indeed by the age of 5, a child who has been exposed to finger plays and poetry can recognize a rhyme. Such a child can demonstrate phonological awareness by filling in the missing rhyming word in a familiar rhyme or rhymed picture book. The procedure of filling in a missing word is called the cloze procedure. It can be used in oral or print literacy activities.

One teaches children phonological awareness by directly pointing out the sounds made by letters singly (as in /b/) or in combination (as in /bl/), and to recognize individual sounds in words.

Phonological awareness skills include but are not limited to the following:

1. Rhyming and syllabification
2. Blending sounds into words, such as *pic-tur-bo-k*
3. Identifying beginning or initial phonemes and ending or final phonemes in short, one-syllable words
4. Breaking words down into sounds, which is also called "segmenting" words
5. Removing initial sounds and substituting others; an example is /bat/ minus the /b/ with an /m/ substituted becomes /mat/

THE ROLE OF PHONOLOGICAL AWARENESS IN READING DEVELOPMENT

Instructional methods to teach phonological awareness may include any or all of the following:

1. Play auditory games, during which children recognize and manipulate the sounds of words, separate or segment the sounds of words, take out sounds, blend sounds, add in new sounds, or take apart sounds to recombine them in new formations.
2. The snap game: The teacher says two words, and the children snap their fingers if the two words share a sound, which might be at the beginning or end of the word. Children hear initial phonemes most easily, followed by final ones. Medial or middle sounds are most difficult for young children to discriminate. One sees this in their oral responses as well as in their invented spelling. Silence occurs if the words share no sounds. Children love this simple game and it also helps with classroom management.
3. Language games model identification of rhyming words. These games help inspire children to create their own rhymes.
4. Read books that rhyme, such as *Sheep in a Jeep* by Nancy Shaw or *The Fox on a Box* by Barbara Gregorich.
5. Share books with children that use alliteration (words that begin with the same consonant sound) such as *Avalanche, A to Z.*

ASSESSMENT OF PHONOLOGICAL AWARENESS

These skills can be assessed by having the child listen to the teacher say two words. Then ask the child to decide if these two words are the same word repeated twice or two different words.

When making this assessment, when using two different words, make certain that they only differ by only one phoneme, such as /d/ and /g/.

Children can be assessed on words that are not real words but are familiar to them, including make-believe words.

THE ROLE OF PHONOLOGICAL PROCESSING IN THE DEVELOPMENT OF INDIVIDUAL STUDENTS

Children who are raised in homes where English is not the first language or where standard English is not spoken may have difficulty with hearing the difference between similar-sounding words like "send" and "sent." Any child who is not in a home, day care, or preschool environment where English phonology operates may have difficulty perceiving and demonstrating the differences between English language phonemes. If children cannot hear the difference between words that "sound the same," like "grow" and "glow," they will be confused when these words appear in a print context. This confusion will, of course, impact their comprehension.

Considerations for teaching phonological processing to ELL children include recognition by the teacher that what works for the English language-speaking child from an English-language-speaking family does not necessarily work in other languages.

Research recommends that ELL children learn to read initially in their first language. It is critical that they learn to speak English before being taught to read English. Research supports that oral language development lays the foundation for phonological awareness.

All phonological instruction programs must be tailored to the children's learning backgrounds. Rhymes and alliteration introduced to ELL children should be read or shared with them in their first language, if at all possible.

STRUGGLING READERS

Students who cannot read by age 9 are unlikely to become fluent readers and have a greater tendency to drop out.

—Beth Antunez

Among the causes of reading difficulties for some children (and adults) are auditory trauma or ear infections that affect their ability to hear speech. Such children need one-on-one support with articulation and perception of different sounds. When a child says a word such as "parrot" incorrectly, repeat it back as a question with the correct pronunciation. If the child gets the sound correct after your question, all is well. Extra support is all that was needed. If the child still has difficulty with pronunciation after repeated instances, then consult with a speech therapist or audiologist. Early identification of medical conditions that affect hearing is crucial to reading development.

Points to Ponder

- Phonological awareness is auditory. It does not involve print.
- It begins before children have learned letter-sound relationships.
- It is the basis for the successful teaching of phonics and spelling.
- It can and must be taught and nurtured.
- It precedes and must be in place before the alphabetic principle can be taught.

PHONEMIC AWARENESS

Phonemic awareness is a specific skill within the broader category of phonological awareness. Probably developing fairly late, it is the knowledge that words are comprised of individual phonemes that can be blended.

Theorist Marilyn Jaeger Adams, who researches early reading, has outlined five basic types of phonemic awareness tasks:

Task 1: Ability to hear rhymes and alliteration
For example, the children listen to a poem, rhyming picture book, or song and identify the rhyming words heard, which the teacher might then record or list on a chart.

Task 2: Ability to do oddity tasks (recognize the member of a set that is different (odd) among the group)
For example, the children look at the pictures of grass, a garden, and a rose, answering, which one starts with a different sound?

Task 3: The ability to orally blend words and split syllables
For example, the children can say the first sound of a word, then the rest of the word, and put it together as a single word.

Task 4: The ability to orally segment words
For example, this is the ability to count sounds. The child is asked to count or clap the sounds in "hamburger."

Task 5: The ability to do phonics manipulation tasks
For example, replace the /r/ sound in rose with a /p/ sound.

THE ROLE OF PHONEMIC AWARENESS IN READING DEVELOPMENT

Children who have problems with phonics generally have not acquired or been exposed to phonemic awareness activities at home or during preschool through second grade. This includes extensive songs, rhymes and read-aloud time.

Instructional Methods

Since the ability to distinguish between individual sounds, or phonemes, within words is a prerequisite to association of sounds with letters and manipulating sounds to blend words—a fancy way of saying "reading," the teaching of phonemic awareness is crucial to emergent literacy (reading instruction from kindergarten through second-grade). Children need a strong background in phonemic awareness in order for phonics instruction (sound-spelling relationship-printed materials) to be effective.

Instructional methods that may be effective for teaching phonemic awareness can include the following:

- Clapping syllables in words
- Distinguishing between a word and a sound
- Using visual cues and movements to help children understand when the speaker goes from one sound to another
- Incorporating oral segmentation activities that focus on easily distinguished syllables rather than sounds
- Singing familiar songs (e.g. "Happy Birthday," "Knick Knack Paddy Wack") and replacing key words with those of a different ending
- Dealing children a deck of picture cards and having them sound out the words for the pictures or calling for a picture by asking for its first and last sound.

CONSIDERATION FOR ELL STUDENTS

Given the demographics of our country with its influx of new Americans, the likelihood is that teachers will have at least some students who are from a non-native English speaking background. Therefore, as a conscientious educator, it is important to understand the special factors involved in supporting children's second language literacy development.

Not all English phonemes are present in various ELL native languages; for example, the sound of /th/ does not appear in Spanish. Some native language phonemes conflict with English phonemes.

It is recommended that all teachers of reading, and particularly those who are working with ELL students, use meaningful, student centered, culturally customized activities. These activities may include language games, word walls, and poems. Some of these activities might, if possible, be initiated in the child's first language and then reiterated in English.

READING AND THE ELL LEARNER

Research has shown that there is a positive and strong correlation between a child's literacy in his/her native language and his/her learning of English. The degree of native language proficiency and literacy is a strong predictor of English language development. Children who are literate and engaged readers in their native language can easily transfer their skills to a second language (i.e. English).

What this means is that teacher educators should not approach the needs of ELL learners in reading the same as they do native speakers. Those children whose families are not from a focused oral literacy and reading culture in the native language will need additional oral language rhymes, read-aloud time, and singing as supports for reading skills development in both their native language and in English.

ASSESSMENT OF PHONEMIC AWARENESS

Teachers can maintain ongoing logs and rubrics for assessment throughout the year of phonemic awareness for individual children. Such assessments would identify particular stated reading behaviors or performance standards, the date of observation of the child's behavior (in this context, phonemic activity or exercise), and comments.

The rubric or legend for assessing these behaviors might include the following descriptors:

- Demonstrates or exhibits reading behavior consistently
- Makes progress/strides toward this reading behavior
- Has not yet demonstrated or exhibited this behavior

Depending on the particular phonemic task the teacher models, the performance task might include the following:

- Saying rhyming words in response to an oral prompt
- Segmenting a word spoken by the teacher into its beginning, middle, and ending sounds
- Counting correctly the number of syllables in a spoken word

Phonological awareness involves the recognition that spoken words are composed of a set of smaller units, such as onsets and rimes, syllables, and sounds.

Phonemic awareness is a specific type of phonological awareness that focuses on the ability to distinguish, manipulate, and blend specific sounds or phonemes within an individual word.

Think of phonological awareness as an umbrella and phonemic awareness as a specific spoke under this umbrella.

Phonics deals with printed words and the learning of sound-spelling correlations, while phonemic awareness activities are oral.

In reviewing reading research and theory, new distinctions and definitions appear often. The body of reading knowledge changes over time. The information and definitions in this guide are those accepted in the year of its publication and the time of its authoring and updating. As changes occur in accepted theories, they will be made in the guides and in the certification exams.

If you believe that you learn to read by reading, you must learn to want to read. Reading to children, therefore models both the "how" and "why" of reading.
—Helen Depree and Sandra Iversen
Early Literacy in the Classroom

The long talk that parents have put off about the ways of the world might need to be an introduction to the facts about the English alphabet.
—Terrence Moore, Ashbrook Center Fellow
Principal of Ridgeview Classical Schools
Fort Collins, Colorado

COMPETENCY 7.0 **UNDERSTAND THE DEVELOPMENT OF CONCEPTS OF PRINT**

The understanding that print carries meaning is demonstrated every day in the elementary classroom as the teacher holds up a selected book to read aloud to the class. The teacher explicitly and deliberately talks aloud about how to hold the book, focuses the class on looking at its cover, points to where to start reading, and sweeps her/his hands in the direction to begin, left to right.

When writing the morning message on the board, the teacher reminds the children that the message begins in the upper left-hand corner at the top of the board to be followed by additional activities and a schedule for the rest of the day.

When the teacher invites children to make posters of a single letter, such as *b*, and list items in the classroom, their home, or outside that start with that letter, the children are concretely demonstrating that print carries meaning.

STRATEGIES FOR PROMOTING AWARENESS OF THE RELATIONSHIP BETWEEN SPOKEN AND WRITTEN LANGUAGE

- Writing down what the children say on a language chart
- Highlighting the uses of print products found in the classroom, such as yellow sticky pad notes, labels on shelves and lockers, calendars, signs, and directions
- Reading big print and oversized books together to teach print conventions such as directionality
- Practicing how to handle a book, including how to turn pages, how to find the top and bottom of pages, and how to tell the difference between the front and back covers
- Discussing and comparing with children the length, appearance, and boundaries of specific words. For example, children can see that the names Dan and Dora share certain letters and a similar shape
- Having children match oral words to printed words by forming an echo chorus as the teacher reads poetry or rhymes aloud and they echo the reading.
- Having the children combine, manipulate, switch, and move letters to change words.
- Working with letter cards to create messages and respond to the messages that they create.

THE ROLE OF ENVIRONMENTAL PRINT IN DEVELOPING PRINT AWARENESS

Containing collaged symbols of their favorite lunch or breakfast foods, an environmental print book can be created by children. The children cut and clip symbols from the packaging of these foods and then place them in alphabetical order in their class-made book. Magazines and catalogues are another source of environmental print that is accessible with ads for child-centered products. Supermarket circulars and coupons from the newspaper are also excellent for engaging children in using environmental print as reading, especially when combined with dramatic play centers or prop boxes. What is particularly effective in using environmental print is that it immediately invites the child from an ELL background into print awareness, through the familiarity of commercial logos and packaging symbols used.

DEVELOPMENT OF BOOK HANDLING SKILLS

Understanding the value and importance of the concepts of print for beginning readers was developed out of the work of Marie Clay in New Zealand. Assessment of these skills typically occurs in kindergarten and into first grade, as necessary. The following skills are part of the assessment process:

- **Print Carries a Message:** The students can demonstrate this skill even if he or she is unable to read the text by pretending to read. This may happen even if the child does not demonstrate any of the other concepts.
- **Book Organization:** Students demonstrate an understanding of the organization of books by being able to identify the title, cover, author, left-to-right progression, top-to-bottom order, and one-to-one correspondence. Students may learn these skills individually as they become more familiar with books.
- **Print Consistencies:** This is the understanding that text is made up of letters, which then form words and are combined to form sentences. As the beginning reader makes these connections, he or she will next develop the concept of capital letters at the beginning of sentences and basic punctuation marks.
- **Letter Identification:** The final stage of the concepts of print assessment involves the identification of both upper- and lower-case letters. More advanced students may begin to recognize some of the most common spelling patterns in beginning texts.

Have the children identify the front cover, back cover, and title page of a specific book.

Model storytelling with the book held so that the audience can see the illustrations shown to them. Then have children demonstrate the skills for their peers.

Have children search through the class libraries for special features on the fronts or backs of books as they help return the books to their bins. Have the children display and talk about the special symbols they have found.

Review with the children, in an age- and grade-appropriate format, additional parts of the book during mini lessons and read-aloud time. These additional parts of the book can include the title page, dedication page, table of contents, copyright date, and glossary.

STRATEGIES FOR PROMOTING AN UNDERSTANDING OF THE DIRECTIONALITY OF PRINT

In order to become proficient readers, young students need to develop a complete understanding that all print is read from left to right and top to bottom. Modeling is one of the most important strategies a teacher can use to develop this understanding in children. The use of Big Books, poems, and charts are strategies teachers can use in both large and small group instruction. Simple questions can engage the students to pay closer attention to these skills (for example, "We are going to read this passage. Where should I put my pointer to start reading?").

Directionality of print should also be taught during the writing process. In language experience stories, interactive writing, and Kidwriting©, the teacher can incorporate explicit modeling and instruction of these skills. Sometimes it may be necessary to provide children with a dot at the top left corner of the paper in order to provide a visual reminder of where to begin.

Techniques for Promoting the Ability to Track Print in Connected Texts

Try model directionality and one-to-one word matching by pointing to words while using a Big Book, pocket chart, or poem written out on a chart. As the teacher repeatedly leads the children in this reading, they can follow along and eventually track the print and make one-to-one matches on the connected text independently. They can also practice by using a pointer (all children love to use the pointer because pleasure becomes associated with the reading) or their fingers to follow the words. Children happily volunteer to be the "point person." Even before Vanna White, the joy of "signifying letters" existed and has tremendous appeal for children.

Copy down a brief, familiar rhyme (perhaps from a favorite book or song) and post it in the room at the children's eye level so they can independently walk around and read it.
Copy down a brief, familiar rhyme or poem on individual word cards. Then challenge the children in small groups or independently to reassemble and display the poem on a pocket chart. As children "play" with constructing and

reconstructing this pocket chart, they will develop an awareness of directionality, one-on-one matching of print to spoken words, spacing, and punctuation.

Model interactive emergent writing with the class. For example, while the teacher is noting down the weather, deliberately ask and have the children suggest if the first word in that report should go at the top or bottom of the board. Ask if the first letter be uppercase or lowercase and what should go at the end of the sentence?

Create with the children sing-song repetitions/rules for using capitals, periods, and commas. Encourage the children to begin reciting these singsongs as soon as they identify specific concepts of print in connected texts.

Model for children how, when pointing at words, they can start at the top and move from left to right. Tell the children that if there are more words to the sentence they are reading under the first line of print, they must go back to the left and under the previous line. Young children enjoy practicing this kinesthetic "return sweep." They can be taught to identify the need to do this by saying, "Don't fall asleep at the page," or "Time to get to the 'return sweep' stage!" Post this saying and encourage them to singsong as they joyously take ownership of their reading.

Have beginning readers "read" through the text to find letters they recognize in the story and then share some of the text that includes these specific letters to whet their appetite for reading.

STRATEGIES FOR PROMOTING LETTER KNOWLEDGE AND LETTER FORMATION

Engage the children in a Tale Trail game. Use a story they have already heard or read. Ask the children to circle certain letters and then reread the story, sharing the letters they have circled.

Give the children many opportunities to do letter sorts. Pass out word cards that have the targeted letter on them. Ask the children to come up to the front of the classroom and display their answers to questions like these about the letter, like *r*.

*R as the first letter—rose, rise, ran
*R as the last letter—car, star, far
*R with a *t* after it—start, heart, part, smart
*R, two *r*s in the middle of a word—carry, sorry, starry

Play "What's in a Name?" Select a student's name, such as William copy it down on a sentence strip. Have the children count the number of letters in the name and how many of them appear twice. Allow them to talk about which letter is uppercase and which letters are lowercase. Have the students chant the name. Then rewrite the name on another sentence strip. Have the strip cut into separate letters and see if someone from the class can put the name back correctly.

As you read a book with or to children, ask that they show you specific letters or lowercase or uppercase letters. Read the text first and encourage as many children to identify the letters as possible. Use a Big Book and have felt and sandpaper letters available for display as well. If grade, age, and developmentally appropriate, have children then write the letter they identified themselves, or for even more fun, construct it using pipe cleaners, play dough, or coded colored markers (different colors for upper- and lowercase letters).

Play "letter leap" with the children and have them look carefully at the room to identify labeled items that begin with a specific letter by "leaping" over to the items and placing a large lettered placard next to them. Children who are advanced in letter formation can then be challenged to "leap" through the classroom when called upon to literally "letter" unlabeled objects.

RECOGNITION THAT PHONEMES ARE REPRESENTED BY LETTERS AND LETTER PAIRS

As young children begin to learn to read, they make connections between the printed letters on the page and the sounds they have heard in language. Phonemic awareness activities are crucial for building this bridge. Students have engaged in many auditory activities. At this time, it is important the teacher use explicit and systematic methods to demonstrate to the students how these auditory sounds are represented on a page by letters or sometimes letter pairs. As this occurs, students can begin to decode text and move toward becoming proficient readers.

USE OF READING AND WRITING STRATEGIES FOR TEACHING LETTER-SOUND CORRESPONDENCE

Provide children with a sample of a single letter book (or create one from environmental sources, newspapers, coupons, circulars, magazines, or other text ideas). Make sure that the already published or created sample includes a printed version of the letter in both upper- and lowercase forms. Make certain that each page contains a picture of something that starts with that specific letter and also has the word for the picture. The book should be a predictable one in that when the picture is identified, the word can be read.

Once the children have been provided with the sample and have listened to it being read, challenge them to each make a one-letter book. Often it is best to focus on familiar consonants for the single-letter book or the first letter of the child's first name. Using the first letter of the child's first name invites the child to develop a book that tells about him or her and the words that he or she finds. This is an excellent way to have the reading and writing workshop enhance the teaching of the alphabetic principle. Encourage children to be active writers and readers by finding words for their book on the classroom word wall, in alphabet books in the special alphabet book bin, and in grade- and age-appropriate pictionaries (dictionaries for younger children that are filled with pictures).

Of course, the richest resource within the reading and writing workshop classroom for teaching and fostering the alphabetic principle lies in the use of alphabet books as anchors for inspiring students writing. While young children in kindergarten and first grade will do better with the one-letter book authoring activity, children in grades 2 and beyond can truly be inspired and motivated by alphabet books to enhance their own reading, writing, and alphabetic skills. Furthermore, use of these books, which are being produced in a variety of formats to enhance social studies, science, and mathematical themes, provide an opportunity for even young children to create a meaningful product that authenticates their content study as it enhances alphabetic skills and, of course, print awareness.

An annotated bibliography of selected alphabet books has been provided in the bibliography section of this guide. It was limited by space considerations, but the teacher can, with no expense and with much pleasure, catch up on the latest titles and identify those most appropriate for the grade taught by visiting a bookstore. Hold the print book in hand and then consider selecting an alphabet book that has a particularly inviting concept, art style, or adaptable format within the children's capacity to use as a model.

For instance, Tina Hoban uses actual color photographs of letters in her *26 Letters and 99 Cents*. Children may want to make clay letters or create letter sculptures that develop their own alphabet book similar to Hoban's. If nutrition is the science topic, children might want to examine Ehlert's very accessible *Eating the Alphabet: Fruits and Vegetables from A to Z*. This, combined with an examination of the fruits and vegetables in a local store (perhaps a pleasant walk from the school and a quick break from the routine) can yield a wonderful alphabet book on fruits and vegetables that can also include those eaten in various cultures (for example, mangos, plantains, and pomegranates).

The alphabet book can also offer the class a chance to work collaboratively using a template page created by the teacher. Completion of this collaborative work can be shared with peers in another class and parents and be kept in the classroom library as a model for the following year's class with their recognition and acceptance of the authors.

ASSESSMENT THROUGHOUT THE YEAR OF GRAPHOPHONEMIC AWARENESS

The teacher will want to maintain individual records of children's reading behaviors demonstrating alphabetic principle/graphophonemic awareness.

The following performance standards should be part of a record template form for each child in kindergarten through first grade and beyond, as needed (depending on ELL or special needs):

- Match all consonant and short vowel sounds.
- Read one's own name.
- Read one-syllable words and high-frequency words.
- Demonstrate ability to read and understand that as letters in words change, so do the sounds.
- Generate the sounds from all letters, including consonant blends and long vowel patterns. Blend those different sounds into recognizable words.
- Read common sight words.
- Read common word families.
- Recognize and use knowledge of spelling patterns when reading, such as run/running, hop/hopping.

The following template can be used by teachers to record student progress for each child in kindergarten through first grade and beyond, as needed (depending on ELL or special needs):

Reading Progress

Skill Area	Mastered	Making Progress	Not Yet	Comments
Matches all consonant and short vowel sounds				
Reads one's own name				
Reads one-syllable words and high-frequency words				
Demonstrates ability to read and understand that as letters in words change, so do the sounds				
Generates the sounds from all letters, including consonant blends and long vowel patterns. Blends those different sounds into recognizable words				
Reads common sight words				
Reads common word families				
Recognizes and uses knowledge of spelling patterns when reading, such as run/running, hop/hopping				

Any record kept of an individual child's progress should include each date of observation and some legend or rubric detailing the level of performance, standard acquisition, or mastery.

DEVELOPMENT OF ALPHABETIC KNOWLEDGE IN INDIVIDUAL STUDENTS

Researchers Laura M. Justice and Helen K. Ezell (2002) evaluated alphabetic knowledge and print awareness in preschool children from low-income households. In their post-tests, children who had participated in shared reading sessions that emphasized a print focus outperformed their control group peers (other Head Start children) on three measures of print awareness: words in print, print recognition, and alphabetic knowledge.

Other researchers, including Chaney (1994[TAR8]), have demonstrated a statistically significant and inverse relationship between household income and children's performance on measures of print awareness and the alphabetic principle. Lonigan (l999) [TAR9]found that substantial group differences existed on a variety of preliteracy tasks administered to 85 preschool children from lower- and middle-income households. The researchers looked at environmental print, print and book reading conventions, and alphabet knowledge. Results showed that preschool children from middle-income households showed significantly higher levels of skill across all print awareness tasks in comparison with preschoolers from low-income households.

Obviously this data highlights the importance of extensive alphabetic knowledge activities and print awareness opportunities for some children from low-income households in kindergarten through first grade and even beyond, if necessary.

Two other studies undertaken by Ezell and Justice (2000) suggested that structuring adult-child shared book reading interactions to include an explicit print awareness and alphabetic principle focus resulted in a substantial increase in children's verbal interactions with print.

This work highlights the importance of not only classroom and preschool emphasis on print awareness and alphabetic principle routines but also the need for teachers to reach out to parents and to model for them these shared reading experiences so that family life can parallel classroom experiences. Many schools currently have parent volunteers and reading buddy programs. Training of these volunteers, particularly in high need, low-income communities is certainly warranted.

David J. Chard and Jean Osborn (l999) [TAR10]have reflected on the guidelines necessary for teachers to use in selecting supplemental phonics and word-recognition materials for addressing students with learning disabilities.

They note that an important way to help children with reading disabilities figure out the system underlying the printed word is leading them to understand the alphabetic principle. Children with learning disabilities (LD) in particular benefit from organized instruction that centers on letters and sounds and the relations between them. They also benefit from word-recognition patterns instruction, which offers practice with word families that share similar letter patterns.

Children who are LD also benefit from opportunities to apply what they are learning to the reading and rereading of stories and other texts. Such texts contain a high portion of words that reflect the letters, sounds, and spelling patterns the children are learning.

For special needs children, a beginning reading program should include the following elements of alphabetic knowledge instruction:

1. A variety of alphabetic knowledge activities in which the children learn to identify and name both upper- and lowercase letters
2. Games, songs, and other activities that help children to learn to name the letters quickly
3. Writing activities that encourage children to practice the letters that they are writing
4. A sensible sequence of letter introduction that can be adjusted to the needs of the children.

COMPETENCY 8.0   UNDERSTAND THE DEVELOPMENT AND APPLICATION OF PHONICS SKILLS

SEQUENCE OF PHONICS SKILLS

- Letter naming
  - Lowercase letters
  - Uppercase letters
- Letter sounds
  - Continuous sounds
  - Stop sounds
  - Both consonant and vowel sounds
- Short vowels in CVC[TAR11] (consonant-vowel-consonant) words
- Short vowels with digraphs and –tch trigraph
- Short vowels and consonant blends
- Long vowels
- Variant vowels and diphthongs
- R- and l- controlled vowels
- Multi-syllabic words

EXPLICIT AND IMPLICIT STRATEGIES FOR TEACHING PHONICS

Uta Frith has identified three phases that describe the progression of children's phonic learning from ages 4 through 8:

Logographic Phase

Children recognize whole words that have significance for them, such as their own names or the names of stores they frequent or products that their parents buy. Examples are McDonald's, SuperValu, and the like. Strategies that nurture development in this phase include explicit labeling of classroom objects, components, furniture and materials, and showing the children's names in print as often as possible. Toward the end of this phase, children start to notice initial letters in words and the sounds that they represent.

Analytic Phase

During this phase, the children begin to make associations between the spelling patterns in the words they know and new words they encounter. Children in this phase of reading development are able to generalize that hat and cat are going to be read in a similar manner because they recognize that the /at/ portions of the words are the same. This is helpful with word families and can be transferred to encoding words through many activities. Some teachers find it helpful to add word families or family houses to their word walls around the room. In this way, students can begin to make these generalizations more rapidly. As the students find more complex words that fall into the family/house, they add them.

Orthographic Phase

In this phase, children recognize words almost automatically and can rapidly identify an increasing number of them. Students are able to apply many different strategies in a seamless manner to help decode unknown words. This may include phonics, structural analysis, syntax, semantics, and contextual clues. Students at this level are fluent readers with good prosody. They are reading to make the shift from learning to read to reading to learn. It is a critical shift for children.

To best support these phases and the development of emergent and early readers, teachers should focus on elements of phonics learning, which help children analyze words for their letters, spelling patterns, and structural components. Children need to be involved in activities in which they use what they know about words to learn new ones.

The teacher needs to build on what the children know to introduce new spelling patterns, vowel combinations, and short and long vowel investigations. The teacher must do this and be aware that these will be reintroduced again and again as needed.

Keep in mind that children's learning of phonics and other key components of reading is not linear, but rather falls back to review and then flows forward to build new understandings.

The following are among suggested activities to support phonics instruction to address the needs of these three phases of phonics learning:

(These activities have specifically been provided in detail so that the educator can study them and use them in the sample constructed response questions that have been provided at the end of the guide. Since the role of phonics in promoting reading development is so crucial, it is highly likely that a constructed response question on the certification test will focus on the use of such strategies. Therefore it is a good idea for the certification candidate to study them closely. As a bonus, the detail with which these strategies are set forth also makes them readily useful with classes the teacher is currently teaching).

Sorting words

This activity allows children to focus closely on the specific features of words and to begin to understand the basic elements of letter-sound relationships. Start with one syllable (monosyllabic) words. Have the children group them by their length, common letters, sound, and/or spelling pattern.

Prepare for the activity by writing 10 to 15 words on oaktag strips and place them randomly on the sentence strip holder. These words should come from a book previously shared in the classroom or a language experience chart. Next begin to sort out the words with the children, perhaps by where a particular letter appears in a word. While the children sort the place of a particular letter in a given word, they should also be coached (or facilitated) by the teacher to recognize that sometimes a letter in the middle of the word can still be the last sound heard and that some letters at the end of a word are silent (such as "e").

Children should be encouraged to make their own categories for word sorts and to share their own discoveries as they do the word sorts. The children's discoveries should be recorded and posted in the rooms with their names so they have ownership of their phonics learning.

Spelling pattern word wall

One of the understandings emergent readers come to about a word is that if they know how to read, write, and spell one word, they can write, read, and spell many other words as well.

Create a spelling pattern word wall in the classroom. This can be created by stapling a piece of 3" x 5" butcher block paper to the bulletin board. Then attach spelling pattern cards around the border with thumbtacks so that the cards can be easily removed to use at the meeting area.

Once a spelling pattern for instruction has been decided on, remove the corresponding card from the word wall. Then take a 1"x 3" piece of a contrasting color of butcher block paper and tape the card to the top end of a sheet the children will use for their investigation.

After the pattern is identified, the children can try to come up with other words that have the same spelling pattern. The teacher can write these on the spelling pattern sheet, using a different color marker to highlight the spelling pattern within the word. The children have to add to the list until the sheet is full, which might take two days or more. After the sheet is full, the completed spelling pattern is attached to the wall.

Letter holder making words

Use a 2" x 3" piece of foam board to make a letter holder. On the front of the board, attach 16 library pockets—one for each letter from A to P. Use the back of the board to attach another 10 pockets for the rest of the alphabet.

Write the letter name on each pocket and use clear bookbinding tape to secure each row of cards. Make 12 cards for each letter. On the front of each 2" x 6" strip, make a capital letter, and on its back write that letter in lowercase. Write consonants in black marker and vowels in red marker, or any other two colors.

Through use of this letter holder, children can experience how letters can be rearranged, added, or removed to make new words. They can use these cards also to focus as needed on letter sequences and to support them in recognizing spelling patterns in words.

The words chosen for this activity can be selected from Patricia Cunningham and Dorothy P. Hall's *Making Words* (l994). Select a word that is called the "secret word." Build up toward the creation of that word through a focus on the smaller words within it. Words should be chosen that reflect the spelling patterns being studied by the class.

Letter holders can be created for the children by folding up the bottom third of a used manila file folder and taping the ends to form a shallow pocket. Give them letter cards that are made of 2" x 6" oaktag. So, for example, if the secret word is bicycle, the children would be given the separate letter cards that would make up that word. The children keep the letters on the floor in front of them and only place them in the holder when they are actually making a word.

Making words should begin with making two-letter words, progressing as each individual child is ready to make larger ones. The teacher provides the instruction of which two letters the children are to use to make a word. After the instruction is given, the children select the correct letters and make the word in the folder. The teacher then writes the word down and the children check their letter holder word against it. The teacher goes around checking through and reviewing the letter holders to see which children are "getting it" and then continues to build up words with more letters if the children are ready.

Word splits

Through working with compound words, children can actually experience bigger words that are often made up of smaller words. By working with five to ten compound words on oaktag cards, children can analyze letter-sound relationships and meaning.

Before children meet in a group, write five to ten words on oaktag cards and arrange them on the sentence strip holder. After the words have been read, cut each of the words into its two smaller words and randomly arrange them on the sentence strip holder. Allow the children to randomly take turns arranging the small words back into the original compound words. Also, encourage them to form new compound words. For example, if one of two original compound words is "rainbow" and the other is "dropping," the children should be able to come with "raindrop." The new words the children come up with should be written on blank oaktag cards with the names of the children who came up with them attached. In this way the children can add to their growing bank of new words and have ownership of the words that they have added.

ROLE OF PHONICS IN DEVELOPING RAPID, AUTOMATIC WORD RECOGNITION, DECODING, AND READING COMPREHENSION

To decode means to change communication signals into messages. Reading comprehension requires that the reader learn the code within which a message is written and be able to decode it to get the message.

Although effective reading comprehension requires identifying words automatically (Adams 1990, Perfetti 1985[TAR12]), children do not have to be able to identify every single word or know the exact meaning of the every word in a text to understand it. Indeed, Nagy (1988[TAR13]) says that children can read a work with a high level of comprehension even if they do not fully know as many as 15% of the words within a given text.

Children develop the ability to decode and recognize words automatically. They then can extend their ability to decode to multi-syllabic words.

Cooper (2004) and other advocates of the balanced literacy approach feel that children become literate, effective communicators who are able to comprehend by learning phonics and other aspects of word identification through the use of engaging reading texts. Engaging text, as defined by the balanced literacy group, are those texts that contain highly predictable elements of rhyme, sound patterns, and plot. Researchers, such as Chall (1983) [TAR14]and Flesch (1981[TAR15]), support a phonics-centered foundation before the use of engaging reading texts. This is at the crux of the phonics versus whole language/ balanced literacy/ integrated language arts, teaching of reading controversy.

It is important for the new teacher to be informed about both sides of this controversy, as well as the work of theorists who attempt to reconcile these two perspectives, such as Kenneth Goodman (1994[TAR16]). There are powerful arguments on both sides, and each approach works wonderfully with some students and does not succeed with others.

As far as the examinations go, all that is asked of the teacher is the ability to demonstrate that familiarity with these varied perspectives. If asked on a constructed response question, the teacher needs to be able to show that he or she can talk about teaching some aspect of reading using strategies from one or the other or a combination of both approaches.

This guide is designed to provide teachers with numerous strategies representing both approaches.

The working teacher can, depending on the perspective of his /her school administration and the needs of the particular children he or she serves, choose from the strategies and approaches that work best for the children concerned.

Blending Letter Sounds

Prompts for graphophonic cues

- You said (the child's incorrect attempt). Does that match the letters you see?
- If it were the word you just said (the child's incorrect attempt), what would it have to start with?
- If it were the word you just said (the child's incorrect attempt), what would it have to end with?
- Look at the first letter/s, look at the middle letter/s, look at the last letter. What could it be?
- If you were writing (the child's incorrect attempt) what letter would you write first? What letters would go in the middle? What letters would go last?

A good strategy to use in working with individual children is to have them explain how they finally correctly identified a word that was troubling them. If prompted and habituated through one-on-one teacher/tutoring conversations, they can be quite clear about what they did to "get" the word.

If the children are already writing their own stories, the teacher might say to them, "You know when you write your own stories, you would never write any story which did not make sense. You wouldn't and probably this writer didn't either. If you read something that does make sense, but doesn't match the letters, then it's probably not what the author wrote. This is the author's story, not yours right now, so go back to the word and see if you can find out the author's story. Later on, you might write your own story."

Letter-sound correspondence and beginning decoding

Use this procedure for letter-sound investigations that support beginning decoding.

1. Focus on a particular letter/s that you want the child to investigate. It is good to choose one from a shared text that the children are familiar with. Make certain that the teachers' directions to the children are clear and either focus them on looking for a specific letter or on listening for sounds.
2. Begin a list of words that meet the task given to the children. Use chart paper to list the words that the children identify. This list can be continued into the next week as long as the children's focus is maintained on the list. This can be easily done by challenging the children with identifying a specific number of letters or sounds and "daring" them as a class team to go beyond those words or sounds.
3. Continue to add to the list. Focus the children at the beginning of the day on the goal of their individual additions to the list. Give them an adhesive note (sticky pad sheet) on which they can individually write down the words they find. Then they can attach their newly found words with their names on them to the chart. This provides the children with a sense of ownership and pride in their letter-sounding abilities. During shared reading, discuss the children's proposed additions and have the group decide if these meet the directed category. If all the children agree that they do meet the category, include the words on the chart.
4. Do a word sort from all the words generated and have the children put the words into categories that demonstrate similarities and differences. They can be prompted to see if the letter appeared at the beginning or the end of the word. They might also be prompted to see that one sound could have two different letter representations. The children can then "box" the word differences and similarities by drawing colors established in a chart key.
5. Before the children go off to read, ask them to look for new words in the texts that they can now recognize because of the letter-sound relationships on their chart. During shared reading, make certain that they have time to share the words they were able to decode because of their explorations.

Strategies for helping students decode single-syllable words that follow common patterns and multi-syllable words

(*This activity is presented in detail so it can actually be implemented with children in an intermediate classroom and also to provide detail for a potential constructed response question on a certification examination.*)

Developed by Jackie Montierth, a computer teacher in South San Diego for use with fifth- and sixth-grade students, the CVC phonics card game is a good one to adapt to the needs of any group with appropriate modifications for age, grade level, and language needs.

The children use the vehicle of the card game to practice and enhance their use of consonants and vowels. Their fluency in this will increase their ability to decode words. Potential uses beyond whole classroom instruction include use as part of small group word work and as part of cooperative team learning. This particular strategy also is particularly helpful for English language learners grade 4 and beyond who are in a regular English language classroom setting.

The card game works well because the practice of the content is implicit for transfer as the children continue to improve their reading skills. In addition, the card game format allows "instructional punctuation," using a student-centered high interest exploration.

Card design

The teacher can use the computer, 5" x 8" index cards, or actual card deck-sized oaktag cards to create a deck. For repeated use and durability, it is recommended that the deck be laminated.

The deck should consist of the following:

- 44 consonant cards (including the blends)
- 15 vowel cards (including 3 of each vowel)
- 5 wild cards (which can be used as any vowel)
- 6 final *e* cards

The design of this project can also focus on specific CVC words that are part of a particular book, topic, or genre format. In advance of playing the game, children can also be directed to review what is on the word wall or a word map.

Procedure

The game is best introduced first as part of a mini-lesson with the teacher reading the rules and a pair of children demonstrating step by step when the game is played before the class for the first time. Have the children divide into pairs or small groups of no more than four per group. Each group needs one deck of CVC cards.

Have each group choose a dealer. The dealer shuffles the cards and deals five cards to each player. The remaining cards are placed face down for drawing during the play. One card is turned over to form the discard pile. Players may not show their cards to the other players. The first player to the left of the dealer looks at his/her cards and, if possible, puts down three cards that make a consonant-vowel-consonant word. For more points, four cards forming a consonant-vowel-consonant word can be placed down. The player must then say the word and draw the number of cards he or she laid down. If he or she is unable to form a word, he or she draws a card from either the draw or discard pile. The player then discards one card. All players must have five cards at all times. Play moves to the left.

The game continues until one or more of the following happens:

1. There are no more cards in the draw pile
2. All players run out of cards.
3. All players cannot form a word

The winner is the player who has laid down the most cards during the game. Players may only lay down words at the beginning of their turn. Proper names may not be counted as words.

Other ways the game may be played

The game can be played with teams of individuals in a small group of four or fewer competing against one another (this is excellent for special needs or resource room students). It can also be done as a whole-class activity where all the students are divided into cooperative teams or small groups who compete against one another. This second approach will work well with a heterogeneous classroom that includes special needs and/or ELL children.

Teachers of ELL students can do this game in the native language first and then transition it into English, facilitating native language reading skills and second language acquisition. They can develop their own appropriate decks to meet the vocabulary needs of their children and to complement the curricula.

Using phonics to decode words in connected text

Identifying new words

Some strategies to share with children during conferences or as part of shared reading include the following prompts:

- Look at the beginning letter/s. What sound do you hear?
- Stop to think about the text or story. What word with this beginning letter would make sense here?
- Look at the book's illustrations. Do they provide you with help in figuring out the new word?
- Think of what word would make sense, sound right, and match the letters that you see. Start the sentence over, making your mouth ready to say that word.
- Skip the word, read to the end of the sentence, and then come back to the word. How does what you've read help you with the word?
- Listen to whether what you are reading makes sense and matches the letters (ask the child to self-monitor). If it doesn't make sense, see if you can correct it on your own.
- Look for spelling patterns you know from the spelling pattern wall.
- Look for smaller words you might know within the larger word.
- Read on a little and then return to the part that confused you.

TEACHER CERTIFICATION STUDY GUIDE

COMPETENCY 9.0

COMPETENCY 9.0   UNDERSTAND A VARIETY OF WORD
                      IDENTIFICATION STRATEGIES

USE OF SEMANTIC AND SYNTACTIC CUES TO HELP DECODE WORDS

Semantic Cues

Students will need to use their base knowledge of word meanings, or semantics, to help them decipher unknown words or text as well as to clarify reading when it does not seem to make sense. Some prompts the teacher can use that will alert the children to semantic cues include the following:

- Does that sentence make sense?
- Which word in that sentence does not seem to fit?
- Why doesn't it fit?
- What word might make sense in that sentence?

Syntactic Cues

The first strategy good readers use from their own knowledge base to help determine misreading is syntactic cues. Syntactic cues use the order of words and the student's knowledge of the oral English language to help determine if what was read is accurate. Some prompts the teacher can use to encourage and develop syntactic cues in reading include the following:

- You read (child's incorrect attempt). Does that sound right?
- You read (child's incorrect attempt). When we talk, do we talk that way?
- How would we say it?
- Recheck that sentence. Does it sound right the way you read it?

SPECIFIC TERMINOLOGY ASSOCIATED WITH PHONICS

It is important to have a clear understanding of the terms associated with phonics. Here are some definitions that are helpful in having a clear understanding of phonic development in children.

Phoneme: A phoneme is the smallest unit of sound in the English language. In print, phonemes are represented by the letter and a slash. So, /b/ represents the sound the letter *b* would make.

Morpheme: A morpheme is the smallest unit of grammar in the English language. In other words, it is the smallest unit of meaning, not just sounds.

Consonant Digraph: A consonant digraph are two consonants of the English language, which, when placed together in a word, make a unique sound that neither makes when alone. Examples are ch, th, sh, and wh.

Consonant Blend: A consonant blend is when two consonants are put together, but each retains its individual sound. The two sounds go together in a seamless manner to produce a blended sound. Examples are st, br, cl.

Schwa Sound: Schwa sound is a vowel sound that is neutral. It typically occurs in the unaccented syllable of a word. An example would be the sound of the *a* at the end of the word sofa, or the *e* in the word *the*. It is represented in print by an upside down *e*.

DEVELOPMENT OF PHONICS SKILLS WITH INDIVIDUAL STUDENTS

In *On Solid Ground*, Taberski said that it is much harder for children from ELL backgrounds and children from homes where other English dialects are spoken to use syntactic cues to attempt to self-correct.

These children, through no fault of their own, do not have sufficient experience hearing standard English spoken to use this cueing system as they read. The teacher should sensitively guide them through by modeling the use of syntactic and semantic cues.

Highly proficient readers can be paired as buddy tutors for ELL or special needs classroom members, or to assist the resource room teacher during their reading time. They can use the CVC game developed by Montrieth to support their peers and can even modify the game to meet the needs of other students. Of course, this also offers the highly proficient reader the opportunity to do a service learning project while still in elementary school. It also introduces the learner to another dimension of reading—the role of the reader as trainer and recruiter of other peers into the circle of readers and writers.

If the highly proficient readers are so motivated or if their teachers so desire, the peer tutors can also maintain an ongoing reading progress journal for their tutees. This will be a wonderful way to realize the goals of the reading and writing workshop.

There are many different strategies to help children who are struggling with their phonics skill development. A beginning step is to identify the area of difficulty within phonics. A simple assessment to help determine the exact area of difficulty is the CORE Phonics Survey, which can be downloaded at http://www.scholastic.com/dodea/Module_2/resources/dodea_m2_tr_core.pdf Once the area of deficit has been identified, small-group instruction can be developed around these areas to increase specific skills.

When working on specific phonics skills, it is important to utilize decodable texts. There are numerous publishers who have available a variety of different skills and texts for use within the classroom. If students continue to struggle, it may be necessary to utilize a more specific systematic and explicit phonics program. Some examples of these include Wilson Reading, Early Intervention Reading, and Open Court.

DEVELOPMENT OF WORD ANALYSIS SKILLS AND STRATEGIES, INCLUDING STRUCTURAL ANALYSIS

Structural analysis is a process of examining words in the text for meaningful word units (affixes, base words, inflected endings). There are six word types that are formed and therefore can be analyzed using structural analysis strategies. They include the following:

1. Common prefixes or suffixes added to a known word ending with a consonant
2. Adding the suffix –ed to words that end with consonants
3. Compound words
4. Adding endings to words that end with the letter *e*
5. Adding endings to words that end with the letter *y*
6. Adding affixes to multi-syllabic words

When teaching and using structural analysis procedures in the primary grades, teachers should remember to make sound decisions on which to introduce and teach. Keeping in mind the number of primary words in which each affix appears and how similar they are will help the teacher make the instructional process smoother and more valuable to the students.

Adding affixes to words can be started when students are able to read a list of one-syllable words by sight at a rate of approximately 20 words correct per minute. At the primary level, there is a recommended sequence for introducing affixes. These are the steps in this process:

- Start by introducing the affix in the letter-sound correspondence format
- Practice the affix in isolation for a few days
- Provide words for practice that contain the affix (word lists, flash cards, and so on)
- Move from word lists to including passage reading, which include words with the affix (and some from the word lists/flash cards).

Word Study Group

This involves the teacher taking time to meet with children from grades 3 to 6 in a small group of no more than six children for a word study session. Taberski (2000) suggests that this meeting take place next to the word wall. The children selected for this group are those who need to focus more on the relationship between spelling patterns and consonant sounds.

It is important that this not be a formalized traditional reading group that meets at a set time each week or biweekly. Rather the group should be spontaneously formed by the teacher based on the teacher's quick inventory of the selected children's needs at the start of the week. Taberski has templates in her book *Guided Reading Planning Sheets.* These sheets essentially include targeted word and other skills with her written, dated observations of children who are in need of support to develop a given skill.

The teacher should try to meet with this group for at least two consecutive 20-minute periods daily. Over those two meetings, the teacher can model a *making words* activity. Once the teacher has modeled making words the first day, the children would then make their own. On the second day, the children would "sort" their words.

Other topics for a word study group within the framework of the balanced literacy approach that Taberski advocates are inflectional endings, prefixes and suffixes, and/or common spelling patterns. These are covered later in this chapter.

It should be noted that this activity would be classified by theorists as a structural analysis activity because the structural components (for example, prefixes, suffixes, and spelling patterns) of the words are being studied.

Discussion Circles

Cooper (2004) believes that children should not be "taught" vocabulary and structural analysis skills. Flesch and E. D. Hirsch, who are key theorists of the phonics approach and advocates of cultural literacy (a term coined by and associated with Hirsch), believe that specific vocabulary words at various grade and age levels need to be mastered and must be explicitly taught in schools. As far as Cooper is concerned, all the necessary and meaningful (for the child and ultimately adult reader) vocabulary can't possibly be taught in schools (no apologies to Hirsch). To Cooper, it is far more important that the children be made aware of and become interested in learning words by themselves. Cooper feels that through the child's reading and writing, he or she develops a love for and a sense of "ownership" of words. All of Cooper's suggested structural analysis word strategies are therefore designed to foster the child's love of words and a desire to "own" more of them through reading and writing.

Discussion circles fit nicely into the balanced literacy lesson format. After the children conclude a particular text, Cooper suggests responding to the book in discussion circles. Among the prompts, the teacher-coach might suggest that the children focus on words of interest they encountered in the text. These can also be words that they heard if the text was read aloud. Children can be asked to share something funny or upsetting or unusual about the words they have read. Through this focus on children's response to words as the center of the discussion circle, peers become more interested in word study.

Banking, Booking, and Filing It: Making Words My Own

Children can literally realize the goal of making words their own and exploring word structures through creating concrete objects or displays that demonstrate the words they own. Children can create and maintain their own files of words they have learned or are interested in learning. The files can be categorized by the children according to their own interests. They should be encouraged to develop files using science, history, physical education, fine arts, dance, and technology content. Newspapers and Web resources that the teacher has approved are excellent sources for such words. In addition, this provides the teacher with the opportunity to instruct the child in appropriate age- and grade-level research skills. Even children in grades 2 and 3 can begin simplified bibliographies and webliographies for their "found" words. Children can learn how to annotate and note the page of a newspaper, book, or URL for a particular word.

They can also copy down the word as it appears in the text (print or electronic). If appropriate, the child can place the particular words found for a given topic or content, in an actual bank of the child's own making. The words can be printed on cards. This allows for differentiated word study and appeals to those children who are kinesthetic and spatial learners. Of course, children can also choose to create their own word books that include their specialized vocabulary and descriptions of how they identified or hunted down their words. Richard Scarry, watch out! Scarry books can be anchor books to inspire this structural analysis activity.

ELL learners can share accounts in their native language first and then translate (with the help of the teacher) these accounts into English with both the native language and the English language versions of the word exploration posted.

Write out Your Words, Write with Your Words

Ownership of words can be demonstrated by having the children use them as part of their writings. The children can author a procedural narrative (a step-by-step description) of how they went about their word searches to compile what they found for any of the activities. If the children are in kindergarten or first grade, or if the children are struggling readers and writers, their procedural narratives can be dictated. They can then be posted by the teacher.

ELL students can share their accounts in their native language first and then translate (with the help of the teacher) these accounts into English with both the native language and the English language versions of the word exploration posted.[tac917]

Children with special needs may model a word box on a specific holiday theme, genre, or science/social studies topic with the teacher. Initially this can be done as a whole class. As the children become more confident, they can work with peers or with a paraprofessional to create their own individual or small team/pair word boxes.

Special needs children can create a storyboard with the support of a paraprofessional, their teacher, or a resource specialist. They can also narrate their story of how they all found the words, using a tape recorder.

Word Study Museum within the Classroom

This strategy has been presented in detail so it can be used by the teachers within their own classrooms. In addition, the way the activity is described and the mention at the end of the description of how the activity can address family literacy, ELL, and special needs children's talents provides an example of other audiences a teacher should consider in curriculum design.

Almost every general education teacher and reading specialist will have to differentiate instruction to address the needs of special education and ELL learners. Family or shared literacy is a major component of all literacy instruction.

Children can create single or multiple museum-style exhibits within their classrooms to celebrate their word study. They can build actual representations of the type of study they have done, including word trees (made out of cardboard or foam board), elaborate word boxes and games, word history timelines or murals, and word study maps. They can develop online animations, Kids Spiration graphic organizers, quick movies, digital photo essays, and PowerPoint presentations to share the word they have identified. The classroom, the gym, or the cafeteria can be transformed into a gallery space. Children can author brochure descriptions for their individual, team, or class exhibits. Some children can volunteer to be tour guides or docents for the experience. Other children can work to create a banner for the museum. The children can name the museum themselves and send out invitations to its opening. Invitations can be sent to parents, community, staff members, peers, or younger classes.

Depending on their age and grade level, children can also develop interactive games and quizzes focused on particular exhibits. An artist or a team of class artists can design a poster for the exhibit, while other children can choose to build the exhibits. Another small group can work on signage and a catalogue or register of objects within the exhibit. Greeters who will welcome parents and peers to the exhibit can be trained and can develop their own scripts.

If the children are in grades 4–6, they can also develop their own visitor feedback forms and design word-themed souvenirs. The whole museum within the school or classroom can be captured digitally or with a regular camera. The record of this event can be hung near the word walls. Of course, the children can use many of their newly recognized and owned words to describe the event.

The word study museum activity can be used with either a phonics-based or a balanced literacy approach. It promotes additional writing, researching, discussing, and reading about words.

It is also an excellent family literacy strategy in that families can develop their own word exhibits at home. This activity can also support and celebrate learners with disabilities. It can be presented in dual languages by children who are ELL learners and fluent in more than one language.

COMPETENCY 10.0 UNDERSTAND THE DEVELOPMENT OF VOCABULARY KNOWLEDGE AND SKILLS

RELATIONSHIP BETWEEN WORD ANALYSIS SKILLS AND READING COMPREHENSION

The explicit teaching of word analysis requires that the teacher preselect words from a given text for vocabulary learning. These words should be chosen based on the storyline and main ideas of the text. The educator may even want to create a story map for a narrative text or develop a graphic organizer for an expository text. Once the story mapping and/or graphic organizing have been done, the educator can compile a list of words that relate to the storyline and/or main ideas.

The number of words that require explicit teaching should only be two or three. If the number is higher than that, the children need guided reading, and the text needs to be broken down into smaller sections for teaching. When broken down into smaller sections, each text section should only have two to three words that need explicit teaching.

Some researchers, including Tierney[TAR18] and Cunningham[TAR19], believe that a few words should be taught as a means of improving comprehension.

It is up to the educator whether the vocabulary selected for teaching needs review before reading, during reading, or after reading.

Introduce vocabulary *before reading* if

- The children are having difficulty constructing meaning on their own after previewing the text and indicating words they want to know.
- The teacher has seen that there are words within the text that are definitely keys necessary for reading comprehension.
- The text, in the judgment of the teacher, contains difficult concepts for the children to grasp.

Introduce vocabulary *during reading* if

- The children are already doing guided reading.
- The text has words that are crucial to its comprehension and the children will have trouble understanding them if they are not helped with the text.

Introduce vocabulary *after reading* if

- The children have shared words that they found difficult or interesting.
- The children need to expand their vocabulary.
- The text itself is one that is particularly suited for vocabulary building.

Strategies to support word analysis and enhance reading comprehension include the following:

- Use of a graphic organizer, such as a word map
- Semantic mapping
- Semantic feature analysis
- Hierarchical and linear arrays
- Preview in context
- Contextual redefinition
- Vocabulary self-collection

Note that these terms are in the Glossary.

IDENTIFICATION OF COMMON MORPHEMES, PREFIXES, AND SUFFIXES

This aspect of vocabulary development is to help children look for structural elements within words that they can use independently to help them determine meaning.

Some teachers choose to directly teach structural analysis. In particular, those who teach by following the phonics-centered approach for reading do this.

Other teachers, who follow the balanced literacy approach, introduce the structural components as part of mini-lessons that are focused on the students' reading and writing.

Structural analysis of words as defined by Cooper (2004) involves the study of significant word parts. This analysis can help the child with pronunciation and constructing meaning.

The term list below is generally recognized as the key structural analysis components.

Root Words

This is a word from which another word is developed. The second word can be said to have its "root" in the first, such as *vis* (to see) in visor or vision. This structural component can be illustrated by a tree with roots to display the meaning for children. Children may also want to literally construct root words using cardboard trees to create word family models.

ELL learners can construct these models for their native language root word families, as well for the English language words they are learning. ELL students in the fifth and sixth grade may even appreciate analyzing the different root structures for contrasts and similarities between their native language and English.

Learners with special needs can focus in small groups or individually with a paraprofessional on building root word models.

Base Words

These are stand-alone linguistic units that cannot be deconstructed or broken down into smaller words. For example, in the word *re-tell*, the base word is *tell*.

Contractions

These are shortened forms of two words in which a letter or letters have been deleted. These deleted letters have been replaced by an apostrophe.

Prefixes

These are beginning units of meaning that can be added (the vocabulary word for this type of structural adding is "affixed") to a base word or root word. They cannot stand alone. They are also sometimes known as "bound morphemes," meaning that they cannot stand alone as a base word. Examples are *re-*, *un-*, and *mis-*.

Suffixes

These are ending units of meaning that can be "affixed" or added on to the ends of root or base words. Suffixes transform the original meanings of base and root words. Like prefixes, they are also known as "bound morphemes," because they cannot stand alone as words. Examples are *-less*, *-ful,* and *-tion*.

Compound Words

These occur when two or more base words are connected to form a new word. The meaning of the new word is in some way connected with that of the base word. Examples are *firefighter*, *newspaper*, and *pigtail*.

Inflectional Endings

These are types of suffixes that impart a new meaning to the base or root word. These endings in particular change the gender, number, tense, or form of the base or root words. Just like other suffixes, these are also termed "bound morphemes." Examples are *–s* or *-ed*.

Comments on the Certification Test[tac920]

Definitions are included because the structural analysis components are explicitly taught in schools that advocate the phonics-centered approach and are also incorporated into the word work component of the schools that advocate the balanced literacy approach for instruction.

Definition questions, or multiple choice questions that have only a single right answer, test whether the teacher candidate has memorized the appropriate terminology. They constitute no less than 15% of the multiple choice questions on the test. Therefore, by taking the time to memorize these easy definitions, scores are likely to improve.

Some of these activities are presented in detail to help answer the constructed response questions of the test.

KNOWLEDGE OF GREEK AND LATIN ROOTS THAT FORM ENGLISH WORDS

Knowledge of Greek and Latin roots that comprise English words can measurably enhance children's reading skills and can also enrich their writing.

Word Webs

Taberski (2000) does not advocate teaching Greek and Latin derivatives in the abstract to young children. However, when she naturally comes across specific Greek and Latin roots while reading to children, she uses that opportunity to introduce children to these rich resources.

For example, during readings on rodents (a favorite of first and second graders), Taberski draws her class's attention to the fact that beavers gnaw at things with their teeth. She then connects the "dent" root or derivative to other words the children are familiar with or have experiences in their lives. The children then volunteer "dentist," "dental," "denture." Taberski begins to place these in a graphic organizer or word web.

When she has tapped the extent of the children's prior knowledge of "dent" words, she shares with them the fact that *dens/dentis* is the Latin word for teeth. Then she introduces the word "indent," which she has already previewed with them as part of their conventions of print study. She helps them to see that the "indenting" of the first line of a paragraph can even be related to the "teeth" Latin root in that it looks like a "print" bite was taken out of the paragraph.

Taberski displays the word web in the word wall chart section of her room. The class is encouraged throughout, for example, about a week's time to look for other words to add to the web. Taberski stresses that for her, as an elementary teacher of reading and writing, the key element of the Greek and Latin word root web activity is the children's coming to understand that if they know what a Greek or Latin word root means, they can use that knowledge to figure out what other words mean.

She feels the key concept is to model and demonstrate for children how fun and fascinating Greek and Latin root study can be.

Greek and Latin Roots Word Webs with an Assist from the World Wide Web

Older children in grades 3–6 can build on this initial print activity by searching online for additional words with a particular Greek or Latin root that has been introduced in class.

They can easily do this in a way that authentically ties in with their own interests and experiences by reading reviews online for a book that has been read aloud or by just reading the summaries of the day's news and printing out those words that appear in the stories online that share the root discussed.

The children can be encouraged to circle these instances of the word's Latin or Greek root and also to document the exact date and URL for the citation. These can be posted as part of their own online web in the word wall section study area. If the school or class has a Web site or Web page, the children can post this data there as a special Greek and Latin root word page.

Expanding the concept of the Greek and Latin word web from the printed page to the World Wide Web nicely inculcates the child in the habits of lifelong reading and researching online. This beginning expository research will serve them well in intermediate-level content area work and beyond.

Use of Syllabification as a Word Identification Strategy

Strategy: Clap hands, count those syllables as they come!!

The objective of this activity from Taberski is for children to understand that every syllable in a polysyllabic word can be studied for its spelling patterns in the same way that monosyllabic words are studied for their spelling patterns.

The easiest way for the kindergarten to third-grade teacher to introduce this activity to the children is to share a familiar poem from the poetry chart (or to write out a familiar poem on a large experiential chart).

First the teacher reads the poem with the children. As they are reading it aloud, the children clap the beats of the poem and the teacher uses a colored marker to place a tic (/) above each syllable.

Next, the teacher takes letter cards and selects one of the polysyllabic words from the poem that the children have already "clapped" out. The children use letter cards to spell that word on the sentence strip holder or it can be placed on a felt board or up against a window on display. Together the children and teacher divide the letters into syllables and place blank letter cards between the syllables. The children identify spelling patterns they know.

Finally, and as part of continued small-group syllabification study, the children identify other polysyllabic words they clapped out from the poem. They make up the letter combinations of these words, and then they separate them into syllables with blank letter cards between the syllables.

Children who require special support in syllabification can be encouraged to use many letter cards to create a large butcher paper syllabic (in letter cards with spaces) representation of the poem or at least a few lines of the poem. They can be told that this is for use as a teaching tool for others. In this way, they authenticate their study of syllabification with a real product that can actually be referenced by peers

Techniques for identifying compound words

The teaching of compound words should utilize structural analysis techniques. (See above section on structural analysis).

Here are some other strategies for helping students to identify and read compound words:

- Use songs and actions to help children understand the concept that compound words are two smaller words joined together to make one bigger word.
- Use games like concentration, memory, and go fish for students to practice reading compound words.
- Use word sorts to have students distinguish between compound words and non-examples of compound words.

Identification of Homographs

Homographs are words that are spelled the same but have different meanings. A subgroup within this area includes words that are spelled the same, have different meanings, and are pronounced differently. Some examples of homographs include:

- Lie
- Tear
- Bow
- Fair
- Bass

Teaching homographs can be interesting and fun for the students. Incorporate them into passages where the students can use the context clues to decipher the different meanings of the homographs. Games are also a good strategy for helping students understand multiple meaning words. Jokes and riddles are usually based on homographs, and students love to make collections or books of these.

Semantic Feature Analysis

This technique for enhancing vocabulary skills by using semantic cues is based on the research of Johnson and Pearson (1984[TAR21]) and Anders and Bos (1986). It involves young children in setting up a feature analysis grid of various subject content words that is an outgrowth of their discussion about these words.

For instance, Cooper (2004) includes a sample of a Semantic Feature Analysis grid for vegetables.

Vegetables	Green	Have Peels	Eat Raw	Seeds
Carrots	-	+	+	-
Cabbage	+	-	+	-

Note the use of the + for yes, - for no, and possible use for + and - if a vegetable like squash could be both green and yellow.

Teachers of children in grade 1 and beyond can design their own semantic analysis grids to meet their students' needs and to align with the topics the students are learning. Select a category or class of words (could be planets, winter words, or weather words).

Use the left side of the grid to list at least three if not more items that fit this category. The number of actual items listed will depend on the age and grade level of the children, with three or four items fine for kindergarten and first grade, and up to ten to fifteen for grades 5 and 6. Brainstorm with the children, or if better suited to the class, the teacher may list his/her own features that the items have in common. As can be noted from the example excerpted from *Cooper's Literacy: Helping Children Construct Meaning (*2004), common features, such as vegetables' green color, peels, and seeds are usually fairly easy to identify.

Show the children how to insert the notations +, -, and even ? (if they are not certain) on the grid. The teacher might also explore with the children the possibility that an item could get both a + and a -. For example, a vegetable like broccoli might be eaten cooked or raw, depending on taste, and squash can be green or yellow.

Whatever the length of the grid when first presented to the children (perhaps as a semantic cue lesson in and of itself tied in to a text being read in class), make certain that the grid, as presented and filled out, is not the end of the activity.

Children can use it as a model for developing their own semantic features grids and share them with the whole class. Child-developed grids can become part of a word work center in the classroom or even be published in a word study games book by the class as a whole. Such a publication can be shared with parents during open school week and evening visits and with peer classes.

CONTEXTUAL REDEFINITION

This strategy encourages children to use the context more effectively by presenting them with sufficient context *before* they begin reading. It models for the children the use of contextual clues to make informed guesses about word meanings.

To apply this strategy, the teacher should first select unfamiliar words for teaching. No more than two or three words should be selected for direct teaching. The teacher should then write a sentence in which there are sufficient clues supplied for the child to successfully figure out the meaning. Among the types of context clues the teacher can use are compare/contrast, synonyms, and direct definition.

Then the teacher should present the words only on the experiential chart or as letter cards. Have the children pronounce the words. As they pronounce them, challenge them to come up with a definition for each word. After more than one definition is offered, encourage the children to decide as a whole group what the definition is. Write down their agreed upon definition with no comment as to its accurate meaning.

Next, share with the children the contexts (sentences the teacher wrote with the words and explicit context clues). Ask that the children read the sentences aloud. Then have the students come up with a definition for each word. Make certain that as they present their definitions, the teacher does not comment. Ask that they justify their definitions by making specific references to the context clues in the sentences. As the discussion continues, direct the children's attention to the previously agreed upon definition of the word. Facilitate their discussing the differences between their guesses about the word when they saw only the word itself and their guesses about the word when they read it in context. Finally, have the children check their use of context skills to correctly define the word by using a dictionary.

DEVELOPMENT OF WORD ANALYSIS SKILLS BY INDIVIDUAL STUDENTS

This type of direct teaching of word definitions is useful when the children have dictionary skills and the teacher is aware of the fact that there are not sufficient clues about the words in the context to help the students define them. In addition, struggling readers and students from ELL backgrounds may benefit tremendously from being walked through this process that highly proficient and successful readers apply automatically

By using this strategy, the teacher can also "kid watch" and note the students' prior knowledge as they guess the word in isolation. The teacher can also actually witness and hear how various students use context skills.

Through their involvement in this strategy, struggling readers gain a feeling of community as they experience the ways in which their struggles and guesses resonate with other peers' responses to the text.

CONTEXTUAL VOCABULARY STRATEGIES

Vocabulary Self-Collection

This strategy is one in which children, even on the emergent level from grade 2 and up, take responsibility for their learning. It is also by definition a student-centered strategy that demonstrates student ownership of their chosen vocabulary.

This strategy is one that can be introduced by the teacher early in the year, perhaps even the first day or week. The format for self-collection can then be started by the children. It may take the form of a journal with photocopied template pages, and it can be continued throughout the year.

To start, ask the children to read a required text or story. Invite them to select one word for the class to study from this text or story. The children can work individually, in teams, or in small groups. The teacher can also do the self-collecting so that this becomes the joint effort of the class community of literate readers. Tell the children that they should select words that particularly interest them or that are unique in some way.

After the children have had time to make their selections and to reflect on them, make certain that they have time to share them with their peers as a whole class. When each child shares the word that he or she has selected, have them provide a definition for the word. Each word that is given should be listed on a large experiential chart or even in a Big Book format, if that is age and grade appropriate. The teacher should also share the word he or she selected and provide a definition. The teacher's definition and sharing should be somewhere in the middle of the children's recitations.

The dictionary should be used to verify the definitions. When all the definitions have been checked, a final list of child-selected (and single teacher-selected) words should be made.

Once this final list has been compiled, the children can record it in their word journals, or they may opt to record only those words they find interesting in their individual journals. It is up to the teacher at the onset of the vocabulary self-collection activity to decide whether the children have to record all the words on the final list or can eliminate some. The decision made at the beginning by the teacher must be adhered to throughout the year.

To further enhance this strategy, children, particularly those in grades 3 and beyond, can be encouraged to use their collected words as part of their writings or to record and clip the appearance of these words in newspaper stories or online. This type of additional recording demonstrates that the child has truly incorporated the word into his/her reading and writing. It also habituates children to be lifelong readers, writers, and researchers.

One of the nice things about this simple but versatile strategy is that it works equally well with either expository or narrative texts. It also provides children with an opportunity to use the dictionary.

Assessment is built into the strategy. As the children select the word for the list, they share how they used contextual clues, and through the children's response to the definitions offered by their peers, their prior knowledge can be assessed.

What is most useful about this strategy is that it documents that children can learn to read and write by reading and writing. The children take ownership of the words in the self-collection journals, and that can also be the beginning of writer observation journals as they include their own writings. They also use the word lists as a start for writers' commonplace books. These books are filled with newspaper, magazine, and functional document clippings using the journal words.

This activity is a good one for demonstrating the balanced literacy belief that vocabulary study works best when the words studied are chosen by the child.

THE RELATIONSHIP BETWEEN ORAL VOCABULARY AND THE PROCESS OF IDENTIFYING AND UNDERSTANDING WRITTEN WORDS

One way to explore the relationship between oral vocabulary and the comprehension of written words is through the use of oral records (which are discussed at length in the appendix).

In *On Solid Ground: Strategies for Teaching Reading K-3*, Taberski (2000) discusses how oral reading records can be used by the kindergarten through third grade teacher to assess how well children are using cueing systems. She notes that the running record format can also show visual depictions for the teacher of how the child "thinks" as the child reads. The notation of miscues in particular shows how a child "walks through" the reading process. They indicate if and in what ways the child may require "guided" support in understanding the words he or she reads aloud. Taberski notes that when children read, they need to think about several things at once. First, they must consider whether what they are reading makes sense (semantic or meaning cues). Next, they must know whether their reading "sounds right" in terms of standard English (syntactic and structural cues). Last, they have to weigh whether their oral language actually and accurately matches the letters the words represent (visual or graphophonic cues).

In taking the running record and having the opportunity first-hand to listen to the children talk about the text, the teacher can analyze the relationship between the child's oral language and word comprehension. Information from the running record provides the teacher with a road map for differentiated cueing system instruction.

For example, when a running record is taken, a child often makes a mistake but then self-corrects. The child may select from various cueing systems when he or she self-corrects. These include: "M" for meaning, "S" for syntax, and "V" for visual. The use of a visual cue means that the child is drawing on his or her knowledge of spelling patterns. Of course, Taberski cautions that any relationship between oral language and comprehension that the teacher draws from an examination of the oral-reading records must be drawn using a series of three or more of the child's oral reading records, taken over time, not just once.

A teacher can review a child's running records over time to note his or her pattern of miscues and which cues are used most in self-corrections. Whichever cueing system the child uses to the greatest extent, it is necessary for the teacher to offer support in also using the other cueing systems to construct correct meaning. Taberski suggests that while assessing running records to determine the relationship between oral language and meaning, the child reads from "just right" books.

STRATEGIES FOR PROMOTING ORAL LANGUAGE DEVELOPMENT AND LANGUAGE COMPREHENSION

Read-Aloud Time

(*This is the corner piece of the balanced literacy approach for teaching reading. Therefore it is advised that the teacher candidate and new teacher read this material carefully. This may well appear as an essay topic in the Constructed Response section.*)

Comments on the Certification Test

Within the context of the balanced literacy approach and the literacy block, the read aloud is part of whole-class activities. The book selected should be one taken from the classroom library. Before reading the book to the class, the teacher needs to be familiar with it. The teacher should also "plan" or at least "know" what nuances of content, style, rhythm, and vocabulary that will be emphasized in the reading.

In addition, specifically for the younger grades, the teacher should select a text that also enhances the development of phonemic awareness. This might include a text that can be used to teach rhyming, alliteration, or poetry. Sometimes, read-aloud texts are selected for their tie-ins with the science, social studies, and mathematics curriculum.

Generally teachers aim to teach one strategy during read-aloud time, which the children will practice in small groups or independently. For the first grader, this could include print strategies and talking about books.

While reading aloud, the teacher's voice quality should highlight his or her enjoyment of the read-aloud time and involvement with its text. Often in a balanced literacy classroom, the teacher reads from a specially decorated reader's chair, as do the guest readers. This chair's decorativeness, complete with comfortable throwback pillows or rocking chair–style frame, is meant to set an atmosphere that will promote the children's engagement in and love for lifelong reading.

The balanced literacy approach also advocates that teachers select books that children will enjoy reading aloud. Collections of poetry are particularly accessible texts for elementary school classroom read-aloud times.

Teachers must allow time for discussion during and after each read-aloud period. After the children have made comments, the teacher should also talk about the reading.

KNOWLEDGE OF FOREIGN WORDS AND ABBREVIATIONS COMMONLY USED IN ENGLISH (E.G. RSVP)

Strategy: RSVP Your Foreign Language In English Literacy

The English language is replete with abbreviations that are shortened forms of words from other languages. Not only can this be used for expanding children's vocabulary and writing variety; but also it can help to positively highlight the bilingual and sometimes trilingual abilities of ELL students.

The teacher should develop a word strip mix and match game with commonly found foreign words and abbreviations. These items should, if possible, be cut out of newspapers and flyers to highlight their authenticity as part of everyday life objects. Those common words and abbreviations might include perfume, liqueur (chocolate, of course), latte, cappuccino, panini, brioche, and latkes. Food, the local Starbucks, coffee houses, and bakeries are excellent sources of these abbreviations. To get sufficient material to cut out to start the game, just get an extra Sunday newspaper or pick up a few circulars from a large supermarket.

Model for the children how to play the game and find out the common words' or abbreviations' meaning and foreign derivation using the dictionary.

Next have the children as a whole class or in small groups work to identify the derivations of the foreign words and even map them on a world map.

As part of additional, foreign word center activities, children can choose from a number of choices, including maintaining a Big Book of foreign words or abbreviations. Many can contribute by using the weekly food circulars and collecting labels with foreign words. These can then be collaged with an accompanying product list, authored stories[tac922], and true accounts, featuring as many foreign words as possible.

What is productive about this strategy is that it enhances vocabulary development while also highlighting the extent to which the English language as spoken, used, and written in the United States currently and is embedded with foreign language words and terms. This, of course, makes the native language talents of the ELL child positive and important ones.

EXTENDING A READER'S UNDERSTANDING OF FAMILIAR WORDS

Dictionary Use

Dictionaries are useful for spelling, writing, and reading.

It is very important to initially expose and habituate students to enjoy using the dictionary.

Cooper (2004) suggests that the following be kept in mind as the teacher of kindergarten through sixth grade introduces and then habituates children to a lifelong fascination with the dictionary and vocabulary acquisition.

Requesting or suggesting that children look up a word in the dictionary should be an invitation to a wonderful exploration, not a punishment or busy work that has no reference to their current reading assignment.

Model the correct way to use the dictionary for children, even as late as the third through the sixth grade. Many have never been taught proper dictionary skills. The teacher needs to demonstrate to the children that as an adult reader and writer, he or she routinely and happily uses the dictionary and learns new information that makes him or her better at reading and writing.

Cooper believes in beginning dictionary study as early as kindergarten, which is now very possible because of the proliferation of lush picture dictionaries that can be introduced at that grade level. He suggests that children not only look at these picture dictionaries but also begin to make their own filled with pictures and beginning words at this grade level. As children join the circle of lexicographers, they will begin to see themselves as compilers and users of dictionaries. Of course, this will support their ongoing vocabulary development.

In early grade levels, use of the dictionary can nicely complement the children's mastery of the alphabet. They should be given whole class and small-group practice in locating words.

As the children progress with their phonetic skills, the dictionary can be used to show them phonetic respelling using the pronunciation key.

Older children in grades 3 and beyond need explicit teacher demonstrations and practice in the use of guide words. They also need to begin to learn about the hierarchies of various word meanings. In the upper grades, children should also explore using special content dictionaries and glossaries in the backs of their books.

COMPETENCY 11.0   UNDERSTAND READING COMPREHENSION SKILLS AND STRATEGIES

THE RELATIONSHIP BETWEEN ORAL AND WRITTEN VOCABULARY DEVELOPMENT AND READING COMPREHENSION

Biemiller[TAR23]'s 2003 research documents that children entering fourth grade with significant vocabulary deficits demonstrate increasing reading comprehension problems. Evidence shows that these children do not catch up, but rather continue to fall behind.

Strategy One: Word Map

This strategy is useful for children in grades 3–6 and beyond. The target group of children for this strategy includes those who need to improve their vocabulary acquisition abilities. The strategy is essentially teacher-directed learning where children are "walked through" the process. They are helped by the teacher to identify the type of information that makes a definition. They are also assisted in using context clues and background understanding to construct meaning.

The word map graphic organizer is the tool teachers use to complete this strategy with children. Word map templates are available online from the Houghton Mifflin Web site and from READWRITETHINK, the Web site of the NCTE (see webliography section). The word map helps the children to visually represent the elements of a given concept.

The children's literal articulation of the concept can be prompted by three key questions: What is it? What is it like? What are some examples?

For instance, the word "oatmeal" might yield a word map with the question "What is it?" and the answer that it is a hot cereal one eats in the morning; "What is it like?" and the answer, hot, mushy, and salty; "What are some examples?" and the answer instant oatmeal you make in a minute, apple-flavor oatmeal, or Irish Oatmeal.

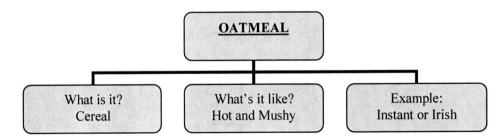

The procedure to be used in sharing this strategy with children is to select three concepts the children are familiar with. Then show them the template of a word map. Tell them that the three questions asked on the map and the boxes to fill in beneath them helps readers and writers to see what they need to know about a word. Next, help the children to complete at least two word maps for two of the three concepts that were preselected. Then have the children select a concept of their own to map either independently or in a small group. As the final task for this first part of the strategy, have the children, in teams or individually, write a definition for at least one of the concepts using the key things about it listed on the map. Have the children share these definitions aloud and talk about how they used the word maps to help them with the definitions.

For the next part of this strategy, the teacher should pick up an expository text or a textbook the children are already using to study mathematics, science, or social studies. The teacher should either locate a short excerpt where a particular concept is defined or use the content to write model passages of definition on his or her own.

After the passages are selected or authored, the teacher should duplicate them. Then they should be distributed to the children along with blank word map templates. The children should be asked to read each passage and then to complete the word map for the concept in each passage. Finally, have the children share the word maps they have developed for each passage. Give them a chance to explain how they used the word in the passage to help them fill out their word map. End by telling them that the three components of the concept—class, description, example—are just three of the many components for any given concept.

This strategy has assessment potential because the teacher can literally see how the students understand specific concepts by looking at their maps and hearing their explanations. The maps the students develop on their own demonstrate whether they have really understood the concepts in the passages. This strategy serves to ready students for inferring word meanings on their own. By using the word map strategy, children develop concepts of what they need to know to begin to figure out an unknown word on their own. It assists the children in grades 3 and beyond to connect prior knowledge with new knowledge.

This word map strategy can be adapted by the teacher to suit the specific needs and goals of instruction. Illustrations of the concept and the comparisons to other concepts can be included in the word mapping for children grades 5 and beyond. This particular strategy is also one that can be used with a research theme in other content areas.

Strategy Two: Preview in Context

This is a direct teaching strategy that allows the teacher to guide the students as they examine words in context prior to reading a passage. Before beginning the strategy, the teacher selects only two or three key concept words. Then the teacher reads carefully to identify passages within the text that evidence strong context clues for the word.

The teacher presents the word and the context to the children. As the teacher reads aloud, the children follow along. Once the teacher has finished reading aloud, the children reread the material silently. After the silent rereading, the children will be coached by the teacher to a definition of one of the key words selected for study. This is done through a child-centered discussion. As part of the discussion, the teacher asks questions that get the children to activate their prior knowledge and to use the contextual clues to figure out the correct meaning of the selected key words. Make certain that the definition of the key concept word is finally made by the children.

Next, help the children to begin to expand the word's meaning. Do this by having them consider the following for the given key concept word: synonyms, antonyms, other contexts or other kinds of stories/texts where the word might appear. This is the time to have the children check their responses to the challenge of identifying word synonyms and antonyms by having them go to the thesaurus or the dictionary to confirm their responses. In addition, have the children place the synonyms or antonyms they find in their word boxes or word journals. The recording of their findings will guarantee them ownership of the words and deepen their capacity to use contextual clues.

The main point to remember in using this strategy is that it should only be used when the context is strong. It will not work with struggling readers who have less prior knowledge. Through listening to the children's responses as the teacher helps them to define the word and its potential synonyms and antonyms, the teacher can assess their ability to successfully use context clues. The key to this simple strategy is that it allows the teacher to draw the child out and to grasp through the child's responses the individual child's thinking process. The more talk from the child, the better.

Strategy Three: Hierarchical and Linear Arrays

The complexity of the vocabulary used in this strategy description may be unnerving for the teacher. Yet this strategy, included in the Cooper (2004) literacy instruction, is really very simple once it is outlined directly for children.

By using the term "hierarchical and linear" arrays, Cooper really is talking about how some words are grouped based on associative meanings. The words may have a "hierarchical" relationship to one another. Classification is the thinking process behind hierarchical arrays. For instance, an undergraduate or a first grader is lower in the school hierarchy than the graduate student and second grader. Within an elementary school, the fifth grader is at the top of the hierarchy and the preschooler or kindergartener is at the bottom of the hierarchy. By the way, the term for this strategy obviously need not be explained in this detail to children in kindergarten through third grade but might be shared with some grade- and age-appropriate modifications with children in grades 3 and beyond. It will enrich their vocabulary development and ownership of arrays they create.

Words can have a linear, or serial, relationship to one another in that they run a spectrum from bad to good. For example, for kindergarteners through third graders, words that describe their experiences could be pleased, happy, and overjoyed. These relationships can be displayed in horizontal boxes connected with dashes. Seriation is the thinking process behind linear arrays. Below is another way to display hierarchical relationships.

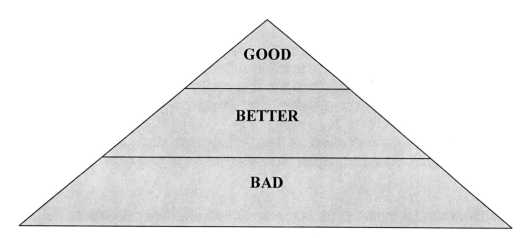

Once you get past the seemingly daunting vocabulary words, the arrays turn out to be another neat graphic organizer tool that can help children "see" how words relate to one another.

To use this graphic organizer, the teacher should preselect a group of words from read-aloud time or from the children's writing. Show the children how the array will look using arrows for the linear array and straight lines for the hierarchy. Invite some children up to draw the straight hierarchy lines as the model is presented so that they have a role in developing even the first hierarchical model.

Do one hierarchy array and one linear array using the preselected word with the children. Talk them through filling out (or helping the teacher to fill out) the array. After the children have had their own successful experience with arrays, they can select the words from their independent texts or familiar, previously read favorites to study. They will also need to decide which type of array, hierarchical or linear, is appropriate. For fifth and sixth graders, this choice can and should be voiced using the now-"owned" vocabulary words "hierarchical array" and "linear array."

This strategy is best used after reading, since it will help the children to expand their word banks.

KNOWLEDGE OF COMMON SAYINGS, PROVERBS AND IDIOMS

Strategy: The Fortune Cookie Strategy

The Fortune Cookie Strategy is discussed by Reissman (1994[TAR24]). It is appropriate for grades 3 and up.[TAR25]

Distribute fortune cookies just before snack time to the children. Allow them to eat the cookies and then draw their attention to the fortunes that are enclosed.

First, the teacher will model by reading aloud and sharing his or her own fortune. After reading the fortune aloud, the teacher will explain what the fortune means, using its vocabulary as a guide. Then the teacher can share whether or not he or she agrees with the statement made in the fortune.

Children can either volunteer to share their fortunes or each can read the fortune aloud, explain the saying, and tell whether he or she agrees with the proverb.

Next, children can be asked to go home and interview their parents or community members to get family proverbs and common sayings.

Once the children return with the sayings and proverbs, they can each share them and explain their meaning. The class as a whole can discuss to what extent these sayings are true for everyone. Proverbs and sayings can become part of a word wall or be included in a special literacy center. The teacher can create fill-in, put together, and writing activities to go with the proverbs. They tie in nicely with cultural study on grades 3–6 levels, including Asian, Latin American, and African nations.

What makes proverbs particularly effective for vocabulary development are their limited number of words and the fact these short texts allow for guided and facilitated reading instruction.

This strategy also highlights in a positive way the uniqueness and commonality of the family proverbs that are contributed by children from ELL backgrounds. If possible, their proverbs can also be posted in their native languages as well as in English.

To write like a Babylonian, see http://www.penn.museum/cgi/cuneiform.cgi

To write like an Egyptian, see http://www.penn.museum/cgi/hieroglyphsreal.cgi

KNOWLEDGE OF READING AS A PROCESS TO CONSTRUCT MEANING

If there were two words synonymous with reading comprehension as far as the balanced literacy approach is concerned, they would be "constructing meaning."

Cooper, Taberski, Strickland[TAR26], and other key theorists and classroom teachers conceptualize the reader as interacting with the text and bringing his or her prior knowledge and experience to it. Writing is interlaced with reading and is a mutually integrative and supportive parallel process. Hence the division of literacy learning by the balanced literacy folks into reading workshops and writing workshops, with the same anchor "readings" or books being used for both.

Consider the sentence, "The test booklet was white with black print, but very scary looking."

According to the idea of constructing meaning as the reader reads this sentence, the schemata (generic information stored in the mind) of tests the reader had experienced was activated by the author's notion that tests are scary. Therefore the ultimate meaning that the reader derives from the page is from the reader's own responses and experiences coupled with the ideas the author presents. The reader constructs a meaning that reflects the author's intent and also the reader's response to that intent.

It is also to be remembered that generally readings are fairly lengthy passages, composed of paragraphs that in turn are composed of more than one sentence. With each successive sentence, and every new paragraph, the reader refocuses. The schemata are reconsidered, and a new meaning is constructed.

KNOWLEDGE OF LEVELS OF READING COMPREHENSION AND STRATEGIES FOR PROMOTING COMPREHENSION OF IMAGINATIVE LITERARY TEXTS AT ALL LEVELS

Taberski (2000) recommends that strategies for promoting comprehension of imaginative literary texts can initially be done with the whole class.

Here are Taberski's four main strategies for promoting comprehension of imaginative literary texts. She feels that if repeated sufficiently during kindergarten through third grade and even if introduced as late as fourth grade, these strategies will serve the adult lifelong reader in good stead.

Strategy One: Stop to think and reflect on the text as a whole.

As part of this strategy, the reader is challenged to come up with the answer to these three questions:

- What do I think is going to happen? (inferential)
- Why do I think this is going to happen? (evaluative and inferential)
- How can I prove that I am right by going back to the story? (inferential)

Taberski recommends that teachers introduce these key instructive strategies with books that can be read in one sitting, including picture books.

Taberski also suggests that books that are read aloud and used for this strategy also contain a strong storyline, some degree of predictability, a text that invites discussion, and a narrative with obvious stopping points.

Strategy Two: Story mapping is used for promoting comprehension of imaginative/literary texts.

For stories to suit this strategy, they should have distinct episodes, few characters, and clear-cut problems to solve. In particular, Taberski tries to use a story where a single, central problem or issue is introduced at the beginning and then resolved or at least followed through by the close of the story. To make this kind of story map, Taberski divides the class into groups and asks one to illustrate the characters in the book. Another group of children are asked to draw the setting, while the third and fourth groups tackle the story's problem and its resolution. The story map may also help children hold together their ideas for writing in the writing workshop, as they take their reading of an author's story to a new level.

Strategy Three: The character mapping strategy also used by Taberski focuses the children as readers on the ways in which the main character's personal traits can determine what will happen in the story. Character mapping works best when the character is a non-stereotypical individual, has been featured perhaps in other books by the same author, has a personality that is somewhat predictable, and is capable of changing behavior as a consequence of what happens.

Using writing to share, deepen, and expand understanding of literary texts is a cornerstone of the balanced literacy approach.

Strategy Four: Taberski advocates reading sections of stories aloud and then having the teacher pause to reflect on what's happened in the story and model writing down a response to it. The teacher can use a chart to record his or her response to the events or characters of a particular story being read and the children can contribute their comments as well. Later on, the children can start reflective reader's notebooks or journals recording their reactions to their readings independently.

The best texts for this type of response are those that include age-appropriate issues for young children (for example, themes such as homework, testing, bullies, and friendship), a plot that can be interpreted in different ways, a story that is filled with questions, and suspense or wonder.

DEVELOPMENT OF LITERARY RESPONSE SKILLS

Literary response skills are dependent on prior knowledge, schemata, and background. Schemata (the plural of schema) are those structures that represent concepts stored in our memory.

Without schemata and experiences to call upon as they read, children have little ability to comprehend. Of course, the reader's schemata and prior knowledge have more influence on the comprehension of plot or character information that is implied rather than directly stated.

Prior Knowledge

Prior knowledge can be defined as all of an individual's prior experiences, learning, and development that precede his or her entering a specific learning situation or attempting to comprehend a specific text. Sometimes prior knowledge can be erroneous or incomplete. Obviously, if there are misconceptions in a child's prior knowledge, these must be corrected so that his or her overall comprehension skills can continue to progress. Children's prior knowledge could include their accumulated positive and negative experiences both in and out of school.

These might come from wonderful family travels, watching television, and visiting museums and libraries to visiting hospitals, prisons, and surviving poverty. Whatever the prior knowledge that children bring to the school setting, the independent reading and writing that they do in school immeasurably expands their prior knowledge and hence broadens reading comprehension capabilities.

As the teacher prepares to begin any imaginative/literary text, he or she must consider the following about the students' level of prior knowledge:

1. What prior knowledge needs to be activated for the text, theme, or writing to be done successfully?
2. How independent are the children in using strategies to activate their prior knowledge?

Holes and Roser (1987[TAR27]) have suggested five techniques for activating prior knowledge before starting an imaginative/literary text:

1. **Free recall:** Tell us what you know about . . .
2. **Unstructured discussion:** Let's talk about. . .
3. **Structured question:** Who exactly was Jane Aviles in the life of the hero of the story?
4. **Word association:** When you hear the words hatch, elephant, who, and think, what author do you think of?
5. **Recognition:** When you think of Mulberry Street, what author comes to mind?

Previewing, predicting, and story mapping are also excellent strategies for activating prior knowledge.

DEVELOPMENT OF LITERARY ANALYSIS SKILLS

There are many exciting ways to sensitize and teach children about the features and formats of different literary genres.

Strategy One: Genre Switch, Reader and Writer Transformation

This strategy should be introduced during read-aloud time with young children, with those who are struggling readers, or with ELL learners. Older children in grades 3–6 might just be started off by a teacher prompt and do the required reading on their own.

To begin, the teacher selects a particular genre book. If it is close to Halloween, a goblin or suspense story will do well. The teacher begins to read the story with the open invitation to the students to determine what type of story it is and what makes it that type of story.

Older children can take notes in their reading journals, while younger children and those more in need of explicit teacher support can contribute their ideas and responses as part of the discussion in class. Their responses are recorded on a chart.

As the reading continues, the story type components are listed on the chart (most of the responses are those that have been elicited from the children).

At some point during either read-aloud time, guided reading, or independent reading, the teacher directs the children's attention to the components that have emerged on the chart. They then use these components that are generally components of story—character, setting, plot, style, conflict, and language—to identify the story genre.

The teacher provides the children with an opportunity to expound at length on why this story is an example of the genre that they have identified. Once they have done so, the teacher challenges them to consider how this story, with its set of given characters, plot, and setting, would be changed if the genre were different. The teacher can challenge the class as a whole with the idea of changing the story to a radically different genre, for example, from suspense to a fairy tale or a comedy, or allow the children to come up another genre.

Then depending on the children's developed writing abilities, they might be given time to rewrite the story on their own or retell it in class prior to writing and illustrating it.

In the balanced literacy approach, this transformation of the story into another genre is done as part of the writing workshop component that uses the same reading material as the source for writing. This strategy results in the children having had the experience of an in-depth analysis of a particular genre as well as hands-on writing (or telling, if they cannot yet write or cannot yet write in English) experience of restyling the basic plot and characters into another genre. This authenticates the children's participation as readers and writers.

Strategy Two: Analyzing Story Elements

Story elements include plot (conflict and resolution), setting (time and place), characters (flat and round or static and dynamic), and theme (the main idea of the story). Students can use graphic organizers such as story maps, compare/contrast displays, and sequence boxes to display their understanding of these critical features of fiction.

Strategy Three: Analyzing Character Development

Characters in children's literature may be flat or round. A flat character is one-dimensional and is often defined by one characteristic. Rosie in *Rosie's Walk* is an example. A round character seems like someone familiar, such as Jesse in *Bridge to Terabithia*. Static characters do not change from the beginning to the end of the story, while dynamic ones do. Characters reveal themselves through their actions, their interactions, and by what they say.

Strategy Four: Interpreting Figurative Language

Similes are direct comparisons between two things using "like" or "as." "Her eyes were like stars" is a simile. Metaphors are indirect comparisons, such as "The earth is a big blue marble." Personification is giving human characteristics to non-animal beings. Frances, Shrek, or the animals in *Mr. Gumpy's Outing* are all examples of personification.

Strategy Five: Identifying Literary Allusions

Children can understand allusions best when they read a lot. When it appears in a story, a literary allusion is also called *intertextuality*. That is when a reference, character, or symbol from one story appears or is alluded to in another. Recently, many popular children's books used literary allusions, from the Ahlbergs' *Each Peach Pear Plum* to Jon Scieszka's *The True Story of the Three Little Pigs*. Note that any character or plot element can become an allusion, not just references from fairy tales.

Strategy Six: Analyzing the Author's Point of View

In fiction, point of view is the vantage point from which the narrator tells the story. We determine point of view by asking questions, such as, where is the narrator standing in relation to the characters? Is the narrator inside or outside of the story? If inside, is the narrator one of the characters? This is called *first person point of view*. If outside, can the narrator "see" into anyone else's mind besides his or her own? If the narrator cannot see into the mind and heart of other characters, then the point of view is *third person limited*. Narrators who can see what other characters are thinking and feeling are using *third person omniscient point of view*.

USE OF COMPREHENSION STRATEGIES BEFORE, DURING, AND AFTER READING

Cooper (2004), Taberski (2000), Cox (2005) and other researchers recommend a broad array of comprehension strategies before, during, and after reading.

Cooper suggests a broad range of classroom posters on the walls plus explicit instruction to give children prompts to monitor their own reading. The following is his "My Strategic Reading Guide."

1. Do I infer/predict important information, use what I know, think about what may happen or what I want to learn?
2. Can I identify important information about the story elements?
3. Do I generate questions and search for the answers?
4. Does this make sense to me? Does this help me meet my purpose in reading?
5. If lost, do I remember fix-ups?
6. Reread, read further ahead, look at the illustrations, ask for help, think about the words, and evaluate what I have read.
7. Do I remember to think about how the parts of the stories that I was rereading came together?

Storyboard panels, which are used by comic strip artists, artists who do advertising campaigns, and television and film directors, are perfect for engaging children in kindergarten through sixth grade in a variety of comprehension strategies before, during, and after reading. They can storyboard the beginning of a story, read it aloud, and then storyboard its predicted middle or end. Of course, after they experience or read the actual middle or ending of the story, they can compare and contrast what they produced with its actual structure. They can play familiar literature identification games with a buddy or as part of a center by storyboarding one key scene or characters from a book and challenging a partner or peer to identify the book and characters correctly.

USE OF ORAL LANGUAGE ACTIVITIES TO PROMOTE COMPREHENSION

Retelling

Retelling needs to be very clearly defined so that the child reader does not think that the teacher wants him or her to spill the *whole* story back in the retelling. A child should be able to talk comfortably and fluently about the story he or she has just read. He or she should be able to tell the main things that have happened in the story.

When a child retells a story to a teacher, the teacher needs ways to help the child assess his or her understanding. Ironically, the teacher can use some of the same strategies he or she suggests to the child to assess the child's understanding of a book that is not familiar to the teacher. These strategies include the following: back cover reading, scanning the table of contents, looking at the pictures, and reading the book jacket.

If the child can explain how the story turned out and provide examples to support these explanations, try not to interrupt him or her with too many questions.

Children can use the text of the book to reinforce what they are saying and they can even read from it if they wish. It is also important to note that some children need to reread the text twice, which is out of enjoyment.

When the teacher plans to use the retelling as a way of assessing the child, then the following ground rules have to be set and made clear to the child.

The teacher explains the purpose of the retelling to determine how well the child is reading at the outset of the conference.

The teacher maintains in the child's assessment notebook or in his or her assessment record what the child is saying in phrases, not sentences.

Just enough is recorded to indicate whether the child actually understood the story. The teacher also tries to analyze from the retelling why the child cannot comprehend a given text. If the child's accuracy rate with the text is below 95%, then the problem is at the word level, but if the accuracy rate for the text is above 95%, the difficulty lies at the text level.

DEVELOPMENT OF THE READING COMPREHENSION SKILLS AND STRATEGIES OF INDIVIDUAL STUDENTS

ELL students bring to their classrooms different prior knowledge concerns than do their native English language speaking peers. Some of the ELL students have extensive prior knowledge in their native language and can read well on or above their chronological age level in their native language. Other ELL students come to the United States from cultures where reading was not emphasized or circumstances did not give families native language literacy opportunities.

Rigg and Allen (1999[TAR28]) offer the following four principles regarding the literacy development and prior knowledge of ELL/second-language learners:

1. In learning a language, one learns to do the things with people who are speaking that language.
2. A second language, like the first, does not develop linearly, but rather globally.
3. Language can develop in rich context.
4. Literacy develops parallel to language, so as speaking and listening for the second language develop, so do writing and reading.

As far as retelling, it needs to be noted that English language learners have the problem of not bringing rich oral English vocabulary to the stories they are decoding. Therefore, often they "sound the stories out" well but cannot explain what they are about because they do not know what the words mean.

USE OF ORAL READING FLUENCY IN FACILITATING COMPREHENSION

At some point it is crucial that just as the nervous, novice bike rider finally relaxes and speeds happily off, so too must the early reader integrate graphophonic cues with semantic and structural ones. Before this is done, the oral quality of early readers has a stilted beat to it, which of course does not promote reading engagement and enjoyment.

The teacher needs to be at his or her most dramatic to model for children the beauties of voice and nuance that are contained in the texts whose print they are tracking so anxiously. Children love nothing more than to mimic their teacher and can do so legitimately and without hesitation if the teacher takes time each day to recite a poem with them. The poem might then be posted on chart paper and put up on the wall for a week.

First, the teacher can model the fluent and expressive reading of the poem. Then with a pointer, the class can recite it with the teacher. As the week progresses, the class can recite it on their own.

USE OF WRITING ACTIVITIES TO PROMOTE LITERARY RESPONSE AND ANALYSIS

In addition to the activities already mentioned, the ones listed below will promote literary response and analysis:

- Have children take a particular passage from a story and retell it from another character's perspective.
- Challenge children to suggest a sequel or a prequel to any given story they have read.
- Ask the children to recast a story in which the key characters are male into one where the key characters are female (or vice versa). Have them explain how these changes alter the narrative, plot, or outcome.
- Encourage the children to transform a story or book into a reader's theater format and record it, complete with sound effects, for the audio-cassette center of the classroom.
- Have the children produce a newspaper as the characters of a given story would have reported the news in their community.
- Transform the story into a ballad poem or a picture book version for younger peers.
- Give ELL children an opportunity to translate stories into their native language or to author in English with a buddy a favorite story that was originally published in their native language.

COMPETENCY 12.0   UNDERSTAND READING SKILLS ASSOCIATED WITH CONTENT-AREA LITERACY

STRATEGIES FOR PROMOTING COMPREHENSION ACROSS THE CURRICULUM BY EXPANDING KNOWLEDGE OF CONTENT AREA VOCABULARY

Key Words

Cooper (2004) feels that it is up to the teacher to preview the content area text to identify the main ideas. Then the teacher should compile a list of terms related to the content thrust. These terms and words become part of the key concepts list.

Next, the teacher sees which of the key concept words and terms are already defined in the text. These will not require direct teaching. Words for which children have sufficient skills to determine their meaning through base, root, prefixes, or suffixes also will not require direct teaching.

Instruction in the remaining key words, which should not be more than two or three in number, can be provided before, during, or after reading. If students have previewed the content area and identified those words they need support on, the instruction should be provided before reading. Instruction can also easily be provided as part of guided reading support. After reading support is indicated, the text offers the children an opportunity to enrich their own vocabularies.

Having children work as a whole class or in small groups on a content-specific dictionary for a topic regularly covered in their grade level social studies, science, or mathematics curriculum offers an excellent collaborative opportunity for children to design a dictionary/word resource that can celebrate their own vocabulary learning. Such a resource can then be used with the next year's classes as well.

DEVELOPMENT OF VOCABULARY KNOWLEDGE AND SKILLS IN INDIVIDUAL STUDENTS

Hierarchical and linear array vocabulary development strategies lend themselves well to support the struggling learners or second language learners. The use of the arrays allows these learners to use a visual format to "see" and diagram word relationships. Furthermore the diagrams are easy to make, and they can be illustrated. With sufficient support and modeling, many special needs children can do simple linear and hierarchical arrays on their own. The arrays can also be attractively displayed in resource rooms and in regular education classrooms as a demonstration of these individual students' ownership of their words.

English language learners should first demonstrate their capacity to fill out hierarchical and linear arrays in their native language and then work with this same format to hone their English language vocabulary development. Their native language hierarchical relationships and arrays can be displayed in their general education classrooms. Teachers may also want to encourage children grades 3 and beyond to make connections between some of the native words and words derived from them in English. This could be a rich "buddy" (ELL child and native English language speaker) investigation or it could be one for ELL children alone. At any rate, use of the array with the ELL child's native language makes that child a second language vocabulary owner, which immediately includes the child positively in ongoing vocabulary development.

Cooper (2004) suggests that teachers who have children from different language backgrounds use any unscheduled or "extra" time that emerges for read-aloud time.

USING THE SEMANTIC FEATURE ANALYSIS GRID

Highly proficient readers can be asked to help same-grade peers or younger peers with their word analysis skills by having them work with these struggling readers on filling out teacher-developed semantic analysis grids. Some fifth and sixth grade highly proficient readers may also evidence the aptitude and desire to create their own semantic analysis grids for their same grade or younger peer tutees. In this way, highly proficient readers can gain insights into the field of teaching reading at an early age, and younger struggling readers can have the edge taken off their struggles by working with a peer or an older student. For both individual students, the experience is one that promotes and celebrates word analysis skills and nurtures the concept of a literate and caring community of readers.

ELL students can also add in items to the categories that reflect their cultures. For instance, Latino children can add in plantains and guava to the fruits their non-Latino peers might list. This provides the ELL children with an opportunity to enrich the knowledge base of their peers' inventory and puts them in a positive spotlight. The easy notations on the grid make it accessible for even ELL children with limited English language writing and speaking capacities.

Special needs learners can benefit from the grid. It can be developed by teachers, paraprofessionals, and tutors. It can be notated by the children themselves. They can also illustrate it. It can be posted or kept in the word center. The grid provides these learners who are often spatial learners with a concrete demonstration of their word analysis achievement.

Biemiller's research indicates that the listening vocabulary for a sixth grader who tests at the 25th percentile in reading is equivalent to that attained by the 75th percentile third grader. This deficit in vocabulary presents a formidable challenge for the sixth grader to succeed, not only on reading tests but also in various content subjects in elementary school and beyond.

KNOWLEDGE OF LEVELS OF READING COMPREHENSION (LITERAL, INFERENTIAL, AND EVALUATIVE) AND STRATEGIES FOR PROMOTING COMPREHENSION OF INFORMATIONAL/EXPOSITORY TEXTS AT ALL THREE LEVELS

There are five key strategies for child reading of informational/expository texts:

1. Inferencing is a process that involves the reader making a reasonable judgment based on the information given and engages children to literally construct meaning. In order to develop and enhance this key skill in children, they might have a mini-lesson where the teacher demonstrates this by reading an expository book aloud (such as one on skyscrapers for young children) and then demonstrates for them the following reading habits:

   - Looking for clues
   - Reflecting on what the reader already knows about the topic
   - Using the clues to figure out what the author means/intends

2. Identifying main ideas in an expository text can be improved when the children have an explicit strategy for identifying important information. They can make this strategy part of their everyday reading style, "walking" through the following exercises during guided reading sessions:
   - The child should read the passage so that the topic is readily identifiable to him or her. It will be what most of the information is about.

- Next the child should be asked to be on the lookout for a sentence within the expository passage that summarizes the key information in the paragraph.
- The child should read the rest of the passage or excerpt in light of this information and also note which information in the paragraph is less important. The important information the child has identified in the paragraph can be used to formulate the author's main idea. The child reader may even want to use some of the author's own language in stating that idea.

3. Monitoring means self-clarifying. The reader often realizes that what he or she is reading is not making sense. The reader then has to have a plan for making sensible meaning out of the excerpt. Cooper and other balanced literacy advocates have a stop and think strategy with children. The child reflects, "Does this make sense to me?" When the child concludes that it does not, the child then either rereads, reads ahead in the text, looks up unknown words, or asks for help from the teacher. What is important about monitoring is that some readers ask these questions and try these approaches without ever being explicitly taught them in school by a teacher. However, these strategies need to be explicitly modeled and practiced under the guidance of the teacher by most, if not all child readers.

4. Summarizing engages the reader in pulling together into a cohesive whole the essential bits of information within a longer passage or excerpt of text. Children can be taught to summarize informational or expository text by following these guidelines:

- First they should look at the topic sentence of the paragraph or the text and ignore the trivia.
- Then they should search for information that has been mentioned more than once and make sure it is included only once in their summary. Find related ideas or items and group them under a unifying heading. Search for and identify a main idea sentence.
- Finally, put the summary together using all these guidelines.

5. Generating questions can motivate and enhance children's comprehension of reading in that they are actively involved. The following guidelines will help children generate meaningful questions that will trigger constructive reading of expository texts.

- First children should preview the text by reading the titles and subheadings.
- They should also look at the illustrations and the pictures.
- Then they should read the first paragraph. These first previews should yield an impressive batch of specific questions.

- Next, children should get into a Dr. Seuss mode and ask themselves a "think" question. Make certain that the children write down the question.
- Then have them read to find important information to answer their "think" question. Ask that they write down the answer they found and copy the sentence or sentences where they found the answer. Also have them consider whether, in light of their further reading through the text, their original question was a good one or not.
- Ask them to be prepared to explain why their original question was a good one or not. Once the children have answered their original "think" question, have them generate additional ones and then find their answers and judge whether these questions were good ones in light of the text.

STRATEGIES FOR IDENTIFYING POINT OF VIEW, DISTINGUISHING FACTS FROM OPINIONS AND DETECTING FAULTY REASONING IN INFORMATIONAL/EXPOSITORY TEXTS

Expository texts are full of information that may or may not be factual and may reflect the bias of the editor or author. Children need to learn that expository texts are organized around main ideas. Expository content is commonly found in newspapers, magazines, content textbooks, and informational reference books (such as an atlas, an almanac, or a yearbook of an encyclopedia).

The following five types of expository texts (also called "text structures") should be introduced to the children through modeled reading and a teacher facilitated walk through:

Description Text: This usually gives the characteristics or qualities of a particular topic. It can be depended upon to be factual. Within this type of text, the child reader has to use all of his or her basic reading strategies because these types of expository texts do not have explicit clue words.

Causation or Cause-Effect Text: This text is one where faulty reasoning may come into play and the child reader has to use inferential and self-questioning skills to assess whether the stated cause-effect relationship is a valid one. Clue words to look for are therefore, the reasons for, as a result of, because, in consequence of, and since. The reader must then decide whether the relationship is valid.

Comparison Text: This is an expository text that gives contrasts and similarities between two or more objects and ideas. Many social studies, art, and science textbooks in class and nonfiction books include this contrast. Key words to look out for are like, unlike, resemble, different, different from, similar to, in contrast with, in comparison to, and in a different vein. As children examine texts that are talking about illustrated or photographed entities, it is important that they can review the graphic representations for clues to support or contradict the text.

Collection Text: This text presents ideas in a group. The writer presents a set of related points or ideas. This text structure is also called a listing or a sequence. The author frequently uses clue words, such as first, second, third, finally, and next, to alert the reader to the sequence. Based on how well the writer structures the sequence of points or ideas, the reader should be able to make connections. It is important for the writer to make clear in the expository text how the items are related and why they follow in that given sequence. For example, simple collection texts that can be literally modeled for young children include recipe making. A class of first graders, who were beginning readers and writers, were literally spellbound by a teacher's presentation of a widely known copyrighted collection text. The children were thrilled as the author followed the sequences of this collection text, and the children finally took turns stirring it until it was creamy and smooth. The children enjoyed eating their Cream Farina from a commercial cereal box that had cooking directions on it.

The children had constructed meaning from this five minute class demonstration and would now pay close attention to collection texts on other food and product instruction boxes because this text had become an authentic part of their lives.

Response Structure Expository Texts: These present a question or response followed by an answer or a solution. Of course, entire mathematics textbooks and some science and social studies textbooks are filled with these types of structures. Again it is important to walk the child reader through the excerpt and to sensitize the child to the clue words that signal this type of structure. These words include but are not limited to the problem is, the question is, you need to solve for, one probable solution would be, an intervention could be, the concern is, and another way to solve this would be.

Newspapers provide wonderful features that can be used by the teacher during read-aloud time to introduce children grades 3–6 to point of view distinctions, specifically, editorials, editorial cartoons, and key sports editorial cartoons. Children can also come to understand the distinction between fact and fiction when they examine a newspaper advertisement or a supermarket circular for a product they commonly use, eat, drink, or wear that includes exaggerated claims about what the product can actually do for the individual in question.

Finally the fact versus opinion distinction can be nicely explored if a teacher takes the children online to look at some movie star Web sites and walks them through some exaggerated claims made about their favorite actors. It is very important at some point, if the children have access to the Internet, that the teacher show them how to examine Web sites, look at who developed them, and consider how credible the developers of the site are.

USE OF READING STRATEGIES FOR DIFFERENT TEXTS AND STRATEGIES

As children progress to the older grades (3–6), it is important for the teacher to model for them that in research on a social studies or science exploration, it may not be necessary to read every single word of a given expository information text. For instance, if the child is trying to find out about hieroglyphics, he or she might only read through those sections of a book on Egyptian or Sumerian civilization that dealt with picture writing. The teacher, assisted by a child, should model how to go through the table of contents and the index of the book to identify only those pages that deal with picture writing. In addition other children should come to the front of the room or to the center of the area where the reading group is meeting. They should then, with the support of the teacher, skim through the book for illustrations or diagrams of picture writing that is the focus of their need.

Children can practice the skills of skimming texts and scanning for particular topics that connect with their grade social studies, science, and mathematics content area interests.

USE OF COMPREHENSION SKILLS BEFORE, AFTER, AND DURING READING

Cooper (2004) advocates that the child ask him or herself what a text is about before he or she reads it and again during reading of the text. The child should be continually questioning him or herself as to whether the text confirmed the child's predictions. Of course after completing the text, the child can then review the predictions and verify whether they were correct.

Using another strategy, the child reader looks over the expository text subheadings, illustrations, captions, and indices to get an idea about the book. Then the child, still before reading the text, decides whether he or she can find the answer to his or her question.

USE OF ORAL LANGUAGE ACTIVITIES TO PROMOTE COMPREHENSION

Taberski (2000) advocates using the "Stopping to Think About" strategy with expository texts as well as fictional ones.

This strategy is centered on the reader's using three steps as he or she goes through the expository text. These steps may be expressed as questions.

1. What do I, the reader, think is going to happen?

2. What clues in the text, illustrations, or graphics lead me to think that this is going to happen?

3. How can I prove that I am right by going back to the text to demonstrate that this does happen or is suggested by actual clues in the text?

Taberski deliberately uses expository texts that relate to her grade's social studies and science lessons to model for children how to stop and think about the way an expository text is organized. She sometimes deliberately reads a section of a text or a nonfiction book aloud until the end of its chapter, so that the children can consider what they have learned about the topic and how it is organized. Then together as a whole class or as a whole guided reading group, they make predictions about what is coming next.

DEVELOPMENT OF READING COMPREHENSION SKILLS AND STRATEGIES OF INDIVIDUAL STUDENTS

While all child readers can benefit from explicit expository reading strategies, the English language learner can truly get a gateway for understanding second language materials by working with a native English language speaking buddy on the question-generating strategy. Both the buddy (a peer) and the teacher should alert and walk through with the English language learner student how much of a resource illustrations and pictures can be for constructing meaning.

If the teacher has time to work individually with the English language learner, the day's daily newspaper, which is replete with graphics, photos, and text, is a wonderful tool for honing expository reading skills using these strategies.

The five strategies for enhancing expository reading skills are not beyond use with learners with special needs. However, rather than be offered in an array, these strategies would have to be presented one at a time, probably one on one with explicit teacher modeling and then done as shared reading and shared writing with the specific child.

Highly proficient readers might enjoy sharing their skills with other peers and could serve as the newspaper reading buddies for special needs students. They might not only support special needs grade level or younger peers in reading through a designated newspaper section every day but also collaborate or oversee these peer in designing a word search or crossword puzzle based on that particular section of the newspaper.

Use of editorial sports page cartoons is a good way to introduce special needs learners to opportunities for identifying point of view. They can also create their own takes on the topics of the editorial cartoons using an accessible, non-threatening storyboard format for their commentary.

THE ROLE OF ORAL LANGUAGE FLUENCY IN FACILITATING THE COMPREHENSION OF INFORMATIONAL/EXPOSITORY TEXTS

Children in the middle and secondary levels of education who are studying social studies content have been exposed to what social studies educators call re-enactments. This is a reader's theater version of history and cultural study based completely on fact and established historical texts and documents.

Even young children will enjoy and gain tremendous additional expository comprehension facility when they are asked to dramatize a well-known historical document or song. They may act out the preamble to the Constitution or read aloud as a chorus the Declaration of Independence or dramatize the "Battle Hymn of the Republic." This gives children an opportunity to examine in deep form the vocabulary, syntactic, and semantic clues of these texts. They then have to use their oral instruments (voices) to express the appropriate expression for the texts.

If the children are in grades 4 and above, they can also be asked to "explain" in writing how they used the word, syntactic, and semantic clues to interpret their oral language recitation. Recitation and writing can be a powerful experience for children grades 4 and up as they build their expository reading and writing skills.

USE OF WRITING ACTIVITIES TO PROMOTE COMPREHENSION

K-W-L Strategy

This is a graphic organizer strategy that activates children's prior knowledge and also helps them to target their reading of expository texts. This focus is achieved through having the children reflect on three key questions.

Before the child reads the expository passage:

  1. "What do I *Know*?"
  2. "What do I or we *Want* to find out?"

After the child has read the expository passage:

  3. "What have I or we *Learned* from the passage?"

What is excellent about this strategy, which is broadly used and easily implemented in almost any classroom, is that it is almost totally student-centered and powerfully focuses the child's attention on the actual reading of expository passages. The K-W-L strategy also helps the child prepare for a potential writing task.

When the teacher first introduces the K-W-L strategy, the children should be allowed sufficient time to brainstorm what everyone in the class or small group actually know about the topic. The children should have a three-columned K-W-L worksheet template for their journals and there should be a chart up front to record the responses from class or group discussion. The children can write under each column in their own journal and should also help the teacher with notations on the chart. This strategy involves the children actually gaining experience in note taking and having a concrete record of new data and information they have gleaned from the passage about the topic.

Depending on the grade level of the participating children, the teacher may also want to channel them into considering categories of information they hope to find out from the expository passage. For instance, they may be reading a book on animals to find out more about the animal's habitats during the winter or about the animal's mating habits.

When children are working on the middle section (*Want*) strategy sheet, the teacher may give them a chance to share what they would like to learn further about the topic and help them to express it in question format.

K-W-L is useful and can even be introduced as early as grade 2 with extensive teacher support. It not only serves to support the child's comprehension of a particular expository text but also models for children a format for note taking. Beyond note taking, when the teacher wants to introduce report writing, the K-W-L format provides excellent outlines and question introductions for at least three paragraphs of a report.

Cooper (2004) recommends this strategy for use with thematic units and with reading chapters in required science, social studies, or health textbooks. In addition to its usefulness with thematic unit study, K-W-L is wonderful for providing the teacher with a concrete format to assess how well children have absorbed pertinent new knowledge within the passage (by looking at the *Learn* section). Ultimately it is hoped that students will learn to use this strategy not only under explicit teacher direction with templates of K-W-L sheets but also on their own by informally writing questions they want to find out about in their journals and then going back to their own questions and answering them after reading.

USE OF TEXT FEATURES (INDEX, GLOSSARY), GRAPHIC FEATURES (CHARTS, MAPS), AND REFERENCE MATERIALS

Traditionally, the aspects of expository text reading comprehension have been taught in a dry format using reference books from the school or public library, particularly, the atlas, almanac, and dusty large geography volumes, to teach these necessary and meaningful skills.

Although these worthy library and perhaps classroom library books can still be used, it is much easier to take a simple newspaper to introduce and provide children with daily ongoing, authentic experiences in learning these necessary skills as they also keep up with real world events that affect their daily lives.

They can go on a chronological hunt through the daily newspaper and discover the many formats of schedules contained therein. For instance, some newspapers include a calendar of the week with literary, sports, social, movie, and other public events. Children can also go on scavenger hunts through various sections of the newspaper and on certain days find full-blown timelines detailing famous individual's careers, business histories, and milestones in the political history of a nation or even key movies made by a famous movie director up for an Oscar.

The nature of the newspaper reportage and the public's need to know the why and wherefore behind the story of natural disasters, company takeovers, political downfalls, and uprisings leads newspapers to represent events graphically and to use cause/effect diagramming and comparison/contrast wording If the teacher specifically wants to make certain that the students come away with this material, he or she can pre-clip "teaching" stories from the news for the child and introduce them in a special news center.

After children have been walked through these comparison/contrast news writings and cause/effect diagramming as it has appeared in the newspaper, they can be challenged to find additional examples of these text structures in the news or challenged to reframe or rewrite familiar stories using these text structures. They can even use desktop publishing to re-author the stories using the same text structures.

If a class participates in a local Newspaper in Education program, where the children receive a free newspaper two to three times a week within the classroom, the teacher can teach indexing skills using the index of the newspaper and have children compete or cooperate in small groups to find various features.

Map and chart skills take on much more relevance and excitement when the children work on these skills using sport charts detailing the batting averages and pass completions of their favorite players or perhaps the box scores of their older siblings' football and baseball games. Maps dealing with holiday weather become meaningful to children as they anticipate a holiday vacation.

ABILITY TO APPLY READING SKILLS FOR VARIOUS PURPOSES

What is really intriguing about the use of newspapers as a model and an authentic platform for introducing children into recognizing and using expository text structures, features, and references, is that the children can demonstrate their mastery of these structures by putting out their own newspapers detailing their school universe using some of these text structures. They can also create their own timelines for projects or research papers they have done in class using newspaper models.

APPLICATION OF COMPREHENSION STRATEGIES FOR ELECTRONIC TEXTS

If there are newspapers in the classroom as part of an ongoing Newspapers in Education program, it is natural and easy for the teacher to take the time to show children how the same news is covered online. All of the newspapers have e-news. Children can first do a K-W-L on what they know or think they know about e-news and then actually review their specific daily newspaper's site. With the support of the teacher or an older peer, they can examine the resource and perhaps note the following differences in electronic text:

- Use of moving pictures and video to document events
- Use of sound clips in addition to written text
- Use of music/sound effects not in printed text
- Links to other Web resources and to other archived articles

Of course, this can lead to much rich discussion and to further detailed Web versus print news resource analysis. For children in grades 5 and 6, this might even include a research investigation of a particular news story or event, including broadcast media coverage.

DEVELOPMENT OF READING COMPREHENSION SKILLS AND STRATEGIES OF INDIVIDUAL STUDENTS

Both English language learners and struggling readers can benefit from the structure and format of the K-W-L approach. It allows them to share their prior experiences and knowledge of the topics covered in the expository text through natural conversation, and it provides them with a natural device for the teacher or tutor to customize and to scaffold instruction to meet their linguistic and experiential backgrounds. Through the discussion and sharing of other children's comments, struggling readers and children from ELL backgrounds have an opportunity to learn how to use questions to "walk through" and take notes on expository writing.

Highly proficient readers can do a comparative expository news event study between print accounts, e-news reportage, and broadcast media coverage. They can prepare charts and their own news mock-up to show the similarities and contrasts between what aspects of the event get covered in what media format. They may also want to write to actual reporters and editors from the different media to share their insights and see if they get a response.

If we want children to become strategic readers, then we create classrooms that reinforce the strategies we've demonstrated and allow children to practice on books that match their needs.

—Sharon Taberski

COMPETENCY 13.0 UNDERSTAND THE DEVELOPMENT OF EFFECTIVE STUDY SKILLS

With the advent of the Internet, the art of research and study skills in texts is becoming lost. It is, however, a skill that needs to be emphasized and explained to students. Understanding reference materials will provide the students with the necessary foundational to prepare them for future learning.

Students need to be able to locate the information that they need for projects or to further their learning. In order to be able to find the information they need, students will need knowledge of using indexes, tables of contents, and other time-saving helpers.

Furthermore, students need to be taught how to read and interpret graphs, charts, and maps that will be found within reference materials and content-specific materials. Being able to correctly interpret these types of information will better allow the student to draw appropriate conclusions. It will enhance the knowledge the student gains from reading and provide further clarification.

Once the children understand how to access and interpret the information contained in content-specific materials or reference materials, they can then begin to analyze it to clarify their thinking process and make connections to their own life or information from other texts. Sometimes the students will find conflicting pieces of information that they will be able to then look at in a more in-depth manner.

Processing information in this way takes the level of reading to an even higher level. It also requires students to find their own method for integrating information into their personal schema for later recall.

Teaching students specific study skills like note taking, summarizing, using graphic organizers, semantic mapping, and time management will allow for effective use of the reference materials available to them. Teaching students such techniques as SQ3R (survey, question, read, recite, and review) also helps them comprehend nonfiction texts in the content areas.

COMPETENCY 14.0   **UNDERSTAND THE ROLE OF ORAL AND WRITTEN LANGUAGE IN THE DEVELOPMENT OF READING PROFICIENCY**

See Competencies 10.0, 11.0, 12.0

COMPETENCY 15.0   **UNDERSTAND STRATEGIES FOR PROMOTING THE READING DEVELOPMENT OF STUDENTS WITH READING DIFFICULTIES**

See Competencies 10.0, 11.0, 12.0

SUBAREA III.   THE ROLE OF THE LITERACY PROFESSIONAL

COMPETENCY 16.0   UNDERSTAND HOW TO ORGANIZE EFFECTIVE LITERACY ENVIRONMENTS AND TO MANAGE LITERACY PROGRAMS

See competency 1.0

STRATEGIES FOR PLANNING, ORGANIZING, MANAGING, AND DIFFERENTIATING READING INSTRUCTION TO SUPPORT THE READING DEVELOPMENT OF ALL STUDENTS

The physical set up of your classroom is exceedingly important to support the effective development of all children.

Understanding Our Role and Goals

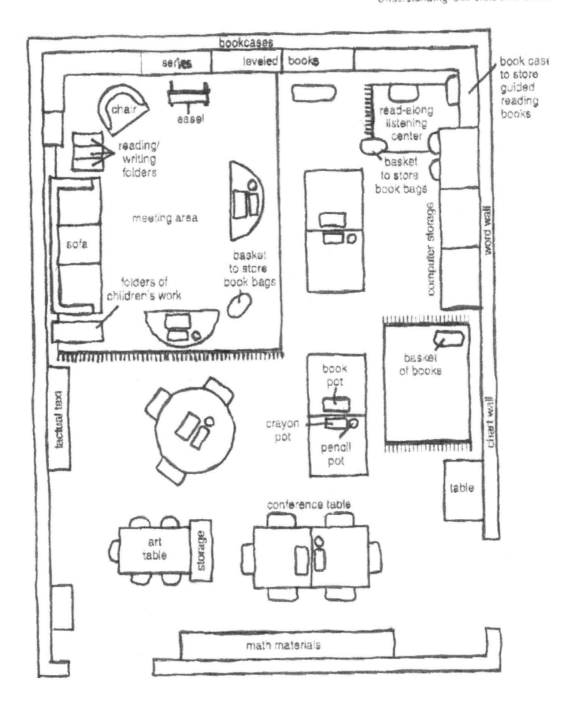

The homey look of the classroom belies its deliberate design as a space where children can experience, practice, share, and learn. Some teachers have done away with the large desk and use smaller tables instead. Taberski advocates for young children in kindergarten through third grade to adjust the height of the table legs so they can use the tables as writing spaces and sit on the floor. She gives each of her children a personal 12" x 9" x 2" tray on which they place their home possessions, books, homework, and folder. This is kept in a small storage unit near the coat closet during the day.

Children put their completed homework in one wire basket and notes from parents or the office in a second wire basket. Supplies such as pencils, markers, crayons, scissors, and erasers are not brought from home but rather are available for all in the class from "community" containers at the center of each of the children's tables.

All the children's reading, writing, and individual math folders are stored together in plastic bins in the meeting area. Every child has an individual book bag that is kept in one of two large wicker baskets set in different areas of the room.

This storing of materials away from children decreases their "fiddling with" personal belongings during class, makes the room look much neater, and frees the children to focus on their learning experiences rather than where their belongings are at any given time of day.

As can be seen on the accompanying diagram, the 10' x 10' meeting area is the center of classroom learning. This is where the whole class is gathered at the beginning of the reading and the writing workshop and for sharing sessions. It is also the demonstration and modeling center for both the teacher and for children.

Generally, the presenter sits on the adult chair (in some balanced literacy classrooms, this is a rocking chair) near the easel with the chart. Generally, this chair and the easel are strategically positioned so that the teacher can see the door and any visitors or urgent messages from the office. Rearranging furniture during the day takes away from instruction time and is disruptive. Have a designated comfortable section of the room that can be a gathering place for a literacy community and then organize the rest of the classroom activities around that center.

The conference table that is at the back of the room (see diagram) is another key piece of classroom space furniture. It is the place where four or five children and the teacher confer, wait, and do their work. Having children come to a set conference table rather than the teacher's going to them (although some teachers do advocate going to the children) saves time as far as Taberski is concerned. It serves to keep her and the children on task.

Taberski keeps two separate trays of supplies that include a small magnetic board, letters, chalkboard, chalk, sentence strips, index cards, and blank books for her demonstrations during her conferences. She believes that teachers should store materials close to where they are used, so the teacher does not have to take time from the child to get up and get the materials.

The Classroom Library

On the tables, Taberski generally has book crates with books that are not leveled. Children choose from these books during the first independent reading session of her day, which is from 8:40–9:00 a.m. During the second reading session, from 9:30–10:20 a.m., the children select books from the leveled reading bins that are stored on the bookcase shelves.

Beyond the leveled books, which have already been discussed, Taberski also maintains a non-leveled, nonfiction library that includes dictionaries, atlases, almanacs, and informational books related to the themes, projects, and investigations that the children will undertake throughout the year.

In addition, Taberski and other balanced literacy advocates generally include at least 10 to 15 Big Books, which they routinely use to engage children with the text.

Since guided reading with groups of six children is a major part of the balanced literacy approach, Taberski and other teacher educators "bundle" up six copies of selected books so that they can distribute them to their guided reading groups whenever they choose to do them. Taberski models the concept of a home library collection for the children by keeping books that she particularly likes in a bookcase behind her chair. She sometimes places her books on the easel so that they can be shared by the children and returned to her.

Wall Works

Much of creating a family atmosphere lies in the use of the room walls to document the children's learning experiences, skills work, and readings.

Generally, at least one wall in a reading classroom is the chart wall. Charts with various spelling patterns discussed in class can be posted. If a child later has issues or concerns with that particular pattern, he or she should be directed to look at and to review the chart.

One of the centerpieces of the kindergarten through second grade classroom is the high-frequency word chart. This is a growing list of commonly used words that the teacher tapes under the appropriate beginning letter according to the children's directions. At the end of each month, the newest high-frequency words go into the children's folders and become part of their spelling words. Therefore reading, writing, and spelling are all intricately connected.

Supplies for children can include the following:

- A red plastic double pocket reading folder
- A blue plastic double pocket reading folder
- A four-sectioned pressed board spelling/poetry folder
- A 4" x 6" assessment notebook for reading
- A 4" x 6" assessment notebook for writing
- A reading response notebook (loose leaf, 60 pages) \
- A handwriting notebook

The reading folder contains the assessment notebooks, the reading response notebooks, a weekly reading log, and the strategy sheets the child may be using that particular week.

The assessment notebook is a key evaluative tool and a recording document for the conscientious balanced literacy specialist. The teacher uses the notebook to record the child's running records, the retellings of stories shared by the child, and summarizing talks about leveled books read. Within the assessment books, the teacher also has notes about the child's progress, the strategies the child has learned to use well, the books he or she has read, and those strategies the child still needs to practice. These assessment notebooks must be kept accessible so that the teacher can use them to confer with the child, parents, and administrator as needed.

The reading response notebook becomes a compilation of reading strategy sheets and children's writings and art in response to literature.

The weekly reading log allows the child to maintain for him or herself the titles of books they have read and written, and a bit about the narrative, style, and genre of that given book.

The book bags are 10" x 12" heavy duty freezer bags that keep three to ten books a child is "working on" during his or her free time. The teacher generally matches the children to the books and changes these books as needed.

Children keep several pieces of writing in their folders at a time. Within the writing folder, a handwriting notebook and a beginning word book can also be found.

The spelling/poetry folder is one that helps children focus on the sequence of letters in words and learn more how words work.

Balanced literacy advocates have a definite schedule for the teaching of reading and writing from which they generally do not deviate. A sample follows.

8:40–9:00 a.m.: First independent reading/word study group

9:00–9:30 a.m.: Whole group session in the meeting area to include reading aloud, shared reading, or shared writing

9:30–10:30 a.m.: Reading workshop, to include reading conferences or guided reading, second independent reading

Reading share 10:20–10:30 a.m.

10:30–10:40 a.m.: Writing mini-lesson or writing share

10:40–11:20 a.m.: Writing workshop, to include writing conferences, guided writing, modeled writing, and independent writing

Writing share 11:10–11:20 a.m.

COMPETENCY 17.0   UNDERSTAND CURRICULUM DEVELOPMENT
                    AND INSTRUCTIONAL PLANNING FOR
                    LITERACY PROGRAMS

ADJUSTMENT OF READING INSTRUCTION BASED ON ONGOING ASSESSMENT

The running records taken of children help the teacher learn about the cueing systems that children use. It is important for the teacher to adjust reading instruction based on the pattern of miscues gathered from several successive reading records. When the teacher carefully reviews a given student's substitutions and self-corrections, certain patterns begin to surface.

A child may use visual cues as he or she reads and adds meaning to self-correct. To the alert teacher, the reliance on visual miscues indicates that the reader may not make sense of what she or he is reading. This means that the teacher needs to check to see what cueing system the child uses when he or she is reading "just right" books. Children who use meaning and structure but not visual/graphophonic cues need to be reminded and facilitated to understand the importance of getting and reconstructing the author's message. They have to be able to share the author's story, not their own.

Not only can and should the teacher use the material in the children's ongoing assessment notebook to adjust his or her current instruction, but the material also serves to document for the child his or her growth as a successful reader over time. In addition, if the same concerns surface over the use of a particular cueing system or high-frequency word, the teacher can adjust the class wall chart and even devote a whole class lesson to the particular element.

INSTRUCTIONAL READING STRATEGIES FOR PROMOTING THE DEVELOPMENT OF PARTICULAR READING SKILLS

Phonemic awareness can be developed through using leveled books that deal with rhyming words and segmenting phonemes into words. Children can also work with word or letter strips to continue the poems from the books and create their own "sequels" to the phoneme-filled story. They can also create an in-style rhyming story using some of the same phonemes from the leveled story they have heard.

Word Identification, Selective Cue Stage

Sometimes children have not yet experienced an awareness of the conventions of print and labeling in their own home environments. The teacher or an aide may have to go on a label adventure and support children in recognizing or affixing labels to parts of the classroom, halls, and school building. A neighborhood walk with a digital or hand-held camera may be required to help children identify uses and functions of print in society. A classroom photo essay or bulletin board could be the outgrowth of such an activity.

Sight Vocabulary

Beginning readers may enjoy outdoing Dolch[TAR29] (1936), who compiled the best-known sight vocabulary word list. They can create their own class version of this list with illustrations and even some comments about why they have nominated certain words for the list.

USES OF LARGE GROUP, SMALL GROUP, AND INDIVIDUALIZED READING INSTRUCTION

The framework for organizing the balanced literacy classroom is referred to as the one book-whole class mode. What this means is that everyone in the class has experiences with the same book, and everyone in the class discusses the literature. The teacher starts by activating prior knowledge and developing the context or background for the piece of literature. Some of the children within the class may have less prior knowledge or context with which to frame the book. The teacher will need to provide a preview of the book or develop key concepts to provide a stronger base for what the class will read together.

Some children will have to work with a paraprofessional or with a reading tutor before the class studies the book. Different modes of reading are accommodated within the class, by the books being read during read-aloud time, as part of shared reading, or as guided reading. Student reader choices can also include cooperative reading, reading with a partner, or independent reading.

Following the reading, the children respond to it. This can be done through a literature circle and/or the whole class or in writing.

COMPETENCY 18.0   **UNDERSTAND HOW TO SELECT AND USE DIVERSE INSTRUCTIONAL MATERIALS TO PROMOTE LITERACY DEVELOPMENT**

STRATEGIES FOR SELECTING AND USING MEANINGFUL READING MATERIALS AT APPROPRIATE LEVELS OF DIFFICULTY

Matching young children with "just right" books fosters their reading independently, no matter how young they are. The teacher needs to have an extensive classroom library of books. Books that emergent readers and early readers can be matched with should have fairly large print and appropriate spacing, so that the reader can easily see where words begin and end, and few words on each page, so that the young reader can focus on all important concerns of top to bottom and left-to-right directionality, as well as the one-to-one match of word to print.

Illustrations for young children should support the meaning of the text and language patterns, and predictable text structures should make these texts appealing to young readers. Most important of all, the content of the story should relate to the children's interests and experiences as the teacher knows them. Only after all these considerations have been addressed can the teacher select "just right" books from an already leveled bin or list. In a similar fashion, when the teacher is selecting books for transitional and fluent readers, the following ideas need to be taken into account:

- The book should take at least two sittings to read, so children can get used to reading longer books. The fluent and transitional reader needs to deal with more complex characters and more intricate plotting. Look for books that set the stage for plot development with a compelling beginning. Age appropriateness of the concepts, plot, and themes is important so that the child will sustain interest in the book. Look for book features such as a list of chapters to help children navigate through the book.
- Series books are wonderful to introduce at this point in the children's development.

CREATION OF AN ENVIRONMENT THAT PROMOTES LOVE OF READING

The aforementioned creation of the meeting area and the reading chair (sometimes a rocking chair) with throw pillows around it promotes a love of reading. Beyond that, some classrooms have adopted an author's hat decorated with the pictures of famous authors and book characters that children wear when they read from their own works.

Many classrooms also have children's storyboards, artwork, story maps, pop-up books, and "in the style of" writing inspired by specific authors. Some teachers buy calendars for the daily schedule that celebrate children's authors or types of literature. Children are also encouraged to bring in public library books and special books from their home libraries. The teacher can model this habit of sharing beautiful books and inviting stories from his or her home library.

In addition, news stories about children's authors, series books, television versions of books, theatrical film versions of books, stuffed toy book character decorations, and other memorabilia related to books can be used to decorate the room.

Various chain book stores, including Barnes and Nobles and Borders, give out free bookmarks and promotional display materials related to children's books that can be available in the room for children to use as they read independently or in their guided groups. They might even use these artistic models to inspire their own book-themed artifacts.

STRATEGIES FOR PROMOTING INDEPENDENT READING IN THE CLASSROOM AND AT HOME

Preselect books for the children that are just right for them. Provide the children with a quiet, relaxing space within the classroom where they can go to read these books. Don't get upset if they seem to take a break or wander around the room after 15 minutes. Adults take breaks as well.

Make certain that the children who are reading independently fill in their weekly logs. Beyond telling what books they were reading and how many pages they have read, have the children respond to the following prompts:

- This week I was successful at . . .
- Next week I plan to . . .

A response can also be an illustration or a sentence or two about the book.

Deliberately assign a child or a pair of children to read Big Books. These are a guaranteed success for the children because they have already been shared in class. Some children enjoy reading these independently using big rulers to point at words. This provides them with a sense of mastery over the words and ownership of their independent reading.

Some children enjoy working on their own strategy sheet, such as a story map, character map, or storyboard panel, to demonstrate how they can apply a strategy to their own independent learning.

COMPETENCY 19.0   UNDERSTAND HOW TO COLLABORATE AND
                   COMMUNICATE WITH COLLEAGUES, PARENTS,
                   CAREGIVERS, AND MEMBERS OF THE
                   EDUCATIONAL COMMUNITY TO PROMOTE
                   STUDENTS' LITERACY DEVELOPMENT

Often times in schools, parents, grandparents, and other people involved in children's lives want to take a more active role in the educational process. Some also may seem to have an opinion on the appropriate method for teaching students how to read. Sometimes this can lead to controversy and misunderstandings.

It is important to provide opportunities for the public to come into the school and participate in activities to encourage reading. During these incentive and fun programs, it is just as important to share tidbits of information about the methodologies and strategies being implemented.

In this way, the public can begin to understand the differences in reading instruction today, in contrast perhaps to what occurred when they attended school. These differences are often the biggest changes observed by adults concerning current educational trends.

Taking the time to educate parents and other family members can not only help to ensure better understanding and open communication, but it can also provide more support for students than the school alone would ever be able to provide. Some strategies for educating parents and family members include the following:

- Bingo games where the correct answer on the bingo board is a fact about reading instruction
- Small-sized parent workshops offered on various topics
- Newsletter pieces or paragraphs
- Individual parent meetings
- Inviting parents in to observe lessons
- Small pieces of information shared during other social times when parents are invited into the school

Communicating general information about reading and appropriate reading instruction is important. It is just as important to share more specific information about students with parents, other school personnel, and the community.

When communicating with parents and colleagues, it is important to remember that adult learners have different characteristics than do children and adolescents. Adults are sometimes impatient with highly theoretical explanations that are not grounded in practical application. Therefore, couching one's explanation of one's literacy philosophy or classroom approach in terms of what the children actually do during literacy blocks is a better way to communicate than to give elaborate definitions of the balanced literacy approach. Furthermore, when discussing school-wide assessments with parents, it is important to communicate what this information means for their child, for them, and for you as the teacher. In that way even formal assessments may take on a less forbidding air for parents. Showing how informal classroom assessments do another kind of job—giving you, the teacher, insights into their child's current literacy functioning—will also show parents how assessment can be most helpful in planning for their child's learning.

Once the reports and information are gathered, the next step involves finding appropriate methods to share this information with the people that need the data. Again, depending on the audience, the amount and type of information may change.

Some ways to share information with parents/guardians include the following:

- Individual parent meetings
- Small group meetings
- Regular parent updates through phone calls
- Charts and graphs of progress sent home
- Notes home

Some ways to share information with school personnel include the following:

- Faculty meetings
- Power Point or other presentations
- E-mail
- Conferences
- School board presentations
- Graphs and charts

COMPETENCY 20.0   UNDERSTAND PROFESSIONAL RESPONSIBILITIES OF LITERACY PROFESSIONALS

Belonging to a professional organization devoted specifically to reading is an effective way to stay in touch with new developments in the field. The IRA publishes journals for elementary, middle, and secondary teachers that one receives as part of the membership dues for joining the organization. The same is true of the National Council of Teachers of English (NCTE). Having access to the writing of other teachers and scholars in the field of reading is an opportunity for professional growth. Some teachers and reading specialists also reach the point of professional expertise at which they themselves begin to write for publication.

All teachers should engage in self-reflection no matter how many years of experience they have or what subject areas they teach. Research is continually changing the materials used in the classroom, and adherence to state standards is vital to ensure that students learn what they are supposed to. Teachers who engage in self-reflection are better able to discover where the instruction was successful and where there was a breakdown in communication with the students. This enables the teacher to determine the areas where students need extra teaching, extra practice, or interventions to help them succeed. They can also make changes to the way they teach in the classroom to meet the needs of all learners. What works for one group of students will not work for other groups. Teachers of the same subject may have to use different instructional techniques with different classes studying the same topic.

Ways that teachers can engage in this reflection process include the following:

- Using a journal to record the events of each day
- Writing a reflection on each lesson to record what worked and what needs to be changed
- Reflecting on how various instructional techniques worked with different students

Within the busy day of school life, teachers often do not have the time for this reflection. However, it does not take a long period of time, and setting aside even 15 minutes before they start planning lessons for the next day can be really worthwhile. Once the practice is established it will become routine.

When administrators provide time for teachers to get together to plan instructional activities geared towards reading, a spirit of collaboration will exist in the school. One way to accomplish this is to provide the teachers with time to visit other schools and observe what is happening in another classroom in the district. Teachers within the same division (for example, primary, elementary, or teachers of one grade in the school) can get together on a regular basis to discuss how they are teaching various concepts and to discuss how to best help students that are struggling with reading. The reading specialist should be part of this team as well as the teacher giving support to the struggling readers. It may mean time after school or during shut down days for the school. Administrators can also schedule the timetable in such a way that these teachers have time off during the school day for this purpose.

Reading specialists, administrators, and teachers are always on the lookout for professional development opportunities that will help them in teaching reading. Many school districts offer professional development in many areas and provide an outline of this to the schools at the beginning of the year. However, this often involves travel, and for schools that manage their own budgets, this is something that has to be looked at carefully.

With the many demands placed on teachers, it is often not feasible to hold professional development sessions after school hours on a regular basis. Teachers do not mind if this is scheduled into the timetable at the beginning of the year and the sessions are only for short periods of time. Using the professional development time allowable by the school district to shut down schools for a half or full day is one way of bringing appropriate professional development to the staff. Schools within close proximity to one another can work together to share the cost of bringing in guest speakers and experts in the field of reading.

Another method that has seen successful is to add 15 minutes to the school day from Monday to Thursday and give teachers Friday afternoons for professional development. When this becomes a district-wide policy, teachers know exactly what is expected of them on Friday. Some of these sessions can be school professional development, where the teachers get time to plan together, discussing how best to teach the children, and how to make sure they are teaching the state-mandated outcomes. Some of these Fridays can be a chance for teachers to get together with those from other schools. For example, there could be a professional development session for grade 1 teachers, those in middle literacy, high school English teachers, and the like. When small groups are formed in this way, there are professional learning communities within the school district.

Professional development opportunities for teacher performance improvement or enhancement in instructional practices are essential for creating comprehensive learning communities. In order to promote the vision, mission, and action plans of school communities, teachers must be given the tools to maximize instructional performances. The development of student-centered learning communities that foster the academic capacities and learning synthesis for all students should be the fundamental goal of professional development for teachers.

The level of professional development may include traditional district workshops that enhance instructional expectations for teachers or the more complicated multiple day workshops given by national and state educational organizations to enhance the federal accountability of skill and professional development for teachers. Most workshops on the national and state level provide clock hours that can be used to renew certifications for teachers every five years. Typically, 150 clock hours is the standard certification number needed to provide a five-year certification renewal, so teachers must attend and complete paperwork for a variety of workshops that range from 1 to 50 clock hours, according to the timeframe of the workshops. Attending state, regional, and national conferences in reading provide ongoing education for both teachers and reading specialists. There is perhaps no better way to continue one's education than to attend these conferences periodically to learn groundbreaking theories and strategies in the teaching of reading.

The research by the National Association of Secondary Principals, "Breaking Ranks II: Strategies for Leading High School Reform" created the following listing of educational practices needed for expanding the professional development opportunities for teachers:

- Interdisciplinary instruction between subject areas
- Identification of individual learning styles to maximize student academic performance
- Training teachers in understanding and applying multiple assessment formats and implementations in curriculum and instruction.
- Looking at multiple methods of classroom management strategies
- Providing teachers with national, federal, state, and district curriculum expectations and performance outcomes
- Identifying the school communities' action plan of student learning objectives and teacher instructional practices
- Helping teachers understand how to use data to impact student learning goals and objectives
- Teaching teachers on how to disaggregate student data in improving instruction and curriculum implementation for student academic equity and access

- Developing leadership opportunities for teachers to become school and district trainers to promote effective learning communities for student achievement and success

In promoting professional development opportunities for teachers that enhance student achievement, the bottom line is that teachers must be given the time to complete workshops at no or minimal costs. School and district budgets must include financial resources to support and encourage teachers to engage in mandatory and optional professional development opportunities that create a win-win learning experience for students.

All teachers will experience many forms of evaluations. Through student teaching to formal evaluations completed by supervisors, ongoing critical looks at performance will be a part of the regular process. One area that is often underutilized but perhaps more valuable than outside evaluations is the self-assessment.

Examining with a critical eye one's own performance is the highest level of reflection. There are several forms that self-assessments can undertake. One format is to videotape yourself completing a lesson with the students and then replaying the tape for yourself at a later time. Before watching the tape, you should have specific questions or areas in mind. Simply watching the tape itself is much less valuable than when you watch it with a purpose. The questions might include, Did I keep the students engaged throughout the lesson? Was I clear in explaining the content I wanted them to understand? What could I do to improve the understanding of this concept for the students?

Another method of self-assessment might include providing your students with surveys to complete. When compiling the data from the questions, you will have a better understanding of how you are perceived by your students and what skills you can work on to improve weak areas. Carefully written questions focused on the items you are interested in learning about is necessary.

SUBAREA IV.   **READING INSTRUCTION AND ASSESSMENT: CONSTRUCTED-RESPONSE ASSIGNMENT**

CONSTRUCTED RESPONSE QUESTIONS

Tips and Reflections for Tackling the Constructed Response Questions:

- Use as many phrases and words from the question as possible in your response.
- Be specific. Mention specific books, authors, theorists, and strategies you have studied. Even though this is a test about the teaching of reading, make specific use of children's trade books and literature if appropriate.
- Use as many details as you are given in the question to make your response. Write no more than five to seven moderately brief paragraphs. The more you write, the larger the margin for error. Check your spelling and grammar, and check to see that you answered everything that was asked but no more than what was asked. Be positive and proactive about your ability to respond to whichever situation is presented.
- Stick with strategies, teaching ideas, and methods that are tried and true.
- Reread your writing at least twice for spelling and grammatical errors.

Constructed Response Question One

Jean is a first-year teacher who is taking over the classroom of a 30-year veteran teacher who is retiring. Jean goes in to meet with the teacher. The teacher, Ms. Banks, talks about the importance of teaching the young first graders the concepts of print.

She gives Jean a list of these concepts and suggests that Jean create some assessment format so that she can be certain that all of her first graders learn these concepts. She also tells Jean that she will be volunteering her time in a neighborhood preschool program close to her home and so she will be taking her private books and materials with her. She suggests that Jean go over the list of concepts of print and consider the needs of her class as she prepares for teaching this crucial set of skills. Before Jean leaves the classroom, Ms. Banks tells her that the kindergarten teacher has let her know that three children who will be in her class next year are from ELL backgrounds, where their families are not involved in oral story telling or reading from native language texts.

Here is Ms. Banks' concepts of print list:

- Starts on left

- Goes from left to right

- Return sweep

- Matches words by pointing

- Points to just one word

- Points to first and last word

- Points to one letter

- Points to first and last letter

- Parts of the book: cover, title page, dedication page, author, and illustrator

Jean thanks Ms. Banks for all of this help and asks if she can send Ms. Banks some of her teaching ideas for concepts of print and the ways she plans to differentiate instruction for her ELL students before the end of the year. Ms. Banks smiles and says she feels good to know that her classroom will be taken over by Jean. She promises to review Jean's response.

Constructed Response Answer One

First, as far as assessment for the key skills of concepts of print, I have decided that it is very important that I have a record of when and how well each of my students masters these concepts. After much thought, I realized that I will be keeping assessment notebooks for all of my students as part of my general reading and teaching. Therefore, I plan to print out all the key concepts of print on an 8" x 11" piece of paper in a grid format. This sheet will be included with other assessment grids for each individual child.

After conferencing with the child and determining the child has demonstrated mastery of a particular concept, I will check it off on the grid and date that mastery. If I have other comments to make about the child's level of mastery or fluency, I will make an anecdotal notation about the child as well. I think that this will guarantee that I have a detailed checklist record and anecdotal record of all my children's individual progress on concepts of print.

I plan to use Big Books and many of the latest picture books, including Caldecott award winners, in demonstrating and sharing with children many of the concepts of print. I will do much of my instruction mini-lessons. In fact, I intend to use some of my own favorite alphabet books to introduce these conventions. With a book like Clare Beaton's *Zoe and her Zebra*, I can easily and naturally cover the title page, cover, illustrator, and also manage to engage the children in the use of repetitive language.

Once I have shared that delightful book with the children during read -aloud time, we will be able to return to it again and use the repetitive language of it in its Big Book format to demonstrate for the children how they can point under each word as if there is a button to push. I can also demonstrate for the children how they should start at the top of the text and move from left to right. I will model going back to the left and under the previous line in a return sweep.

After modeling this as part of the mini-lesson, the children can be divided in small groups or pairs and take other Big Books and practice the "point under each word" and the "return sweep" as part of "shared reading," or buddy reading. I should be able to identify some highly proficient readers who will be happy to serve as buddy reader/tutors for the ELL children. I will ask that these buddies take time in small groups to work on another book from the alphabet book collection to share with the class as a whole. The use of the alphabet books also helps me to get some time in on the alphabetic principle.

I will also do a classroom writing workshop using the original alphabet book I use for the read-aloud time, for example, *Zoe and Her Zebra* as a model for creating our own story. Perhaps we will call it *Barry and his Boxer*. In this way, we will have a concrete literary product that demonstrates the children's mastery of and fluency in the concepts of print as they create an "in style of" story about a peer using illustrations, a title page, a dedication page, numbering of pages, a back and a front cover, and other concepts of print.

I think that using individualized assessments, a group/class collaborative writing project, and an anchor alphabet book will help me successfully teach the concepts of print and address the needs of my ELL learners as well.

Constructed Response Question Two

Marianne has been selected as one of a team of teachers who will start teaching in a brand new school building that has been under construction for several years. While Marianne, a grade 3 teacher, is thrilled to be moving into new facilities, she is a bit overwhelmed to have to "set up her room" all over again at the new site. Her administrator, Mr. Adams, tells her that there are five new teachers with no previous experience teaching primary school–age children who will be on staff. He tells her that these educators could really use help setting up their classrooms.

Marianne smiles and decides that she would very much like to use her set-up of her own grade 3 classroom as a workshop and demonstration for setting up a literacy teaching environment for these new staff members. Mr. Adams thinks that is a great idea and asks Marianne for an agenda and for a general description of what she will cover in her three-hour workshop so that he can give it to the district office.

Marianne is happy to comply because she realizes that she will be assisting new colleagues and getting ten helping hands to help her set up all the materials she has accumulated over a 20-year career.

Constructed Response Answer Two

The concept of sharing with new colleagues how to set up a classroom is very exciting to me. I know, based on my experiences, how crucial a well-planned and conceptualized space is for young learners' literacy learning. Therefore this is an agenda for what I will cover in my three hour in-service session for my new colleagues.

First, I will discuss how whatever the size of the classroom space, it must be sectioned off into the following areas: a meeting area, with a sofa or "soft" setting, a chair, an easel and basket to store book bags, a conference table, children's tables, a bin/basket main area for trade books, and another space for computers.

I may even give out a diagram of my classroom from my old school and some pictures. We will discuss collaboratively how I will set up my own new space as well as how they will want to set up their own spaces to allow for different uses of space within their own classrooms.

I will get into the issue of whether or not they want to have a traditional desk or use smaller tables for everyone. I think that they will need time to consider their own teaching styles in this regard. All teachers need to set up a space where they can easily confer with children and have access to individual assessment notebooks, reading folders (plus poetry/spelling, reading response, and handwriting notebooks) for all their students. I intend to show them how to prepare these folders for each child and how to store them so they can get to them when they need to make additional annotations for each child. Given the fact that I am working with new colleagues, I suspect that this will take at least an hour and a half of our time. I am also going to model for them a weekly reading log.

Most important of all, I am going to spend a major amount of time talking to them about the book bins as I place mine around the classroom. I will show them how to label the books using the Fountas and Pinnell levels and how to arrange the book bins with the spines out so that the children can see the books. Together we will examine how the bookcases should be close to the walls and the expository books should be separated from the narrative texts. I will also get together my audio cassettes and book sets so that they can see how I set up my read-along center for all my children. I will share some dual language tapes I use with ELL students as well. I have some extra "author's hats" and author's chair slipcovers I will share with them.

I also intend to show them how to select Big Books for the easel display and anchor books to be shown there as well. By the way, I will also coach them how to write away for supplies and how to store supplies in common areas so that some children are not missing necessary materials for class activities.

Even though we are focusing on literacy, I am going to show them where to store mathematics materials, other texts, and art supplies. I will end the session by making sure that they know where to place their chart wall and the word wall. If I have time, I will sit down with each of them and start them on the word wall and some key charts for their first day. They will leave my room with an actual experience of setting up a literacy environment, plus viable teaching and reading suggestions for the first day. Most importantly, I will be available for an in-school classroom consultation, if necessary.

GLOSSARY

These definitions are critical for success on all multiple choice questions on the examinations. Proper use of these terms is crucial for success in tackling a constructed response involving balanced literacy.

Ability grouping: This is the grouping of children with similar needs for instructional purposes. Ability groups do not remain constant throughout the year but change as the children's needs within them change.

Alliteration: This occurs when words begin with the same consonant sound, as in "Peter Piper picked a pair of pickled peppers."

Alphabetic principle: This is the idea that written spellings represent spoken words.

Anchor book: This is a balanced literacy term for a book that is purposely read repeatedly and used as part of both the reading and writing workshop. It is a good idea to use certain books that become the children's familiar and cherished favorites for both reading and then to inspire children's writing.

Assonance: This occurs when words begin with the same vowel sound.

Authentic assessment: These are assessment activities that reflect the actual workplace, family community, and school curriculum.

Balanced literacy lesson format: The balanced literacy approach has its own specific format for the delivery of the literacy lesson, whether it is a reading or writing workshop lesson. The format begins with a 10- to 15-minute mini-lesson that the teacher delivers to the whole class. This mini-lesson is then followed by a 30-minute small group (when the children break into small groups to work) lesson. It concludes with a 10-minute share during which the whole class reconvenes to share what they have done in the small groups. One can refer to this format as the whole-small-whole group approach.

Benchmarks: These are school, state, or nationally mandated statements of the expectations for student learning and achievement in various content areas.

Bics-Basic Interpersonal Communication Skills (ELL term, Bilingual Education): To learn second language skills and become proficient in a second language through face-to-face interaction-translation from speaking, listening, and viewing.

Blending: The process of hearing separate phonemes and being able to merge them together to read the word.

Book Features: Children need to be familiar with the following book features: front and back cover, title and half- title page, dedication page, table of contents, prologue and epilogue, and foreword and after notes. For factual books, children need to be familiar with: labels, captions, glossary, index, headings and subheadings of chapters, charts and diagrams, and sidebars.

Checklist: This is an assessment form that lists targeted learning and social behaviors as indicators of achievement, knowledge or skill. They can be professionally or teacher prepared.

Cinquain: This is a five-line poem that can be read and then used as a model for writing. Generally line one of this format is a single word; line two has two words, which describe the title of line one; line three is comprised of three words that are movement words; line four has four words that express feeling; and line five has a single word that is a synonym for line one's single word.

Comprehension: This occurs when the reader correctly interprets the print on the page and constructs meaning from it. Comprehension depends on activating prior knowledge, the cultural and social background of the reader, and the reader's ability to use comprehension-monitoring strategies.

Concepts about Print: This includes how to handle a book, how to look at print, directionality, sequencing, locating skills, punctuation, and concepts of letters and words.

Consonant Diagraphs: These are two consecutive consonants that represent one new speech sound. In the word "digraph," the *ph*, which sounds like /f/, is a digraph.

Contexts: These are sentences deliberately prepared by the teacher that include sufficient contextual clues for the children to decipher meaning.

Contextual Redefinition: This occurs when a reader uses context to determine word meaning.

Cooperative Reading: Children read with a partner or buddy. It can be silent or oral reading.

Crisscrossers: This is an ELL term for second language learners who have a positive attitude toward both first language and second language learning. These second language learners, children from ELL backgrounds, are comfortable navigating back and forth between the two languages as they learn.

Cues: As they self-monitor their reading comprehensions, readers have to integrate various sources of information or cues to help them construct meaning from text and graphic illustrations.

Decoding: The readers sounds out a printed sequence of letters based on knowledge of letter-sound correspondences.

Diphthongs: These are two vowels in one syllable where the two sounds are heard. For instance, in the word "house" both the *o* and the *u* are heard.

Directionality: When readeing, children use their fingers to indicate left-to-right direction and return sweep to the next line.

Differentiated Instruction: This is the need for the teacher, based on observation of individual student's work, progress, test results, fluency, and other reading/literacy behaviors, to provide modified instruction and alternative strategies or activities. These activities are specifically developed by the teacher to address the individual student's different needs.

Early Readers: These children recognize most high-frequency words and many simple words. They use pictures to confirm meaning. Using meaning, syntax, and phonics, they can figure out most simple words. They use spelling patterns to figure out new words and are gaining control of reading strategies. They use their own experiences and background knowledge to predict meanings and occasionally use story language in their writing. This stage follows emergent reading.

Emergent Readers: This is the stage of reading in which the reader understands that print contains a consistent message. The reader can recognize some high-frequency words, names, and simple words in context. Pictures can be used to predict meaning. The emergent reader begins to attend to left-to-right directionality and features of print and may identify some initial sounds and ending sounds in words.

Encode: This occurs when changing a message into symbols. For example, readers encode oral language into writing.

English as a Second Language: This is a way of teaching English to speakers of other languages using English as the language of instruction.

Expository Text:. This is nonfiction that provides information and facts. This text type is what newspapers, science, mathematics, and history texts use. Currently there is much focus, even in elementary schools, on teaching children how to comprehend and author expository texts. They must produce brochures, guides, recipes, and procedural accounts on most elementary grade levels. The teaching of reading of expository texts requires working with a particular vocabulary and concept structure that is very different from that of the narrative text. Therefore time must be taken to teach the reading of expository texts and contrast it with the reading of narrative texts.

First Language: This is an ELL term for the language any child acquires in the first few years of life. It is through this acquired language that the child acquires phonological and phonemic awareness.

Fluent Readers: Fluent readers identify most words automatically. They can read chapter books with good comprehension. They consistently monitor, cross-check, and self-correct reading, and they can offer their own interpretations of text based on personal experiences and prior reading experiences. Fluent readers are capable of reading a variety of genres independently. Furthermore, they can respond to texts or stories by sharing pertinent examples from their lives. They can also readily make connections to other books that they have read. Finally, they are capable of beginning to create spoken and written writings that are in the style of a particular author.

Formal Assessment: This is a test or an observation of a performance task that is done under controlled and regulated conditions.

Functional Reading: This is the reading of instructions, recipes, coupons, classified ads, notices, signs, and other documents that have to be read and correctly interpreted in school and in society.

Grade Equivalent/Grade Score: The is transformed from a raw score on a standardized test into the equivalent score earned by an average student in the norming group.

Graphic Organizers: Graphic organizers express relationships among various ideas in visual form, including sequence, timelines, character traits, fact and opinion, main idea and details, and differences and likenesses. Graphic organizers are particularly helpful for visual learners.

Guided Reading: This is one of the key modes of instruction in the balanced literacy theory approach. During guided reading, the teacher "guides" the child through silent reading of a text by giving them prompts, target questions, and even helping the child start an answer to a specific prompt or question. At the end of each guided reading section or excerpt of the text, the child stops to talk with the teacher about the text. By definition, guided reading is an interactive discussion between the child and the teacher. This mode of reading instruction is generally used when children need extra support in constructing meaning because the text is complex or because their current independent reading capacities are still limited.

High Frequency; These words appear many more times than do other words in ordinary reading material. Examples of such words include as, in, of, and the. These words are also sometimes called service words and are part of sight vocabulary words. A classic best-known high frequency word list was generated by Dolch (1936).

Independent Reading: This is a set period of time within the daily literacy block when children read books with 95% to 100% accuracy on their own. This type of reading without teacher support promotes lifelong literacy and love of learning, which enhances reading mileage, builds fluency, and helps children orchestrate integrated cue strategies.

Informal Assessment: These are observations of children made under informal conditions, including kid watching, checklists, and individual child/teacher conversations.

Informal Reading Inventory (IRI): These are a series of reading excerpts that can be used to determine a child's reading strengths and needs in comprehension and decoding. Many published reading series have an IRI to go with their series.

Justified Print: This is the positioning of print on the page so that each line ends either a sentence or a phrase.

Kid Watching: This term is used within the balanced literacy approach for the teacher's deliberate, detailed, and recorded observations of individual student and class literacy behaviors, often done during small group work. The teacher then reconfigures lessons on experiences to meet the students' individual and group needs.

Kinesthetic: Learning is tactile, as contrasted with an activity where the learner sits still or attempts to sit still in one place. Cutting and moving syllable or word strips or using sandpaper letters are kinesthetic activities.

Language Experience: Children give dictation to the teacher who writes their words on a chart or their drawings. This shows children that words can be written down.

Learning Logs: These are daily records of what students have learned.

Listening Post: These are sets of headphones attached to a single tape player. Children can go to centers where they listen to audiotapes of books while reading the print book. These posts are in many libraries as well.

Literature Circles: This is a group discussion involving four to six children who have read the same work of literature (narrative or expository text). They talk about key parts of the work, relate it to their own experience, listen to the responses of others, and discuss how parts of the text relate to the whole.

Manipulation: This involves moving around or switching sounds within a word or words within a phrase or sentence.

Meaning Vocabulary: These are words whose meanings children understand and can use.

Miscue: This is an oral reading error made by a child that differs from the actual printed text.

Miscue Analysis: The teacher keeps a detailed recording of the errors or inaccurate attempts of a child reader during a reading assessment. These are recorded within a running record. This helps the teacher see whether the cues—syntactic, semantic, or graphophonemic—the child is using are accurate.

Monitoring Reading: These are the various strategies that children use to monitor their readings. A sample are maintaining fluency by bringing prior knowledge to the story to make predictions, using these predictions to do further checking, searching, and self-correcting as the story progresses, and using problem-solving word study skills to make links from known words to unknown words.

Morphemes: These are the smallest units of meaning in words. There are two types of morphemes: free morphemes, which can stand alone, such as *love*; and bound morphemes, which must be attached to another morpheme to carry meaning, such as *ed* in loved.

Narrative Text: This is one of the two basic text structures. The narrative text tells or communicates a story. Narrative texts are novels, short stories, and plays. Some poems are narratives as well. The narrative text needs to be taught differently than the expository text because of its structure.

One-to-One Matching: This is matching one spoken word with one written word.

Onset-Rime Blending–Onset: This is everything before the vowel and RIME (the vowel and everything after it). For example, the word "sleep" can be broken into /sl/ and /eep/. Word families are built using rimes. The /eep/ word family would include jeep, keep, and weep.

Orthography: This is a method of representing spoken language through letters and diacritics.

Percentile: If a child scores at the 56th percentile for his or her grade level, the score is equal to or above that of 56% of the children taking that standardized test and below that of 46% of the children on whose scores the test was normed.

Performance Assessment: This occurs when the teacher has the children do a task that demonstrates their knowledge, skills, and competency. Having children author their own alphabet book on a particular topic would be a performance assessment for knowledge of the alphabet.

Phoneme: These are the speech sound units that make a difference in meaning. The word rope has three phonemes /r/, /o/, and /p/. Change one phoneme, say /r/ to /n/, and you have a different word: nope.

Phonemic Awareness: This is the understanding that words are composed of sounds. Phonemic awareness is a specific type of phonological awareness dealing only with phonemes in a spoken word.

Phonics: This is the study of relationships between phonemes (speech sounds) and graphemes (letters) that represent the phonemes. It is also the decoding or the sounding out of unknown words that are written.

Phonological Awareness: This is the ability to recognize the sounds of spoken language and how they can be blended together, segmented, and switched/manipulated to form new combinations and words.

Phonological Cues: Readers use their knowledge of letter-sound and sound/letter relationships to predict and confirm reading.

Phonology: This is the study of speech structure in language that includes both the patterns of basic speech units (phonemes) and the tacit rules of pronunciation.

Portfolios: These are collections of a child's work over time. They include a cover letter, reflections from the child and teacher, and other supportive documents, such as standards, performance task examples, prompts, and sometimes peer comments.

Primary Language (ELL Term): This is the language an individual is the most fluent in and at ease with. This is usually but not always the individual's first language.

Prompts: This occurs when the teacher intervenes in the child's independent reading to help the child pronounce or comprehend a specific word or prompt. On a reading record, the teacher notes the prompt. When the teacher wants to match a child with a particular book or determine the child's stage of reading/level, the teacher does not use prompts.

Question Generating Strategy for an Expository Text: First the child previews the text by reading titles, subheads, looking at pictures or illustrations, and reading the first paragraph. Next the child asks a "think" question that he or she records. Then he or she reads to find information that might answer the "think" question. The child may write down the information found or think about another question that is answered by what the child is reading. The child continues to read using this strategy.

Reading for Information: This is reading with the purpose of extracting facts and expert opinion from the text. Children should be introduced to the following information reading resources: Web resources that are age and grade appropriate for children, the concept of the table of contents, chapter headings, glossaries, pictures, maps, charts, diagrams, and text structures in an information text. They should be taught to use notes, graphs, organizers, and mind maps to share information extracted from a text.

Recode: To change information from one code into another, such as recoding writing into oral speech.

Recognition Vocabulary: This is a group of words that children are able to correctly pronounce, read orally, and understand on sight.

Record of Reading Behavior (Running Record): This is an objective observation during which the teacher records, using a standard set of symbols, everything the child reader says as he or she reads a book selected by the teacher.

Reflection: This is the analysis, discussion, and reaction to one's learning on any grade or age level.

Retelling: Retelling can be written or oral. Children are expected and encouraged to tell as much of a story as they can remember. Retelling is far more extensive than just summarizing. Children should include the beginning, middle and end plot lines and should be able to tell about the book's characters.

Rubric: This is a set of guidelines or acceptable responses for the completion of any task. Usually a rubric scale ranges from 0 to 4, with 4 being the most detailed response and 0 indicating a response to the task that lacked detail or was in other ways insufficient.

Scaffolding: This refers to the teacher support necessary for the child to accomplish a task or to achieve a goal that the child could not accomplish on his or her own. Vygotsky[TAR30] termed this window of opportunity the "zone of proximal development." Ultimately, as the child becomes more proficient or capable, the scaffold is withdrawn. The goal of scaffolding is to help the child to perform the reading task independently and internalize the behavior. During shared reading, the task is scaffolded by the teacher's reading to the children aloud. As the teacher reads, the teacher scaffolds the initial decoding and helps with the meaning making/construction.

Searching: Children pause to search in the picture, print, or their memory for known information. This can happen as the child tackles an unknown word or after an error.

Second Language (ELL Term): This is a language acquired or learned simultaneously with or after a child's acquisition of a first language.

Segmenting: This is the process of hearing a spoken word and identifying its separate phonemes or syllables.

Self-Correction: This occurs when children begin to correct some of their own reading errors. Generally this behavior is accompanied by the rereading of the previous phrase or sentence.

Semantic Cues: Children use their prior knowledge, sense of the story, and pictures to support their predicting and confirming the meaning of the text.

Semantic Web: This is a visual graphic organizer that the teacher can use to introduce a reading on a specific topic. It visually represents many other words associated with a target word. The web can help activate the children's prior knowledge and extend or clarify it. It can also serve to check new learning after guided or independent reading.

Spatial Learning: This uses images, color, or layout to help readers whose learning style is spatial.

Standard Score: This is how far a child's grade on a standardized test is from the average score (mean) on the test in terms of the standard deviation. If a child scores 70 on a standardized test and the standard deviation is 5 and the average (mean) score is 65, the child is one standard deviation above the average.

Standardized Test: This is a test given under specified conditions, allowing comparisons to be made. A set of norms or average scores on this test will be used for comparisons.

Stop and Think Strategy: This is a balanced literacy strategy for constructing meaning. As the text is being read, the child asks himself or herself, does this make sense to me? If it does not make sense to me, I should then try to reread it or read ahead. I can also look up words that I don't know or ask for help. Generally the teacher models this strategy with the whole class as a mini-lesson and then it is posted prominently in the classroom for continued reference by the children.

Strategic Readers: As defined by researchers Marie Clay and Sharon Taberski, strategic readers are self-improving and do the following as they read: (A lengthy glossary explanation of this term has been provided because it can appear in a variety of multiple choice questions on the examination as well as part of a constructed response question.)

- Monitor their reading to see if it makes sense semantically, syntactically, and visually.
- Look for and use semantic, syntactic, and visual clues.
- Uncover and identify new things about the text.
  Cross check and use one cueing system against another.
- Self-correct their reading when what they first read does not match the semantic, syntactic, and visual clues
- Solve for and identify new words using multiple cueing systems.

Beyond these behaviors, a strategic or self-improving reader uses many strategies to construct meaning. When their reading experience is going well—they know the words and understand the text or story—they are working continuously (even if they are not conscious of it) at maintaining meaning. If and when the strategic or self-improving reader runs into an unfamiliar word, then the reader has many strategies to identify that word. Becoming a successful strategic reader is a goal that can and should be shared with children as early as the middle of the first grade, although the term "self-improving reader" might be used at that point.

Text Features: Children need to be alerted to the following text features that may initially appear strange to them: a period that marks the end of a "telling sentence"; a question mark at the end of a sentence that asks a question; an exclamation mark used to express surprise or excitement at the end of a sentence; capital letters that begin a sentence and the names of persons, places, and things; bold, italicized, or underlined text to highlight key ideas; quotation marks that show dialogue, a hyphen used to break a long word up into its syllables; a dash used to show a break in an idea, or to indicate a parenthetical element or an omission; an ellipse, which shows an omission or break in the text; and a paragraph in nonfiction that shows a new point being made.

Transitional Readers: This occurs when children recognize an increasing number of "hard" words that are content related. They can provide summaries of the stories that they read. They are more at ease with handling longer, more complex, connected text with short chapters. Transitional readers can read independent-level texts with correct phrasing, expression, and fluency. When they encounter unfamiliar words, they have a variety of strategies to figure out the unfamiliar words. Their reading demonstrates that they are able to integrate meaning, syntax, and phonics in a consistent manner so that they can understand the texts they are reading.

Venn Diagram: This is a diagram consisting of two or three intersecting circles to visually represent similarities and differences for texts, characters, and topics. No author study is complete without venn diagrams comparing different authors' works. This is the most commonly used graphic organizer in elementary schools today. It can be used effectively as part of an answer to a constructed response question.

Visual Cues: This occurs when readers use their knowledge of graphemes to predict and confirm text. The graphemes may be words, syllables, or letters.

Word Analysis: This is the analysis of words employing letters, phonic structures, contextual clues, or dictionary skills.

Word Identification: This is how the reader determines the pronunciation and the meaning of an unknown word.

Word Recognition: This is the process of determining the pronunciation and some degree of the meaning of an unknown word.

Word Work: This is the term that the balanced literacy approach uses for the study of vocabulary.

DIRECTORY OF THEORISTS AND RESEARCHERS

Introduction

Many questions on the teacher certification examinations can only be correctly answered if you know the theorist or the research that is referenced. The teaching of reading owes much to the work, principles, and guidelines of teacher educators and university field researchers who have changed the style, methods, and practice of teaching reading. While those listed in this directory are by no means all the major researchers (page constraints would make a complete listing impossible), they are those whose contributions are frequently referenced on the certification tests and whose work is evident in today's elementary classroom teaching and learning of reading.

Phonics-Centered Approach

In 1955, Rudolph Flesch gained national prominence when he published *Why Johnny Can't Read*. This book went on to become a best seller and has now become a classic that is readable and speaks to current concerns. Flesch became the spokesperson for a war that periodically resurfaces in the reading world.

Flesch, Chall (1967[TAR31]), Stahl (1992[TAR32]), Adams (1990), and Johnson and Bauman (1984[TAR33]) believe that a phonics-based approach is crucial for reading success. Flesch and others feel that the balanced literacy advocates are seriously undermining the crucial role that phonics plays in the children's development as successful decoding readers. However, it must be noted that while balanced literacy does emphasize the use of literature-based reading programs, it in no way dismisses phonics from its reading program; indeed phonics is included in the crucial "word work" component of the reading and writing workshop.

The phonics advocates point to the fact that most research shows that early and systematic instruction in phonics skills results in superior reading achievement in elementary school and beyond.

Adams (1990) detailed what type of phonics instruction is needed.

To learn to read skillfully, children need practice in seeing and understanding decodable words in real reading situations and with connected text. Phonics instruction needs to be part of a reading program that provides ample practice in reading and writing. Encouraging children with connected text can also show them the importance of what they are learning and make the lessons in phonics relevant and sensible. Phonics-centered advocates believe that children should begin to learn letter associations in kindergarten, with most useful phonics skills being taught by first grade. These basic skills should then be reviewed in second grade and beyond.

Consonant sounds should be taught first, since they are more reliable in their letter-sound associations.

Short vowel sounds appear more frequently in beginning reading materials, so they should be introduced before long vowels. Phonics advocates believe that most beginning readers need to be taught letter-sound associations explicitly. Phonics advocates also believe that beginning readers need to read stories that have words to which phonics skills apply. This allows them to practice their phonics skills as they write and spell words. They should also play several of letter-sound association games.

Phonics advocates claim that when phonics is abandoned, reading scores drop. Balanced literacy advocates counter with the fact that they have never advocated abandoning the teaching of phonics.

As Jeanne Chall, a professor at Harvard's Graduate School of Education, notes, "A beginning reading program that does not give children knowledge and skill in recognizing and decoding words will have poor results."

Theorists and Researchers

Adams, Marilyn Jager
Noted for her research on early reading, Adams lists five basic types of phonemic awareness tasks that should be covered by the end of first grade. These include ability to hear rhymes and alliterations, ability to do oddity tasks, ability to orally blend words, ability to orally segment words, and ability to do phonemic manipulation tasks.

Clay, Marie M.
A New Zealand–born researcher, Clay specializes in the field of special needs emergent literacy and in the development of assessment tools for these children. Her research in this field is felt throughout the Reading Recovery movement and involves the use of her *Reading Recovery: A Guidebook for Teachers in Training* in the majority of graduate emergent literacy courses and in many classrooms in the United States, including those that do not have a Reading Recovery teacher.

Her doctoral thesis focused on what was to become her life's work: emergent reading behavior. At the crux of her research for the dissertation, Clay reviewed and detailed the progress week by week of 100 children during their first year of school (1966). An important outcome of the dissertation was her development of reliable observation tools for the assessment and analysis of changes over time in children's literacy learning. These assessments are the crux of *An Observation Survey of Early Literacy Achievement* (1993), which is an essential work for the primary school educator. The assessments have been validated and reconstructed for learners from the Spanish, Maori, and French languages. A special appendix in this guide includes the *Record of Reading Behavior* tool she created with Kenneth Goodman.

Reading Recovery is a key Clay contribution to the field of foundations of reading teaching. The movement, which is discussed in detail in this section, was born out of the concerns of classroom educators who were upset that, even with excellent programs and expert teaching, they were not able to positively influence the literacy progress of some of their young children. Clay posed the question of investigating what would happen if the design and delivery of traditional reading education were changed for these struggling young learners.

The whole thrust of the Reading Recovery movement has been to improve the early identification and instructional delivery for these struggling young readers. Her goal was to develop a system that would bring those children scoring the lowest in assessment measures to the level of the average readers within their classes.

With the support of Barbara Watson and others, the program was developed in three years. The first field tests of the program took place in the late 1970s in Auckland, Australia, schools. To date(2005), the program is operating in most English-speaking countries and has been reconstructed for use in Spanish and French.

Janet S. Gaffey and Billie Askew (1991) have said of Clay that her contribution "has been to change what is possible for individual learners when teaching permits different routes to be taken for desired outcomes."

Reading Recovery has been identified by the International Reading Association as a program that not only teaches children how to read but also reduces the number of children who are labeled as "learning disabled." It further lowers the number of children who are placed in remedial reading programs and classes.

Clay Reading Recovery lessons are designed to promote accelerated learning so that children can catch up to their peers and continue to learn independently. The hallmark of the Reading Recovery program is that the Reading Recovery teacher works with one student at a time over a 12- to 20-week period. Each daily 30-minute lesson is tailored to address the needs of the individual student.

Therefore Reading Recovery teachers generally teach no more than four or five students per day in individual lessons.

The Clay Observation of Early Childhood Achievement (1993) is used to assess children's strengths and weaknesses. Reading Recovery teachers devote the first 10 minutes of their sessions with individual children to assessment, as the children engage in reading and writing. A running record of the child's progress is taken every day and is used to plan future lessons.

The lessons include the use of familiar stories. Children engage in assembling and in sequencing cut up stories. They work with letters or write a story. Teaching style involves the teacher demonstrating strategies and the child then developing effective strategies to continue reading independently. Key components of each lesson include phonemic awareness, phonics, spelling, and comprehension study. Much time is devoted to problem solving so that the children's decoding is purposeful. Children are given time to practice and demonstrate fluency skills.

Ultimately what sets Reading Recovery apart[tac934] is the fact that it is one-to-one tutoring. This is also what makes it effective for children. However, what raises issues about it are costs for the school systems that may want to adopt it. Obviously the districts and education systems have to decide whether they want to pay the costs of this and other individualized tutoring systems now in the primary school years or later as these children become adults whose literacy skills are not sufficient for proactive citizenship.

Fountas, Irene C and Gay Su Pinnell

These two researchers have developed a leveling system for reading texts, which arranges them by level of difficulty. Beyond a specific analysis of set titles, the theorists have explained in several published works how to use their leveling system to meet and assess the progress of various readers. They also provide detailed explanations and support for reading teachers of young children in kindergarten through third grade in using reading records and benchmark texts.

They are the key articulators of the balanced literacy model, which includes a reading and writing workshop. Among their other contributions to the field are: guidelines for creating sets of leveled books, assessment rubrics, strategies for fostering "word solver" skills in child readers, and methods for teaching phonics and spelling in the literacy classroom.

Routman, Regie

Routman's contributions to Reading Foundations are the result of over three decades of experience as an elementary school teacher, a reading specialist, a learning disabilities tutor, a Reading Recovery teacher, a language arts and mentor teacher, and a staff developer. Due to these various experiences, her insights into reading resonate with a broad spectrum of school community members.

Routman's works are conversational, teacher-to-teacher sharings of her daily experiences in classrooms. In her books on the teaching of reading (for example, *Reading Essentials*, published by Heinemann in 2002), Routman shows teachers how to teach consistent with the findings in reading research, yet also with highly practical "scripted lessons" and teaching tips that make the classroom come alive. She advocates literature-based teaching and meaning-centered approaches for learning.

In addition, she is a strong advocate of using poetry from grades 1 and beyond as an integral thread for a reading program. She is the author of *Kids' Poems: Teaching Children to Love Writing Poetry* (Scholastic, 2000), which includes separate volumes of poetry for kindergarten through fourth grade.

Routman believes in teaching reading to meet specific children's needs regardless of the particular reading program in place. She is a strong advocate for the use of small, guided reading groups and reading for understanding. Phonics and other word analysis strategies are part of her reading framework but not at its core. Her focus for the reading classroom is on the development and the use of the classroom library as the center for an independent reading program, shared reading, and reading aloud.

Routman has designed informal reading evaluations on books/texts her students are reading (her published works are known for their appendices replete with templates for evaluations, projects, reports, book lists, suggested texts by topics, and so on). Her classroom model includes matching children with specific library books, as well as linking assessment with instruction. Finally, she is a researcher who sees reading as intimately linked to writing.

Routman is also involved with the politics of literacy. This vision of literacy involves the image of the teacher as an informed professional who regularly reads the latest professional books, collaborates with colleagues in school and beyond, and deals with the most recent research developments. Interestingly, Routman is one researcher who also feels that an informed professional can and should know when to question research. Other aspects of the politics of literacy that Routman conceptualizes are communicating effectively with parents and dealing with testing and standards mandates.

Two of her published works, *Conversations: Strategies for Teaching, Learning, and Evaluating* (Heinemann, 2000) and *Invitations: Changing as Teachers and Learners k-12* (Heinemann, 1991 and 1994) are essential for the elementary reading teacher's bookshelf and can take the teacher through several years of work.

Taberski, Sharon

Taberski is an experienced elementary teacher educator who is also a member of the Primary Literacy Standards Committee run by the National Center on Education and the Economy and the University of Pittsburgh. Her works in the field are served up as wonderfully accessible and necessary advice from "the veteran teacher across the hall" who loves her students and is delighted to help a new colleague.

Unlike many theorists in the field of reading, Taberski's work is not focused around a prescribed set of skills but rather around a series of interconnected interactions with the learner.

These interactions are detailed and clearly communicated in her book *On Solid Ground* (Heinemann, 2000):

- *Assessment*: These are procedures for assessing children's reading and to inform teaching, scheduling, and managing reading conferences; taking oral reading records; and using retellings as discussion tools.
- *Demonstration*: Taberski developed and field tested strategies for using shared reading and read-aloud times as platforms for figuring out words and comprehending texts. She is a strong advocate of small group work/guided reading, word-study groups, and teaching children one on one.
- *Practice*: In the Taberski framework, independent reading is used as a time for practice.. Students play key roles in this practice, and Taberski has a set of detailed and easily adaptable guidelines for matching children with books for independent reading. Her work includes booklists and ready-to-use information that is available for reproduction.
- *Response*: It is important for students to know that they are doing well and where they must focus their efforts to improve skills. Taberski explains how her students use writing and dialogue as tools for independent reading.

Vail, Priscilla

Noted for her research in the study of dyslexia and its myths, Vail has articulated ways in which children can develop their reading skills as they cope with this disorder and techniques parents and educators can use to support reading development. She has also worked on specific test-taking skills for children coping with dyslexia and other special needs. Her strategies can be infused in the regular education program to enhance all students' reading achievement schools. She is a proponent of phonics instruction and skills within the context of an integrated whole-language approach (once called integrated language arts).

Another focus of Vail's research is the link between language and thinking. She is concerned with how a child's receptive language, expressive language, and metacognition can be fostered. She has developed assessment methods for each of these capacities and activities to help strengthen them in children in kindergarten through fourth grade.

BIBLIOGRAPHY OF PRINT RESOURCES

Professional Books

Adams, M. 1990. *Beginning to read: Thinking and Learning about Print.* Cambridge, MA: MIT Press.

Anders, P., and C. Bos. l986. "Semantic Feature Analysis: An Interactive Strategy for Vocabulary Development and Reading Comprehension." *Journal of Reading* 29: 610–616.

Blevins, W. l997. *Phonemic Awareness Activities for Early Reading Success.* New York: Scholastic.

Boyd-Bastone, P. 2004. "Focused Anecdotal Record Assessment (ARA): A Tool for Standards Based Authentic Assessment." *Reading Teacher* 58 (3): 230–239.

Calkins, Lucy McCormick. 2001. *The Art of Teaching Reading.* New York: Longman.
> This is the woman who beautifully explains the reading workshop and its relationship to the writing workshop as she shares wonderful snapshots of mini-lessons, conferring, conferencing, independent reading, guided reading, book talks, prompts, coaching, and classroom library use. It is exceedingly readable and direct.

Campbell, Robin. 2004. *Reading and Writing for Real Purposes.* Portsmouth, NH: Heinemann.
> This work focuses on how children who deftly absorb and interconnect symbols and sounds of their universes can be supported in kindergarten and first-grade classes to extend this ability into phonics learning. Campbell demonstrates how immersion in a highly literate classroom filled with print and language stimuli allows kids to build accurate letter-sound relationships. The book provides a framework for teaching phonics using proven field-tested Campbell strategies.
>
> Among these strategies are early mark making, read aloud time, playing with language in rhyme and song, writing and reading in a variety of genres, exploring environmental and classroom print, and using students' own names. Samples of student work are included.

Chancey, C. l994. "Language Development, Metalinguistic Awareness, and Emergent Literacy Skills of 3 Year Old Children in Relation to Social Class." *Applied Psycholinguistics* 15: 371–394.

Clay, Marie M. 1993. *An Observation Survey of Early Literacy Achievement.* Portsmouth, NH: Heinemann.

Clay, Marie M. 1993. *Reading Recovery: A Guidebook for Teachers in Training.* Portsmouth, NH: Heinemann.

Cooper, J. David. 2004. *Literacy-Helping Children Construct Meaning.* Boston, MA: Houghton Mifflin. (5th Edition).
   With numerous charts, tables, templates, and excerpts form actual texts, this book explains what the balanced literacy approach to the teaching of reading and writing is. It offers the new teacher exact schedules, strategies, guidelines, assessment tools, bibliographies, research, and even scripts for conferring with children.

   Cooper is a clear and crisp writer who does not overwhelm, but rather engages the reader. Even veteran teachers would return again and again to this text for support and refreshing insights.

Cox, Carole. 2005. *Teaching Language Arts.* Boston, MA: Pearson.
   A compendium of state-of-the-art lesson plans, Web resources, online case studies, teaching ideas, and extensive templates. All of these materials are aligned to the balanced literacy reading and writing workshop model.

   The book includes teaching ideas for the ELL reader, children with learning disabilities, and speakers of non- standard dialects. The book also features snapshots of second-language learners as well as bi-literacy Web resources.

Cullinan, Bernice E. 1998. *Three Voices-An Invitation to Poetry Across the Curriculum.* New York: Stenhouse.
   In this book for kindergarten through sixth grade and beyond, two classroom educators and a noted researcher in children's literature demonstrate how poetry can be used in the classroom to teach various aspects of reading and to nurture lifelong literacy. Thirty-three grade- and age-appropriate strategies are included that have been field tested in classrooms across the country.

Ezell, H. K., and L. M. Justice. 2000. "Increasing the Print Focus of Adult -Child Shared Book Reading through Observational Learning." *American Journal of Speech Pathology* 9: 36–37.

Flesch, Rudolf. 1985. *Why Johnny Can't Read.* New York: Harper and Row.

Fountas, Irene C. and Gay Su Pinnell. 1999. *Matching Books to Readers Using Leveled Books in Guided Reading K-3.* Portsmouth, NH: Heinemann.
This major contribution to the field has a list of 7,500 grade- and age-appropriate books. In addition, the authors include word counts to be used for keeping running records, text characteristics, guidelines for leveling of additional books, and suggestions for developing classroom library collections.

Fountas, Irene C. and Gay Su Pinnell. 2001. *Guiding Readers and Writers 3-6.* Portsmouth, NH: Heinemann.
This work includes 1,000 leveled books with guidelines for using them as part of a reading and writing workshop. The book explains how to use various genres in the classroom and how to use visual graphic organizers for the teaching of reading and writing.

Other works by these researchers also published by Heinemann include: *Voices on Word matters: Learning about Phonics and Spelling in the Literacy Classroom* (1999) and *Word Matters-Teaching Phonics and Spelling in the Reading/Writing Classroom* (1998).

Fry, Edward Bernard, Jacqueline Kress, Dona Lee Fountakidis. 2000. *The Reading Teacher's Book of Lists.* San Francisco, CA: Wiley Press.
This book is an invaluable one for the working classroom educator. It includes ready-to-use lists that cover a multiplicity of teacher needs. Among them are spelling demons, readability graphs, phonics, useful words, reading math, vowel lists, anagrams, portmanteaus (do you know what they are and how well they can work in word study?), Web sites, classic children's literature, and so on. Even a veteran teacher will find useful and new resources. It is also wonderful for developing independent word study investigations and literature explorations.

Ganske, Kathy. 2000. *Word Journeys-Assessment-Guided Phonics, Spelling, and Vocabulary Instruction.* New York, NY: Guilford Press.
This book offers a practical approach for assessing children's spelling. The author has created a DSA (Development Spelling Analysis) tool that teachers can use to evaluate individual children's spelling progress and to differentiate instruction. The book includes snapshots of children at different levels of spelling development.

Hall, Susan. 1994. *Using Picture Books to Teach Literary Devices.* Westport, CT: Oryx Press.

How to Help Every Child Become a Reader. Just Publishing.[tac935]
> This accessible text for kindergarten through sixth grade and beyond draws on materials developed by the U.S. Department of Education to share research, resources, referrals, and suggestions for supporting all children to become lifelong and engaged readers. It offers specific suggestions and resources for assisting struggling readers, including those with special needs and those from ELL backgrounds.

Labov, L. 2003. When Ordinary Children Fail to Read. *Reading Research Quarterly* 38: 128–31.

Macmillan, B. M. 2002. "Rhyme and Reading. A Critical Review of the Research Methodology." *Journal of Research in Reading* 25 (1): 4–42.

Makor, Barbara. *Primary Phonics Readers.*[tac936]
> These are short storybooks that children in kindergarten through second grade can own and read independently. They feature phonetically controlled texts, sounds, and spellings that are grade and age appropriate, as well as high interest, child-centered themes. As children progress through the series of 20 titles, they review and enhance their mastery of phonetic elements, sight words, and sequences at a more rapid pace. This material is compatible with the majority of phonics programs.

Munro, J. l998. "Phonological and Phonemic Awareness: Their Impact on Learning to Read Prose and Spell." *Australian Journal of Learning Disabilities* 3 (2): 15–21.

Paperback Nursery Rhyme Sampler. Whispering Coyote Press. [tac937]
> Essential for a pre-kindergarten through first-grade classroom and useful even in grade 2; these classic nursery rhymes promote phonemic and phonological awareness and children's ownership of their reading through song and movement.

Routman, Regie. l994. *Invitations: Changing as Teachers and Learners K-12.* Portsmouth, NH: Heinemann.

Routman, Regie. l996. *Literacy at the Crossroads: Crucial Talk About Reading, Writing, and Other Teaching Dilemmas.* Portsmouth, NH: Heinemann.

Routman, Regie. 2000. *Conversations: Strategies for Teaching, Learning, and Evaluating.* Portsmouth, NH: Heinemann.

Routman, Regie. 2002. *Reading Essentials.* Portsmouth, NH: Heinemann.

Statman, Ann. *Handprints-Leveled Storybooks for Early Readers Educators.* Publishing Service. [tac938]

These 50 titles, which come with five teacher's guides, were leveled using the Fountas and Pinnell Guided Reading Leveling System. They are appropriate for kindergarten through second grade. The stories reflect real-world situations and people young readers know. They include sentence structure, pictures, and cues that focus strategic reading. Print size, sentence positioning, and word spacing are appropriate for the level of the particular storybook. The titles build a strong sight vocabulary through the use of high-frequency words. Language used within the series progresses from natural to formal book language.

Schumm, Heanne Shay. *The Reading Tutor's Handbook.* Free Spirit[tac939].

This guide for kindergarten through sixth grade offers step-by-step instructions, templates, and handouts for providing children with differentiated reading support. It is not only helpful for teachers but also can be shared with paraprofessionals, teachers, interns, and parents as a support framework for the classroom reading program.

Taberski, Sharon. 2000. *On Solid Ground: Creating a Literacy Environment in Your K-3 Classroom.* Portsmouth, NH: Heinemann.

Terban, Marvin. *Time to Rhyme-A Rhyming Dictionary.* Boyd Mills Press.[tac940]

This book is easily formatted so that it can be used to introduce children in the early elementary grades (1–3) to the use of a rhyming dictionary as a reference tool. Its simple word groupings encourage writing, which can also reinforce and reciprocally enhance reading skills through the reading and writing workshop.

Vail, Patricia. *Reading Comprehension-Students Needs and Teacher's Tools.* Educators Publishers Service.

This is a compendium of explanations of specific instructional practices, terms, student projects, learning games, and resources that are critical for successfully teaching reading. It is appropriate for kindergarden through sixth grade.

Alphabet Books

A major genre of fiction and nonfiction for the teacher of reading is the alphabet book. These books' appeal, concepts, and efficiency as models for reading and writing merit them a special section in this bibliography. Even those whose text is simple enough for pre-kindergarten through second grade can serve as anchor books and models for writing workshop in grades 3–6.

Aigner-Clark, Julie. 2002. *Baby Einstein- The ABCs of Art*. Illustrations by Nadeen Zaidi. New York: Hyperion Books.

Beaton, Clare. *Zoe and Her Zebra*. Barefoot Books. [tac941]
> This board book features a character young children (pre-kindergarten through first grade) can identify with named Zoe. Her adventures are told in a simple, repetitive text with soft, literally "touchy" felt art.

Bunting, Eve. *Girls A to Z*. Boyd Mills Press. [tac942]
> This book for pre-kindergarten through first grade uses the alphabetic format to promote the opportunity for girls to select various professions and careers, ranging from astronaut to zookeeper. Bunting's text is breezy and rhymes.

Cheney, Lynne. 2002. *America- A Patriotic Primer*. Illustrated by Robin Priess Glasser. New York: Simon and Schuster.

Cheney, Lynne. *A Is For Abigail: An Almanac of Amazing American Women*. New York: Simon and Schuster[tac943]. (Ages 4–8.)

Glaser, Milton. 2003. *The Alphazeds*. Miramax.[tac944] (Ages 4–8.)

Grimes, Nikki. *C is for City*. Illustrated by Pat Cummings. Boyd Mill Press. [tac945]
> This alphabet rhyme book for kindergarten through third grade doubles as a guide to city activities. With its built-in invitations to readers to search for alphabetical items, it is perfect for use as an informal assessment tool or an interactive/paired reading anchor text.

Inkpen, Mick. 2000. *Kipper's A to Z*. San Diego: Harcourt. (Ages 3–7.)

Isadora, Rachel. 1999. *ABC Pops! (Picture Books)*. Disney Press[tac946]. (Ages 4–8.)

Johnson, Stephen. 1995. *Alphabet City*. Penguin Books.[tac947] (All ages.)

Kelley, Marty. *Summer Stinks*. Zino Press. [tac948]
This work describes the summer season in terms of things that "stink" about it, including ants, bugs, and sweat. It is fun to read and add to as the alphabet letters are learned and vocabulary is built up. It is appropriate for pre-kindergarten through first grade.

Martin, Mary Jane. *From Anne to Zach*. Boyd Mills Press.[tac949]
In this captivating book, which can serve as a touchstone text for model collaborative authoring, children learn the letters of the alphabet through other children's names.

Melmed, Laura Krauss and Frane Lesser. 2003. *Capital! Washington DC from A to Z*. New York: Harper Collins.

Musgrove, Margaret. 1976. *Ashanti to Zulu. African Traditions*. Illustrated by Leo and Diane Dillon. New York: Dial Books for Young Readers.
This is a Caldecott-winning book that uses the alphabetic format for a richly detailed and researched study of 26 African peoples. It includes a map, pronunciation guide, and illustrations that were researched in the Schomberg Center and the American Museum of Natural History. Even the frame design for each illustration reflects the African Kano knot, which signifies endless searching.

Paratore, Colleen. *26 Big Things Hands Do*. Minneapolis, MN: Free Spirit. [tac950]
What is delightful about this alphabet book is that it presents the alphabet letters as positive actions children can perform with their own small hands to help others. These actions include applauding, giving gifts, planting, and volunteering. Of course, alphabet study can continue with adding other "helping actions" to the word wall or substituting them in the text.

Pelham, David, 1991. *A is for Animals*. New York: Simon and Schuster.

Seeley, Lorna. *The Book of Shadow Boxes*. Peachtree. [tac951]
Within the shadow of each letter's shadow box lies a hidden treasure for the young reader to find. The book is intricately and exquisitely designed and conceptualized by Seeley. Its visual fascination extends well beyond the elementary grades as it fosters not only the alphabetic principle but also reading comprehension and literacy response.

Sneed, Brad. 2002. *Picture a Letter*. New York: Penguin Books.

Seuss. *ABC*. Random House.[tac952] (Ages 2 and up.)

Thornhill, Jim. *The Wildlife ABC and 123: A Nature Alphabet and Counting Book.* Maple Tree Press.[tac953]
> This is appropriate for kindergarten through first grade, with additional nature notes on the species for the teacher/parent. In addition to fostering the alphabetic principle, the book nicely mixes geographic, multicultural, and scientific knowledge into a beautifully designed text. It uses children's fascination with nature to foster reading and math literacy.

Zschock, Martha. 2001. *Journey Around Boston from A to Z.* Beverly, MA: Commonwealth Editions.

Zschock, Martha and Heather. 2002. *Journey Around New York from A to Z.* Beverly, MA: Commonwealth Editions.

Trade Books

These books foster particular aspects of reading skills, fluencies, and competencies.

Blackstone, Stella. *Where's the Cat?* Barefoot Books[TAR54].
    This book, which focuses its primary school readers on searching for a lost cat, provides excellent use of repetitive language and encourages interactive reading.

Campbell, Bebe Moore. 2003. *Sometimes My Mommy Gets Angry*. New York: G. P. Putnam's Sons.
    This is a moving story about a young girl whose mother suffers from mental illness. It is told in a way that is easy to read, along with beautiful illustrations. The main character is Annie. Sometimes her mother is very happy and other times very angry and sad. Annie has learned what to do when her mom is having a bad episode. She has books to read, a special stuffed animal, and some secret snacks. Annie also has a strong support system in place with friends, neighbors, her teacher, and grandmother.

This book is a good introduction to the issue of mental illness. It is especially important in that students see how this young girl is able to cope with this difficult part of her life. "Sometimes by mommy has a dark cloud inside of her. I can't stop the rain from falling, but I can find sunshine in my mind." Teachers can introduce students to this issue with this poignant book. Students can brainstorm different scenarios and discuss how they can be resolved. They can discuss who their support network includes and what it takes for a person to be strong enough to weather such a storm.

The book is a much needed resource for children in times where Annie's situation is far more common than is generally known. Annie's capacity to make effective, affirming, social decisions makes the work an inspirational touchstone for other peers who need to confront their parents' emotional crises. Children might be inspired to author poetry or create deliberately fictionalized narrative accounts about how they have confronted various crises.

In offering an upper elementary grade and age-appropriate narrative of a peer dealing with an emotionally ill parent, this book provides readers confronting similar family and caregiver issues with an opening for discussion and for hopeful outreach. Just reading this account may well be the first step necessary to assist a youngster in acknowledging a "hidden problem" and getting crucial adult assistance in dealing with the crisis.

Garza, Carmen Lomas. 1990. *Family Pictures Cuadros de familia*. Children's Book Press.

This book tells the story of the author's childhood growing up in a Hispanic community in Texas. The book is written in both Spanish and English, accompanied by the author's most incredible paintings. The paintings are unique, somewhat folksy, colorful, and totally entrancing. They bring you into Carmen's world. Once inside it, you don't want to leave.

There is so much to explore in this book; it works well with the study of "myself and family," community, communities around the world, Mexico, family traditions, and customs. It emphasizes social and emotional learning and how a young girl can find her way in the world. The traditions followed by her community and family were not necessarily accepted or understood by white America. Yet these values gave her the strength to be her own person and to rely on both her relationships and rich inner life to express herself.

There are so many activities that this book inspires. Children can study the origins of the piñata and make one. They can make a cookbook of recipes from Mexico or from their own homes. Children can also be encouraged to design their own book of family pictures. They can emphasize special occasions that they celebrate or focus on family traditions, which reflect their cultural backgrounds. The richness and lushness of the paintings invites the readers to construct meaning and to create their own narratives, procedural accounts, poetry, and dialogues inspired by one or more of the paintings.

Given the Spanish/English text, looking closely at the pictures can be an engaging spatial entry point for descriptive and narrative spoken and written presentations. The lushly detailed illustrations of family rites and celebrations can be springboards for children's literary and artistic renditions of equivalent family pictures and events that are prompted by Carmen's selections.

Use of dual language text for the book validates children's and family member's responses in languages other than English. Obviously, this book and its format are inspirational for ELL/bilingual learners and for special needs learners who can be captivated by the paintings.

The power of this book lies in its accessing and modeling the magic of family rites and rituals for a broad spectrum of linguistics, intrapersonal, spatial, and kinesthetic learners from monolingual, bilingual and special needs backgrounds. Common to all of its audience members are the social and emotionally celebratory components of family pictures.

Glaser, Shirley, and Milton Glaser. 2003. *The Alphazeds Words*. Hyperion Books.

> This book is incredible in so many ways. It is an alphabet book that can be read by or to little ones and not so little ones. It starts with an empty room. One by one, each letter of the alphabet enters the room, each with its own distinct look, fantastic illustrations, and typography by the designer Milton

Glaser. Each of these letters also has its own distinct personality. A is angry, B is bashful, J is jealous, and so on. The room gets quite crowded. How do all of these different personalities manage to get along and coexist? Not too well apparently, as there is shouting, pushing, hitting, and kicking. In the midst of all the chaos, the light in the room goes out and there is silence.

> When the light came back on, something
> extraordinary had happened. Four letters
> had gotten together to comfort one another.
> Together they had managed to create something
> larger and more important than themselves.
> *"They had made the first word."*

This is a great lesson on how each of us can be an individual, yet when we work together, something wonderful can happen. This book illustrates an incredible lesson in social and emotional maturity and helps the child realize that it isn't just about "me."

There are many different activities that a teacher can use with this book. The children can work in groups to make their own alphabet book of emotions. They can then present the book as a group, discussing the roles each of them played, and how they each used their unique talents to make the book.

Older children, grades 3 and up, can research and present as a group some important discoveries that were made more special because they involved people working together. They can also work on a project about cooperative learning, perhaps surveying class and schoolmates on how they feel they learn the best.

Hest, Amy. 1985. *The Purple Coat.* New York: Macmillan Publishing Co.
In the autumn of every year, Gabrielle travels with her mother to New York City to visit her Grandpa who owns a tailor shop. Once there, he always makes her a new coat, but this year Gabrielle decides the usual navy blue coat won't do. The Purple Coat follows Gabrielle in her attempt to establish her own identity.

Lionni, Leo. 1980. *Inch by Inch.* Astor-Honor Publishing Co. Inc.
In *Inch by Inch*, an inchworm (a caterpillar, or larval stage of the fall cankerworm that becomes a moth) keeps itself from being eaten by various birds by proving its worth as a measuring device.

Lupton, Hugh. *The Story Tree- Tales to Read Aloud.* Barefoot Books[TAR55].
These seven multicultural stories are accessible enough to children in kindergarten through third grade to encourage their eventually taking over the read aloud sharing on their own. This book is also a good one for family literacy sessions and for parent volunteers to read aloud in the classroom.

Martin Jr., Bill, and John Archambault. 1966. *Knots on a Counting Rope.* New York: Henry Holt and Company.
This beautifully illustrated book reaches out in so many different directions, and we can all learn so much from it. *Knots on a Counting Rope* is the story of a Native American boy who is blind and is learning from his grandfather how to survive in this world. Boy-Strength-of-Blue-Horses insists on hearing the story of his birth over and over again.

Every time his grandfather retells the story of the boy's birth, he adds a knot to his counting rope. Each time he hears the story, Boy-Strength-of-Blue-Horses gains more confidence in himself. The story emphasizes the Native American tradition of storytelling, and there are numerous art, math, and social studies lessons that offshoot from this book.

Of course, the telling and retelling of the story celebrate the young blind hero's strengths and weaknesses and ability to set goals with optimism. Stories of one's birth related by others are powerful demonstrations of social skills of the highest order.

This book also deals extensively with social and emotional learning. Children learn that those with disabilities need to be treated with sensitivity while learning to find their place in the world. One way in which children's social and emotional learning is strengthened is by understanding themselves and those around them. In order to facilitate this, each child will interview at least one family member about when he/she was born. The accounts collected with appropriate photos or memorabilia can then be shared in class and perhaps even authored into a *Knots on a Counting Rope*–style book format.

Children can also retell the story of the boy using the counting system of cultures other than Native American. This literary response will incorporate cultural study, respect, and empathy into ongoing reading and writing workshop efforts.

McCully, Emily Arnold. 1992. *Mirette on the High Wire*. G.P. Putnam's & Sons.
Mirette helps her mother run a boardinghouse for acrobats, jugglers, actors, and mimes. Her life changes when she discovers a boarder crossing the courtyard on air. She begs him to teach her how he does it. He refuses to teach her, but she begins practicing on her own. As she improves, he begins to help her. In the end, she helps him overcome his fear of the high wire.

Rabe, Bernice. 1981. *The Balancing Girl*. E. P. Dutton.
Margaret, a girl in a wheelchair is excellent at balancing all kinds of objects. Margaret shows her friend Tommy how good she is at balancing at the school carnival.

Ringgold, Faith. 1991. *Tar Beach*. New York: Crown Publishers.
This book is a favorite, and it is moving in its words, art, and the beautiful story it tells. This is an effective book to use for younger grades to connect with yourself, your family, and your community. It can also be used in connection with a mapmaking unit. The children can be encouraged to make a map of their neighborhood from an aerial view.

A starting point for a discussion would be why the author portrayed New York from such a vantage point. In this beautiful book, the narrator, Cassie Louise Lightfoot, lets her dreams and ambitions take her to places in New York City that she ordinarily would not be able to be part of because of her circumstances. As a result of her self-motivation and self-awareness, Cassie is able to go as far as her dreams will let her. In this book, Cassie also shows strengths in the areas of emotional sensitivity, as well as inter- and intrapersonal relationships.

Children can author their own Tar Beach–equivalent night fantasies and then share them with one another through an exhibit or Big Books. Although Cassie's family is obviously poor since they have to picnic on their roof, Cassie's dreamlike, lushly illustrated flight over Harlem validates the beauty of their family life and of the city landscape that is accessible to all. This is an invaluable lesson in the importance of the wealth inherent in the appreciation of family connections and the beauty of nature and public architectural designs. It is a song of family and of the city.

Schories, Pat. *Breakfast for Jack/Jack and the Missing Piece*. Front Street[TAR56].
These wordless stories help pre-literate children, ELL learners new to this country and special needs children explore the basic elements of story-character, setting and plot. The lack of words allows the children to "construct their own meaning," and create their own different stories which "fit" the illustrations.

Steinberg, Laya. *Thesaurus Rex*. Barefoot Books.[TAR57]
This book introduces a dinosaur with an interest in words whose story is told

through a wonderful rhyming text that can be used for fostering phonemic awareness and for choral readings.

Uhlberg, Myron. *The Printer*. Peachtree. [TAR58]
> This story celebrates the conventions of print in that the boy narrator's father is a deaf man who speaks with his hands and as a job chooses to turn lead type letters into words and sentences. It is an excellent book to support family literacy and an appreciation for the conventions of print.

Van Allsburg, Chris. 1988. *Two Bad Ants*. Houghton Mifflin Co. [TAR59]
> In *Two Bad Ants*, news comes to the ant world of a great discovery in a faraway place. A delicious crystal has been found. A group of ants sets out to bring back this crystal to their queen. Two ants are overwhelmed by the treasure and stay behind in this dangerous alien world. It is a tale of choices, consequences, and the discovery of life's real treasures.

Walter, Mildred Pitts. 2004. *Alec's primer*. Illustrated by Larry Johnson. Lebanon, NH: University Press of New England.
> This is the true account of a Virginian slave who was taught to read by his owner's daughter. He later fought in the Civil War on the Union side and became a landowner himself in Vermont. The beautifully written narrative is complemented by the vibrant paintings of Larry Johnson, which include authentic period details.

WEBLIOGRAPHY

Reading Online
http://www.readingonline.org
This online Web resource, which is sponsored by the International Reading Association, is full of specific reading teaching ideas, lessons, and new research. It includes summaries of conference presentations and even tips on how to use technology to teach reading.

Balanced Literacy
http://www.thekcrew.net/balancedliteracy.html
Established in 1996, this site is organized according to the components of the balanced literacy approach. It also has an excellent listing of professional books that can assist with various aspects of teaching reading.

Carol Hurst
http://www.carolhurst.com/index.html
This is a terrific resource for exploring the children's literature works that are at the crux of author and genre study. It can be used for material to supplement period studies and discussions of authors' lives. Older children will be able to explore it on their own.

Read, Write, Think
http://www.readwritethink.org/classroom-resources/lesson-plans/ This resource, maintained by the NCTE (National Council of Teachers of English), has a growing database of age- and grade-specific literacy lesson plans. It also includes all the graphic organizers cited in this book and many more, ready to download.

Inspiration Software
http://www.inspiration.com
http://www.inspiration.com/freetrial/index.cfm
This is the home site for the Inspiration and Kidspiration mind mapping software. These online templates and capacities assist the reading teacher with customizing the various graphic organizers discussed throughout the book and with gaining the ability to design customized graphic organizers for a particular theme, study, or student group. A free trial version of this resource, which is child friendly, can be downloaded.

Visual Thesaurus
http://www.visualthesaurus.com/online/
This is really both an online dictionary and a thesaurus.

Resources for reading aloud, shared reading, and independent reading available on the Internet include the following:

http://www.mightybook.com/parents_and_teachers.html
This is a library of books read aloud by the computer. Children can listen to these books or practice reading with a buddy as the computer broadcasts the text. Of course, this type of reading aloud would only be used *in addition* to the vibrant reading aloud of the teacher.

http://www.enchantedlearning.com/Rhymes.html
These are online nursery rhymes ready for reading to the children and posting throughout for room or for literacy center display.

SEDL-RCI Framework of Reading
http://www.sedl.org/reading/framework/assessment.html
This is an excellent resource for readings in the theories and methods of foundations. There are topic-aligned links to specific theorists that can be included at the close of your lesson planning and may be reviewed before certification tests.

TOOLS TO HELP YOU TEACH THE FOUNDATIONS OF READING AND SUCCEEDING IN CONSTRUCTED RESPONSE CERTIFICATION EXAMINATIONS

Appendix 1: The Record of Reading Behavior: A Close-up Look at a Ley Assessment Tool.

Often in a constructed response question on the foundations of education certification test or on a general elementary certification test; the educator is asked to analyze a record of reading behavior or to construct an appropriate one from data given in an anecdote. Furthermore, with the current climate of accountability, it is a good idea for new teachers and for career changers to examine closely the basic elements of recording reading behavior.

While there are various acceptable formats for emergent literacy assessment used throughout the country, the one selected for use here is based on the work of Marie Clay and Kenneth Goodman. These two are key researchers in the close observation and documentations of children's early reading miscues (reading mistakes).

It is important to emphasize that the teacher should not just "take the Record of Reading Behavior" and begin filling it out as the child reads from a random book prior to beginning of the observation. There are specific steps for taking the record and analyzing its results.

1. Select a text
    If you want to see if the child is reading on instructional level, choose a book that the child has already read. If the purpose of the test is to see whether the child is ready to advance to the next level, choose a book from that level that the child has not yet seen.

2. Introduce the text
    If the book is one that has been read, you do not need to introduce the text other than by saying the title. But if the book is new to the child, you should briefly share the title and tell the child a bit about the plot and style of the book.

3. Take the record
    Generally with emergent readers in grades 1 and 2, there are only 100 to 150 words in a passage used to take a record. Make certain that the child is seated beside you so that you can see the text as the child reads it.

If desired, you may want to photocopy the text in advance for yourself so you can make direct notations on it while the child reads from the book.

After you introduce the text, make certain that the child has the chance to read it independently. Be certain that you do not "teach" or help the child with the text, other than to supply an unknown word that the child requests you supply. The purpose of the record is to see what the child does on his or her own.

As the child reads the text, you must be certain to record the reading behaviors the child exhibits using the following notations.

In taking the record, keep in mind the following: Allow enough time for the child to work independently on a problem before telling or supplying the word. If you wait too long, you could run the risk of having the child lose the meaning and his/her interest in the story as he or she tries to identify the unknown word.

It is recommended that when a child is way off track, you tell him or her to "Try that again" (TTA). If a whole phrase is troubling, put it into square brackets and score it as only one error.

The notation for filling out the Record of Reading behavior involves noting the child's response on the top with the actual text below it.

Comprehension Check

This can and should be done by inviting the child to retell the story. This retelling can then be used to ask further questions about characters, plot, setting, and purpose, which allow you to observe and to record the child's level of comprehension.

CALCULATING THE READING LEVEL AND THE SELF-CORRECTION RATE

Calculating the reading level lets you know if the book is at the level on which the child can read it independently or comfortably with guidance or if the book is at a level where reading it frustrates the child.

Generally, an accuracy score of 95% to 100% suggests that the child can read the text and other books or texts on the same level.

An accuracy score of 90% to 94% indicates that the texts likely will present challenges to the child, but with guidance from you, a tutor, or parent, the child will be able to master these texts and enjoy them. This is instructional level.

However, an accuracy score of less than 89% tells you that the material you have selected for the child is too hard for the child to control alone. Such material needs to be shared with the child in a shared reading situation or by reading to the child.

Keeping Score on the Record

Insertions, omissions, substitutions, and teacher-told responses all count as errors. Repetitions are not scored as errors. Corrected responses are scored as self-corrections.

No penalty is given for a child's attempts at self-correction that results in a finally incorrect response, but the attempts should be noted.. Multiple unsuccessful attempts at a word score as one error only.

The lowest score for any page is zero. If a child omits a line or lines, each word omitted is counted as an error. If the child omits a page, deduct the number of words omitted from the total number of words that you have used for the record.

Calculating the Reading Level

Note the number of errors made on each line on the Record of Reading Behavior in the column marked E (for Error).

Total the number of errors in the text and divide this number into the number of words that the child has read. This will give you the error rate.

If a child reads a passage of 100 words and has made 10 errors, the error rate would be 1 in 10. Convert this to an accuracy percentage of 90%.

Calculating the Self-Correction Rate

Total all the self-corrections. Next, add the number of errors to the number of self-corrections and divide by the number of self-corrections.

A self correction rate of 1 in 3 to 1 in 5 is considered good. This rate indicates that the child is able to help him or herself as problems are encountered in reading.

Analyzing the record

This record should assist the educator in developing a detailed date-specific picture of the child's progress in reading behavior. It should be used to help the educator individualize instruction for the specific child.

As the errors are reviewed, consider whether the child made the error because of semantics (cues from meaning), syntactic (language structure), or visual information difficulties.

As self-corrections are analyzed, consider what led the child to make that self-correction. Check out and consider what cues the child does use effectively and what the child does not use well.

Consider the ways in which the child tackles a word that is unknown. Characterize that behavior and consider how the teacher can assist the child with this issue.

If a child can retell at least three quarters of a story, this is considered adequate for retelling.

Analysis of reading behavior records can and should support the educator in designing appropriate mini-lessons and strategies to help the child with his or her recorded errors and miscues.

SAMPLE TEST

1. **Prioritize these theorists in terms of their contributions regarding young children; intermediate-aged, middle level children; and all children, respectively. (*Rigorous, Competency 1.0*)**

   A) Randolph Caldecott, E.D. Hirsch, John Newbery

   B) Randolph Caldecott, John Newbery, E.D. Hirsch

   C) John Newbery, E.D. Hirsch, Randolph Caldecott

   D) E.D. Hirsch, Randolph Caldecott, John Newbery

2. **In the balanced literacy approach, ability groups are (*Rigorous, Competency 1.0*)**

   A) Abolished

   B) Recommended

   C) Mixed

   D) Changeable

3. **Emergent literacy is: (*Rigorous, Competency 1.0, 2.0, 14.0*)**

   A) An updated term for reading readiness

   B) A stage that follows early reading

   C) A description of children's gradual entry into reading from birth onward

   D) A set of incremental skills that must be mastered before reading

4. **Cues in reading are: (*Average, Competency 1.0*)**

   A) Vowel sounds

   B) Digraphs

   C) Sources of information used by readers to help them construct meaning

   D) None of the above

5. **Rudolf Flesch is to_____ as Marie Clay is to_____** *(Rigorous,* Competency *1.0)*

A) Cultural literacy; balanced literacy

B) Decodable books; leveled books

C) Phonics; Reading Recovery

D) Wordless picture books; picture story books

6. **Ms. Ramirez also wants the children to share their functional reading skills with their families, so she asks that they take the newspapers home to focus on the:** *(Average, Competency 1.0, 14.0)*

A) Advice columns

B) Fill in coupons

C) Metropolitan news briefs

D) Weather section

7. **A theorist who believes that there is a finite body of approved literature children should be taught on various grade levels and has produced books about what everyone needs to know to be literate on various grade levels is:** *(Easy, Competency 1.0)*

A) Rudolf Flesch

B) J. David Cooper

C) John Dewey

D) E. D. Hirsch

8. **A teacher is asking children to look at the beginning letters of words. She then asks the child to connect the beginning letter to the text and story and to think about what word would make sense there. This is an example of:** *(Average, Competency 1.0, 14.0)*

A) A balanced literacy approach

B) A phonemic approach

C) A phonic approach

D) AN ELL differentiated approach

9. **A bound morpheme is:**
    (Average, Competency 1.0)

    A) A word whose meaning stands alone

    B) The smallest unit of sound in the language

    C) An inflectional ending which, when added to a base word, changes it case, gender, or number

    D) A root word whose spelling changes depending on what prefix or suffix one adds to it

10. **Using children's literature trade books plus reader's and writers' workshops best demonstrates the _____ theory of reading.**
    (Average, Competency 1.0, 18.0)

    A) Top-down

    B) Bottom-up

    C) Transactional

    D) Decoding or phonics

11. **A veteran teacher waited for her adult daughter outside of her daughter's first class in the Teaching of Reading. As she and her daughter talked about the first session of the course, the teacher never heard an explicit mention of the teaching of reading. All she heard about was:** *(Easy, Competency 1.0)*

    A) Learning about narratives

    B) Dealing with text structures

    C) Constructing meaning

    D) All of the above

12. **When teaching children to read nonfiction, the knowledge of different text structures will provide them with:**
    (Easy, Competency 1.0, 11.0, 12.0)

    A) Predictable questions for self-correction

    B) The fluency to promote reading speed

    C) Skills to navigate different parts of the text

    D) Schemata that promote comprehension

13. The interrelated skills of reading, writing, listening, and speaking are called the: *(Rigorous, Competency 1.0, 11.0, 12.0)*

    A) Receptive communication arts

    B) Expressive communication arts

    C) Language arts

    D) Communication arts

14. The teacher is watching the children go from oral speech into writing. The teacher says, "Great job:" *(Easy, Competency 2.0)*

    A) A good decoding

    B) A good recoding

    C) A good encoding

    D) All of the above

15. As the child is reading and has made an incorrect attempt, the teacher prompts: *(Rigorous, Competency 2.0, 11.0, 14.0)*

    A) I know you can get it right

    B) Try again, Lila

    C) Does that make sense to you?

    D) That word's a tough one

16. As far as the balanced literacy movement is concerned, the "whole" when referring to a lesson indicates: *(Average, Competency 2.0)*

    A) All the reading themes will be covered that day

    B) The whole class meets for the mini-lesson

    C) The complete unit will be covered over the month

    D) All of the reading and writing work to be done in connection with one book

17. If children are engaged in creating a museum within classroom project to exhibit their work, they are *(Average, Competency 2.0, 18.0)*

    A) Not doing any reading or writing

    B) Doing many authentic reading, writing, and researching tasks

    C) Not likely to visit a real museum.

    D) All of the above

18. The teacher is very concerned about identifying a book that is "just right" for Jay to read independently. This means that Jay should be able to read this book with: *(Easy, Competency 2.0, 4.0, 5.0)*

    A) Below 92% accuracy

    B) 100% accuracy

    C) 95–100% accuracy

    D) 92–97% accuracy

19. All of the following statements are true about the relationship between reading and writing EXCEPT? *(Average, Competency 2.0)*

    A) Both reading and writing must be taught

    B) When taught together, reading and writing improve achievement

    C) Combining reading and writing develops critical thinking

    D) Most children can learn to read and write without any instruction

20. Children's oral language background contributes to their understanding of which of the following aspects of written language? *(Rigorous, Competency 2.0, 14.0)*

    A) Syntax: the order in which sentences are expressed

    B) Semantics: the meaning of words

    C) Phonology: the sounds of language

    D) All of the above

21. **Taking responsibility for a child's own learning, will usually involve the child in:** *(Average, Competency 2.0, 3.0, 18.0)*

    A) Reading and writing on his/her own

    B) Developing a personal literacy project that will later be shared with the teacher and peers and family

    C) Putting away books and materials when directed

    D) both A and B

22. **Arrange these phenomena in the order in which children master them in reading:** *(Rigorous, Competency 3.0, 8.0)*

    A) Environmental print, alphabetic principle, phonological awareness, decoding

    B) Environmental print, phonological awareness, alphabetic principle, decoding

    C) Environmental print, decoding, alphabetic principle, phonological awareness

    D) Environmental print, phonological awareness, decoding, alphabetic principle

23. **Mark Garner has been told that he will have to support some special needs readers in his classroom in addition to the rest of the students. He can expect to have:** *(Easy, Competency 3.0, 15.0)*

    A) Gifted children who are accelerated in reading skills for their grade and age

    B) Children who have disabilities and will need special support in accessing the content and methods he uses with the rest of the class

    C) Children who come from native language backgrounds other than English

    D) Children who display the capacities and needs detailed in A and B

24. **Ability grouping means:** *(Easy, Competency 3.0)*

A) Grouping of children according to the results of an IQ test

B) Grouping of children with similar test results for instructional purposes

C) Grouping of children according to their oral reading accuracy rate

D) Grouping of children with similar needs for instructional purposes

25. **Gracie seems to be struggling with her reading, even in first grade, although her mother works at a publishing firm and her dad is an editor. Her speech is also full of mispronunciations, even though her parents were born in the school neighborhood. Gracie should be checked by:** *(Average, Competency 3.0, 15.0)*

A) A reading specialist

B) A speech therapist or an audiologist

C) A pediatrician

D) A psychologist

26. **Which of the following statements is true concerning individual differences in reading?** *(Rigorous, Competency 3.0)*

A) Gender differences are highly predictive of reading success

B) Young children who were read to by adults in the home have an easier time with beginning reading

C) Socioeconomic class makes no difference in children's early reading efforts

D) Having a brother or sister who reads is predictive of a children's early success at reading

27. The concerned parent whose child had a visual impairment wanted as much help for him as the teacher and the school district could give her. She begged, "Please, he didn't attend pre-school, he has no prior knowledge." Strictly speaking this is: *(Average, Competency 3.0)*

A) Correct, since he didn't get preschool experiences

B) Incorrect, since prior knowledge covers everyone's experiences

C) Incorrect, since he did have prior knowledge experiences but these didn't match those of many of his peers, so he would need to enhance his prior knowledge

D) both B and C

28. Ms. James is seated with a child by her side. The child is reading aloud from an open book. Ms. James is teaching in a school that has embraced the Balanced Literacy Approach. Therefore it is most likely that Ms. James is writing and recording: *(Average, Competency 4.0)*

A) The child's use of expression in reading aloud

B) The child's errors and miscues

C) Her observations of the child's attitude toward reading

D) The child's feelings about the particular passage being read

29. The most important reason to keep ongoing assessments of children's phonological awareness is: *(Rigorous, Competency 4.0, 5.0, 6.0, 17.0)*

A) To be accountable to the principal

B) To compare with teachers of the same grade level

C) To have data for report cards

D) To plan curriculum

30. _____is to the Stanford Achievement Test as_____ is to the Metropolitan Achievement Test. *(Rigorous,4.0, 5.0)*

A) Predictive; diagnostic

B) Individual; group

C) Criterion-referenced; norm-referenced

D) Written; oral

31. A teacher wants to teach her class how to choose a "just right" book to read independently. What should the teacher teach the class? (Easy, Competency 4.0, 5.0)

A) Students should read the summary of the story on the back of the book.
B) Students should read the last page of the story and make predictions about the story.
C) Students should open randomly to the middle of the book and read a page.
D) Students should ask a friend if they had trouble reading the book.

32. Jay really wants to read a book that he can only read with 94% accuracy. He could be able to read this book as: *(Easy, Competency 4.0, 5.0)*

A) An independent reading

B) A guided reading

C) A shared reading

D) All of the above

33. When taking a child's running record, the kinds of self corrections the child makes: *(Average, Competency 4.0)*

A) Are not important, but the percentage of accuracy is important

B) May show something about which cueing systems the child relies on

C) Can be meaningful if analyzed over several records

D) Both B and C

34. **Once a teacher has carefully recorded and documented a running record:** *(Average, Competency 4.0)*

    A) There is nothing further to do as long as the teacher keeps the running record for conferences and documentation of grades

    B) The teacher should review the running record and other subsequent ones taken for growth over time

    C) The teacher should differentiate instruction for that particular student as indicated by growth over time and evidence of other needs

    D) Both B and C

35. **The reliability of a standardized test is measured by:** *(Rigorous, Competency 4.0)*

    A) The percentage of children scoring in a bell-shaped curve

    B) Its lack of bias

    C) Whether it tests what it is supposed to test

    D) Its consistency over time

36. **A quartile on a test is:** *(Easy, Competency 4.0)*

    A) A quarter of the grades grouped

    B) The division of the percentiles into four segments each of which is called a quartile

    C) 25% of the tests scored

    D) both B and C

37. **Validity in assessment means:** *(Average, Competency 4.0)*

    A) The test went off without any previewing of the questions or leaks on its contents

    B) The majority of test takers passed

    C) The correct time was allowed for the children to complete the test

    D) The test assessed what it was supposed to assess and measure

38. **"Bias" in testing occurs when:** *(Average, Competency 4.0)*

A) The assessment instrument is not an objective, fair, and impartial one for a given cultural, ethnic, or special needs participant

B) The testing administrator is biased

C) The same test is given with no time considerations or provisions for those in need of more time or those who have handicapping conditions

D) All of the above

39. **Norm-referenced tests:** *(Rigorous, Competency 4.0)*

A) Give information only about the local samples results

B) Provide information about how the local test takers did compared to a representative sampling of national test takers

C) Make no comparisons to national test takers

D) None of the above

40. **If you get your raw score on a test, you will get** *(Easy, Competency 4.0)*

A) The actual number of points you scored on the test

B) The percentage score of the number of questions you answered correctly

C) A letter grade for your work on the test

D) An aggregated score for your performance on the text

41. **A standardized test will be:** *(Easy, Competency 4.0)*

A) Given out with the same predetermined questions and format to all

B) Not be given to certain children

C) If given out in exactly the same format with the same content, may be taken over a lengthier test period (i.e. four hours instead of three or two)

D) All of the above

42. Bill has been called up to the teacher for an individual conference. She asks him to retell one of the books he has listed on his weekly log. He begins and is still talking seven minutes later. Most probably, Bill: *(Easy, Competency 4.0)*

   A) Told the entire story with all its details and minor characters

   B) May or may not have really gotten the main points and perspectives of the story

   C) May have really liked the story

   D) None of the above

43. What does the phrase, "Assessment drives instruction" mean?

   A) After every unit of study there should be a formal assessment
   B) A teacher should informally assess students everyday
   C) Assessments should be the basis of the following year's curriculum review process
   D) Assessment results should be used and analyzed by the teacher to plan the next unit of study

44. All of the following are characteristics of an effective assessment EXCEPT
   (Rigorous, Competency 4.0)

   A) It should be an ongoing process by the teacher
   B) It should happen every day both informally and formally
   C) It should only measure a small portion of what students know
   D) It should be reflected on by the teacher as a way to improve instruction

45. The data coordinator of the district who is concerned with federal funding for reading will probably want to start aggregating scores immediately because:
   (Rigorous, Competency 5.0)

   A) It is interesting to crunch more data

   B) By aggregating, the individual scores can be combined to view performance trends across groups

   C) This will help the district determine which groups need more remedial instruction

   D) both B and C

46. **The major difference between phonemic and phonological awareness is:** *(Easy, Competency 6.0)*

   A) One deals with a series of discrete sounds and the other with sound-spelling relationships

   B) One is involved with teaching and learning alliteration and rhymes

   C) Phonemic awareness is a specific type of phonological awareness that deals with separate phonemes within a given word

   D) Phonological awareness is associated with printed words

47. **Mr. Sanchez is having his students work with one-syllable words, removing the first consonant and substituting another, as in m/ats to h/ats. What reading skill are they working on?** *(Average rigor) (Skill 6.0, 9.0)*

   A) Morphemic inflections

   B) Pronouncing short vowels

   C) Invented spelling

   D) Phonological awareness

48. **All of the following are true about phonological awareness EXECPT:** *(Easy, Competency 6.0)*

   A) It may involve print

   B) It is a prerequisite for spelling and phonics

   C) Activities can be done by the children with their eyes closed

   D) It starts before letter recognition is taught

49. **Andrew is just starting school, but it looks like he will be successful in reading because:** *(Rigorous, Competency 6.0, 7.0)*

   A) He comes from a family that cares about his progress

   B) He is phonemically aware and knows his alphabet

   C) He has been in preschool

   D) He is well-behaved

50. Ronald's parents are hearing-impaired. What work will this first grader need *most*? *(Rigorous, Competency 6.0, 15.0)*

A) Picture cues to promote visual acuity

B) Sight word mastery to promote fluency

C) Rhymes and reading aloud to promote phonological awareness

D) Letter-sound practice to promote the alphabetic principle

51. A stationery store owner in the neighborhood of the school is amused by the fact that the children on a school walk, are rushing up to various store signs and street signs. The children are probably exploring: *(Average, Competency 6.0)*

A) The alphabetic principle.

B) The principle that print carries meaning.

C) Letter-sound recognition.

D) Phonemic awareness.

52. The purpose of taking dictation is to: *(Easy, Competency 6.0, 7.0, 18.0)*

A) Demonstrate how to copy down speech.

B) Make a connection and promote awareness of the relationship between spoken and written language.

C) Authenticate the children's comments.

D) Raise the children's self esteem.

53. Clapping is the best way to learn syllable divisions because: *(Rigorous, Competency 6.0)*

A) Children enjoy the activity and are motivated to learn.

B) Syllables are rhythmic.

C) The activity is both auditory and kinesthetic.

D) Movement aids memory.

54. The *most important* reason for using children's names in the teaching of concepts of print and the alphabetic principle is: *(Rigorous, Competency 6.0, 7.0)*

A) It appeals to the children's vanity

B) These are among the first letters that children learn

C) These letters are "special" and are highly motivating for the children to use

D) The children will quickly be able to read every other child's name in the classroom

55. The substitute teacher starts reading aloud the Big Book on the easel (which she has never seen before). What do you predict will happen? *(Rigorous, Competency 6.0, 7.0, 18.0)*

A) The children will enjoy hearing the book read by another voice

B) The teacher's unfamiliarity will lead her to ask excellent prediction questions

C) The teacher will be excited by what she spontaneously discovers in the book

D) The teacher will not read very expressively nor will she have a clear purpose for reading the book

56. The value of exposing young children to environmental print is that it *(Rigorous, Competency 7.0, 9.0, 18.0)*

A) Introduces children to the idea that print carries a message

B) Helps children learn to decode

C) Helps children make sense of their world

D) Introduces children to the world of consumerism

57. As visitors from the United Kingdom tour the school, they are pleased to hear a singsong chant "Don't fall asleep at the page, don't forget the _____." Mr. Adams explains to them that the first graders are learning about pointing at words and moving from the left to the right, this is called: *(Easy, Competency 7.0)*

A) Skimming

B) Return sweep

C) Top to bottom

D) Line for line reading

58. Environmental print is available at all of the following EXCEPT: *(Rigorous, Competency 7.0)*

A) Within a newspaper

B) On the page of a library book

C) On a supermarket circular

D) In a commercial flyer

59. Children learn book handling skills best through: *(Rigorous, Competency 7.0)*

A) Teacher modeling during shared reading

B) Parents reading to their children at home

C) Imitation of their book buddies or peer tutors from another class

D) Direct instruction by the teacher

60. The best way for a primary grade teacher to model directionality and one-to-one word matching would be: *(Average, Competency 7.0)*

A) Using a regular library or classroom textbook

B) Using her own person reading book

C) Using a Big Book

D) Using a book dummy

61. An observer enters Julia's first-grade classroom. Children are working with oaktag strips and placing letters on these strips on a sentence strip holder. Then they seem to be involved in some kind of counting. The observer is confused. This activity is taking place during the reading block. Julia explains: *(Average, Competency 8.0, 9.0)*

A) The children are counting letters

B) This is word sorting and the children are grouping words by length, common letters, and sound

C) The children are combining mathematics counting and word study

D) The children are doing a strategy sheet based on a particular word family

62. _____is to letter-sound relationships as_____is to word meanings. *(Rigorous, Competency 8.0, 9.0)*

A) Decoding; syntax

B) Phonological awareness; phonemic awareness

C) Syntax; semantics

D) Graphophonemic awareness; semantics

63. To decode is to: *(Easy, Competency 8.0)*

A) Construct meaning

B) Sound out a printed sequence of letters

C) Use a special code to decipher a message

D) Write out what one hears

64. **By November the first graders have a vocabulary of words that they can correctly pronounce and read aloud. These words are their:** *(Rigorous, Competency 8.0, 10.0, 13.0)*

A) Sight vocabulary

B) Recognition vocabulary

C) Personal vocabulary

D) Working vocabulary

65. **A "decodable text" is:** *(Easy, Competency 8.0, 18.0)*

A) A text that a child can read aloud with correct pronunciations

B) A text that a child can answer comprehension questions about with a high percentage of accuracy

C) Text written to match the sequence of letter-sound relationships that have been taught

D) None of the above

66. **What is the optimum order for teaching these phonics skills?** *(Rigorous, Competency 8.0)*

A) Long vowels, diagraphs and blends, diphthongs, short vowels, and r-controlled words

B) Short vowels, long vowels, digraphs and blends, diphthongs, and r-controlled words

C) Digraphs and blends, diphthongs, long vowels, short vowels, and r-controlled words

D) Short vowels, digraphs and blends, long vowels, diphthongs, and r-controlled words

67. Mr. Adams has complained to Mr. Mark that there are too many newspapers piled up in his classroom. Mr. Mark has responded that he does not want to throw away these piled-up newspapers because: *(Average, Competency 8.0, 18.0)*

A) They can be used for letter-sound correspondence

B) They represent environmental print

C) They can be used to create print-meaning signs.

D) All of the above

68. What is the most important value of allowing children to use invented spelling? *(Rigorous, Competency 9.0, 14.0)*

A) It frees up the teacher to get around to many children during writing workshop

B) It ultimately contributes to good spelling skills

C) It helps children listen to the sounds of words they are attempting to write

D) It makes children feel proud of their writing

69. A word wall is to _____ as a story board is to ___. *(Rigorous, Competency 9.0)*

A) Spelling; characterization

B) The dictionary; the book

C) Word families; plot sequence

D) Sight words; picture cues

70. The word "bat" is a _____ word for "batter-up." *(Rigorous, Competency 9.0)*

A) Suffix

B) Prefix

C) Root word

D) Inflectional ending

71. _____ is a compound word, while _____ is a contraction. *(Rigorous, Competency 9.0)*

A) Trenchcoat; its

B) Flip chart; whose

C) Big top; it is

D) Ballgame, who's

72. As Mr. Adams exits his school building, he notices that Mr. Mark, a new teacher, is leading a group of happy looking fifth graders back into the building. They are carrying all kinds of free pamphlets and circulars from a local coffee house. Mr. Adams immediately asks Mr. Mark why the class went to that coffee house during the lunch break. When he hears Mr. Mark's answer, he is delighted: *(Average, Competency 9.0, 18.0)*

A) Mr. Mark says they went looking for environmental print and words with a café and latte root

B) Mr. Mark says they didn't spend any money and got free hot chocolate

C) The children will have to summarize a pamphlet as homework

D) All of the above

73. In the following sentence, identify the underlined words: "The tourniquet was <u>wound</u> around the <u>wound</u>." *(Average, Competency 9.0)*

A) Homophones

B) Homodicts

C) Homonyms

D) Homographs

74. To promote word study, children can: *(Average, Competency 10.0)*

A) Be required to go to the dictionary at least once or twice a day

B) Collect and share words of interest they find in their readings

C) Do vocabulary work sheets from a basal reader or commercial vocabulary book

D) Do all of the above

75. In order to get children to compile specialized vocabulary, they can use: *(Average, Competency 10.0)*

    A) Newspapers

    B) Internet resources and approved Web sites that focus on the special interest

    C) Experts they can interview

    D) All of the above

76. Teachers should select at least ___words for pre-reading vocabulary discussion: *(Easy, Competency 10.0)*

    A) 12

    B) 15

    C) 2–3

    D) 8–10

77. Pre-teaching vocabulary is to___as choral reading is to____. *(Rigorous, Competency 10.0)*

    A) Comprehension; letter-sound relationships

    B) Fluency; articulation

    C) Esthetic appreciation; comprehension

    D) Comprehension; fluency

78. Two steps a teacher might take before selecting words for study are: *(Easy, Competency 10.0)*

    A) Reading the story and story mapping

    B) Asking advice from a veteran teacher and the grade leader

    C) Looking in a teacher's guide and copying out the words listed there

    D) All of the above are correct

79. In a balanced literacy classroom, new vocabulary would most likely appear on: *(Average, Competency 10.0)*

    A) An experiential chart

    B) A class newspaper

    C) The word wall

    D) Outside the room on a bulletin board

80. An effective way to build vocabulary and to make connections with mandated science and mathematics material is to teach Greek and Latin roots using: *(Average, Competency 10.0, 11.0, 12.0)*

    A) Semantic maps

    B) Hierarchical arrays

    C) Linear arrays

    D) Word webs

81. Cause-and-effect is to __as chronological is to _____. *(Rigorous, Competency 11.0)*

    A) Nonfiction; fiction

    B) Text structure; story

    C) Comprehension; appreciation

    D) Writing; reading

82. Asking a child if what he or she has read makes sense to him or her, is prompting the child to use: *(Average, Competency 11.0, 14.0)*

    A) Phonics cues

    B) Syntactic cues

    C) Semantic cues

    D) Prior knowledge

83. When you ask a child if what he or she has just read "sounds right" to him or her, you are trying to get that child to use: *(Average, Competency 11.0, 14.0)*

    A) Phonics cues

    B) Syntactic cues

    C) Semantic cues

    D) Prior knowledge

84. As part of study about the agricultural products of their state, children have identified 22 different types of apples produced in the state. They can use a _____to compare and contrast these different types of apples: *(Rigorous, Competency 11.0, 12.0)*

    A) Word web

    B) Semantic map

    C) Semantic features analysis grid

    D) All of the above

85. One of the many ways in which a child can demonstrate comprehension of a story is by: *(Average, Competency 11.0)*

A) Filling in a strategy sheet

B) Retelling the story orally

C) Retelling the story in writing

D) All of the above

86. The technique SQ3R is an aid to students' comprehension when used with nonfiction texts. The steps are as follows: *(Average, Competency 11.0, 13.0)*

A) Start Questioning, then Read, Remember, and Report

B) Survey, Question, Read, Recite, and Review

C) Stay Quiet, Read for 3 minutes, and then Remember main points

D) Start with a Question, find 3 Answers, and then Read on

87. The Stop and Think Strategy means that the child reader will: *(Average, Competency 11.0)*

A) Read through until the end of the story or text

B) Ask himself or herself if what he or she has read makes sense to him or her

C) Stop after reading some text and write down his/her concerns

D) All of the above

88. An excellent research project that can combine dictionary study with science research would be: *(Average, Competency 11.0, 12.0, 18.)*

A) A student-authored dictionary terms and phrases about earthworms

B) A teacher-developed specialized dictionary of words and phrases about earthworms

C) A collection of articles on earthworms put together by the school librarian

D) both B and C

89. **Mr. Mark is a brand new teacher who is not from the neighborhood where his school is located. He is a bit nervous as this is his first teaching assignment. He does not yet know how to relax enough to get his students to activate prior experience. He should:** *(Rigorous, Competency 11.0)*

A) Try a free recall question: Tell us what you know about...

B) Try an unstructured question: Let's talk about...

C) Use word association: What do you associate X with?

D) All of the above

90. **Among the literary strategies that teachers can use to activate prior knowledge are:** *(Average, Competency 11.0)*

A) Predicting and previewing a story

B) Story mapping

C) Venn diagramming

D) Linear arrays

91. **Ms. Ancess used to take time to have her children memorize major poems and even had an assembly for parents and school staff where the children dramatically recited various poems. Now that she is worried about the children's reading scores, she doesn't want to waste time with this memorization. Actually if she still includes this high interest, child-centered experience:** *(Rigorous, Competency 11.0)*

A) The children can use their oral fluency and her modeling as a bridge for enhanced comprehension

B) The children can get a sense of "ownership" of the words

C) Children and parents will have a "break" from worrying about the test

D) None of the above

92. To help children with "main idea" questions, the teacher should: *(Average, Competency 11.0)*

    A) Give out a strategy sheet on the main idea for children to place in their reader's notebooks

    B) Model responding to such a question as part of guided reading

    C) Have children create "main idea questions" to go with their writings

    D) All of the above

93. The teacher is working on a life science unit in grade 5 and using many print and electronic sources for information. Some of the words in the unit have a serial and others a categorical relationship to one another. To help the children's comprehension, the teacher could now: *(Rigorous, Competency 11.0, 12.0, 18.0)*

    A) Use a root family diagram or tree

    B) Work with base words

    C) Use hierarchical and linear arrays

    D) Create separate semantic maps of each word

94. When teaching children how to comprehend different text structures, two techniques that work well are: *(Average, Competency 11.0, 12.0, 13.0)*

    A) Small group work and story maps

    B) Semantic features analysis and Venn diagrams

    C) Word webs and "clue words"

    D) Cloze procedure and Kid Pix

95. As part of a study for a unit on the history of Massachusetts, Mr. Gentry is using the early childhood book *26 Letters and 99 Cents* by Tina Hoban. He wants his readers to study it and create a more detailed guide to their state using its concept. This is a technique frequently used in: *(Average, Competency 12.0, 18.0)*

    A) Reading and writing workshop

    B) Writing process instruction

    C) Readers workshop

    D) Technical writing

96. The science fair is coming up and Ms. Gardner is trying to find time in her busy schedule to work on her class's earth worm diary project. With all of the mandated tests and assemblies, she has not found time to start her students on their earth worm research. Within the context of reading instruction, she can: *(Average, Competency 12.0, 18.0)*

A) Begin a thematic study unit

B) Start with reading aloud of the *Diary of an Earth Worm* by Doreen Cronin

C) Scaffold the research process by going online with her children using an approved search engine to find matches for earthworm sites

D) All of the above

97. Study guides can often help students navigate nonfiction or expository text. Find the false statement about study guides in this group: *(Rigorous, Competency 13.0)*

A) They may be successfully used at any grade level

B) The more structured and directive they are, the most support study guides provide

C) They help students construct meaning

D) They are most effective in grades 4 and up

98. One of the most important features in nonfiction books that children should learn to read includes: *(Rigorous, Competency 13.0)*

A) Page numbers

B) Picture cues

C) Characterization

D) Captions

99. When they are in sixth grade, children should be able to independently go through an unfamiliar collection and: *(Average, Competency 13.0)*

    A) Use only the table of contents

    B) Use the first line indices and find a poem by author and subject

    C) Use only the glossary

    D) None of the above

100. In Ms. Francine's class, dictionary use is a punishment. Mr. Adams is: *(Average, Competency 13.0)*

    A) Pleased with the way that Ms. Francine approaches dictionary use

    B) Unconcerned with this approach to the use of the dictionary

    C) Convinced that the teacher should model her own fascination and pleasure in using the dictionary for the children

    D) Delighted by the fact that children are being forced to use the dictionary

101. Dictionary study: *(Average, Competency 13.0)*

    A) Can begin in grades 1 or 2

    B) Can begin in prekindergarten using the lush picture dictionaries

    C) Should start on grade 3 level

    D) both A and B

102. "Beautiful Beth is the Best Girl in the Bradley Bay area." This sentence could be used to help children learn about: *(Average, Competency 14.0)*

    A) Assonance

    B) Alliteration

    C) Rhyming pairs

    D) None of the above

103. **Is it easier for ELL students who read in their first language to learn to read in English?** *(Rigorous, Competency 14.0, 15.0)*

   A) No, because the letter-sound relationships in English are unique

   B) Yes, because this will give the children confidence

   C) No, because there is often interference from one language to the next

   D) Yes, because the process is the same regardless of the language

104. **A very bright child in a grade 1 class came from a family that did not a have a strong oral story telling or story reading tradition in its native language. This child would need support in developing:** *(Rigorous, Competency 14.0)*

   A) Letter-sound correspondence skills

   B) Schemata for generic concepts most children have in their memories and experiences based on family oral traditions and read a loud

   C) Oral expressiveness

   D) both B and C

105. **By definition, which children in a classroom will have trouble with syntactic cues?** *(Rigorous, Competency 14.0, 15.0)*

   A) Those from families who do not have household libraries

   B) Those not in a top reading group

   C) Those from ELL backgrounds

   D) All of the above

106. **The clearest predictor of a child's early reading achievement is:** *(Rigorous, Competency 14.0, 19.0)*

   A) Parents who read to their children at home.

   B) Number of books and magazines a family owns

   C) The child's attendance at a good preschool

   D) Parents' educational levels

107. Most of the children in first-year teacher Ms. James's class are really doing well in their phonemic awareness assessments. However, Ms. James is very concerned about three children who do not seem to be able to distinguish between spoken words that "sound alike" but are different. Since she is a first-year teacher, she feels her inexperience may be to blame. In truth, the reason these three children have not yet demonstrated phonemic awareness is most likely that: *(Rigorous, Competency 14.0, 15.0)*

A) They are not capable of becoming good readers

B) They are bored in class

C) They may be from an ELL background

D) Ms. James does not pronounce the different phonemes clearly enough

108. Chard and Osborn (1999) found that children with reading disabilities need to learn the alphabetic principle because: *(Rigorous, Competency 15.0)*

A) The alphabet has predictable letter-sound relationships

B) Learning sight words is harder for the disabled reader

C) Knowing the alphabet will give these readers confidence

D) The relationship between letters and sounds is central to early reading

109. While the supervisor is pleased overall with Barbara's first year of teaching, he feels that given the fact that two of her students are transfers from Mexico and one student has a hearing impairment, she has to plan for: *(Rigorous, Competency 15.0, 17.0)*

    A) Extra homework for all of them

    B) Extra time for the hearing impaired child

    C) A buddy to work with the two students from Mexico

    D) Differentiated instruction to meet these students' varied special needs

110. Advantages of the basal reading series include all of the following except: *(Rigorous, Competency 16.0, 17.0, 18.0)*

    A) A clearly sequenced set of skills to teach

    B) Highly interesting stories that appeal to children

    C) A continuum of scope and sequence across grade levels

    D) Daily lesson plans available for the teacher

111. In terms of a balanced literacy classroom, a "leveled bin" indicates: *(Easy, Competency 16.0, 18.0)*

    A) A bin of paperback books set at the child's eye level for reading choices.

    B) A bin with books the child has selected for him or herself.

    C) A bin with books leveled by the teacher

    D) A bin with different reading materials, including magazines, at a child's level

112. A natural role for a highly proficient reader would be: *(Average, Competency 16.0, 17.0)*

    A) To assist the teacher with cleaning the classroom and organizing the student folders

    B) To develop charts for the teacher by copying needed poems for full class study

    C) Tutor and support struggling readers

    D) Work on his/her own interests while the teacher works with the rest of the class

113. When displaying children's books in the classroom, the best way to display them for younger readers is: *(Rigorous, Competency 16.0, 18.0)*

A) In a reading center called the "library," with the books shelved alphabetically

B) In crates that display various reading levels

C) Face-up in order to see the title and cover page

D) Placed strategically throughout the room in various learning centers

114. The virtue of teaching integrated units of study (rather than separate subjects) is: *(Rigorous, Competency 17.0)*

A) It is easier for a teacher to organize

B) It results in more purposeful learning

C) It allows more children's literature to be used in the curriculum

D) Embedding skills in integrated curriculum aids transfer of knowledge, and content is more interesting and motivating to study

115. A teacher discovers after considering his class's prior knowledge of the story material that he would need to teach 12 words at least before he starts teaching the story to the whole group. This indicates: *(Average, Competency 17.0)*

A) The children will need read-aloud time

B) The children will need independent reading

C) The children will need guided reading

D) The children will need shared reading

116. A district observer notes that fifth graders are showing younger peers in the first grade how to hold a book and walk around with it, they assume: *(Average, Competency 17.0)*

A) That the fifth graders are particularly theatrical

B) That the fifth graders are proud of how they read stories aloud

C) That the fifth graders are training the younger children in book holding

D) That this has nothing to do with instruction

117. It is 4:00 p.m., yet Francine is still in her classroom. The seats in her classroom are filled with adults of various ages who are holding books. They are seated two by two with both holding copies of the same book. Francine probably is: *(Average, 17.0, 19.0)*

    A) Explaining to parents how she will teach a particular story

    B) Demonstrating shared reading with a buddy for volunteer parents

    C) Hosting a parents' organization meeting for her grade level

    D) Distributing old books from the class library to parents

118. SSR and DEAR have one thing in common. It is: *(Easy, Competency 17.0, 18.0)*

    A) Both are r-controlled words

    B) Both refer to everyone in the school reading at the same time

    C) Both are bottom-up approaches to reading

    D) Both could be located on a map 20 years ago

119. Randy is proud of how many new vocabulary words he has learned. He enjoys playing with a device his teacher has, since it helps him to show all the words he can create from various letters. The device is a: *(Average, Competency 18.0)*

    A) Word strip

    B) Letter holder for making words

    C) Word mask

    D) None of the above

120. It is likely one could use the newspaper to teach all of the following except: *(Easy, Competency 18.0)*

    A) Functional reading

    B) Lifelong reading

    C) Reading charts and graphs

    D) Literary criticism

121. Mr. Adams was pleased with Ms. Ramirez's reading lesson, but he realized that she would have visually represented the comparisons she was trying to get the children to make better, if she had used: *(Average, Competency 18.0)*

    A) A Big Book

    B) More expressive language

    C) A better literary example

    D) A graphic organizer

122. The most effective way to communicate with parents about current thinking about literacy development is: *(Easy, Competency 19.0)*

    A) A monthly classroom newsletter

    B) A Power Point presentation on the teacher's Web site

    C) Parent-teacher conferences

    D) Face-to-face parent-teacher meetings

123. When teaching adults (whether parents or colleagues), what will appeal most to them? *(Average, Competency 19.0)*

    A) Anecdotes that demonstrate theories and practical information

    B) Theoretical background that demonstrates the why of what we do in teaching reading

    C) Facts displayed through charts, pictures, and other graphic displays

    D) Humor and light-hearted banter to help them relax

124. The most important reason to attend professional conferences is: *(Rigorous, Competency 20.0)*

    A) To meet new colleagues from other communities and share one's teaching stories

    B) To keep up-to-date with new theories and strategies about teaching reading

    C) To stimulate and re-inspire oneself about teaching

    D) To relax and reflect about one's professional direction in life in a new environment

125. **The reading specialist should be familiar with which of the following professional organizations on reading?** *(Average, Competency 20.0)*

   A) International Reading Association and National Council of Teachers of English

   B) National Council of Teachers of Mathematics and the National Science Association

   C) National Council of Reading Professionals and National Council of Teachers of English

   D) International Reading Association and the National Reading Association

ANSWER KEY

1. B	43. D	85. D
2. B	44. C	86. B
3. C	45. D	87. B
4. C	46. C	88. A
5. C	47. D	89. D
6. B	48. A	90. A
7. D	49. B	91. A
8. C	50. C	92. D
9. C	51. B	93. C
10. A	52. B	94. C
11. C	53. C	95. A
12. D	54. C	96. D
13. C	55. D	97. A
14. B	56. A	98. D
15. C	57. B	99. B
16. B	58. B	100. C
17. B	59. A	101. D
18. D	60. C	102. B
19. D	61. B	103. D
20. D	62. D	104. B
21. D	63. B	105. C
22. B	64. B	106. A
23. D[TAR60]	65. A	107. C
24. D	66. D	108. D
25. B	67. D	109. D
26. B	68. C	110. B
27. D	69. C	111. C
28. B	70. C	112. C
29. D	71. D	113. C
30. C	72. A	114. D
31. C	73. D	115. C
32. C	74. D	116. C
33. D	75. D	117. B
34. D	76. C	118. B
35. D	77. D	119. B
36. C	78. D	120. D
37. D	79. C	121. D
38. D	80. D	122. D
39. B	81. B	123. A
40. A	82. C	124. B
41. D	83. B	125. A
42. A	84. D	

RATIONALE FOR SAMPLE TEST

1. **Prioritize these theorists in terms of their contributions regarding young children; intermediate-aged, middle-level children; and all children, respectively.**
    (Rigorous, Competency 1.0)

    A) Randolph Caldecott, E.D. Hirsch, John Newbery

    B) Randolph Caldecott, John Newbery, E.D. Hirsch

    C) John Newbery, E.D. Hirsch, Randolph Caldecott

    D) E.D. Hirsch, Randolph Caldecott, John Newbery

    Answer: B. Randolph Caldecott, John Newbery, E.D. Hirsch.
    Randolph Caldecott gave his name to the medal given yearly to the best-illustrated picture book for young children; John Newbery's name is given to the yearly medal for the best book written for intermediate, middle-level children. E.D. Hirsch conceived of "cultural literacy," which is a set of ideas considered critical for children's, adolescents', and adults' reading comprehension.

2. **In the balanced literacy approach, ability groups are**
    (Rigorous, Competency 1.0)

    A) Abolished

    B) Recommended

    C) Mixed

    D) Changeable

    Answer: B. Recommended
    Unlike the Robins and Wrens of the past, ability groups are formed for relatively short periods of time (two to three weeks to a month) and are then changed as children's skills and needs change.

3. **Emergent literacy is:**
   (Rigorous, Competency 1.0, 2.0, 14.0)

   A) An updated term for reading readiness

   B) A stage that follows early reading

   C) A description of children's gradual entry into reading from birth onward

   D) A set of incremental skills that must be mastered before reading

   Answer: C. A description of children's gradual entry into reading from birth onward.
   The concept of emergent literacy has supplanted reading readiness in the current thinking about reading. From birth onward, children engage in behaviors that lead to reading.

4. **Cues in reading are:**
   (Average, Competency 1.0)

   A) Vowel sounds

   B) Digraphs

   C) Sources of information used by readers to help them construct meaning

   D) None of the above

   Answer: C. Sources of information used by readers to help them construct meaning
   While reading, students will use several cueing systems to help comprehend text. These cueing systems include: semantics, syntax, and graphophonic. Semantics depend on context; which words will fit based on their meaning. Syntax is which words will work grammatically within a sentence. Graphophonics is decoding through the letter/sound relationship. Good readers will use and combine all three cueing systems to create meaning.

5. **Rudolf Flesch is to_____ as Marie Clay is to_____**
    (Rigorous, Competency 1.0)

    A) Cultural literacy; balanced literacy

    B) Decodable books; leveled books

    C) Phonics; Reading Recovery

    D) Wordless picture books; picture story books

    Answer: C. Phonics; Reading Recovery
    This analogy expresses the relationship of association. Answer A is incorrect because E.D. Hirsch originated the idea of "cultural literacy." Answer B is incorrect because Flesch has nothing to do with decodable books, while leveled books are an outcome of Marie Clay's work with Reading Recovery. D is incorrect because neither answer relates to either person.

6. **Ms. Ramirez also wants the children to share their functional reading skills with their families, so she asks that they take the newspapers home to focus on the:** *(Average, Competency 1.0, 14.0)*

    A) Advice columns

    B) Fill in coupons

    C) Metropolitan news briefs

    D) Weather section

    Answer: B. Fill in coupons
    The focus on functionality, or utilizing the text for a practical purpose, is best answered by B.

7. A theorist who believes that there is a finite body of approved literature children should be taught on various grade levels and has produced books about what everyone needs to know to be literate on various grade levels is:
(Easy, Competency 1.0)

A) Rudolf Flesch

B) J. David Cooper

C) John Dewey

D) E. D. Hirsch

Answer: D. E. D. Hirsch
E.D. Hirsch conceived of "cultural literacy", which is a set of ideas considered critical for children's, adolescents', and adults' reading comprehension.

8. A teacher is asking children to look at the beginning letters of words. She then asks the child to connect the beginning letter to the text and story and to think about what word would make sense there. This is an example of: *(Average, Competency 1.0, 14.0)*

A) A balanced literacy approach

B) A phonemic approach

C) A phonic approach

D) An ELL differentiated approach

Answer: C. A phonic approach
Phonics is the study of relationships between phonemes (speech sounds) and graphemes (letters) that represent the phonemes. It is also the decoding or the sounding out of unknown words that are written.

9.   **A bound morpheme is:**
      (Average, Competency 1.0)

      A) A word whose meaning stands alone

      B) The smallest unit of sound in the language

      C) An inflectional ending, which, when added to a base word, changes it case, gender, or number

      D) A root word whose spelling changes depending on what prefix or suffix one adds to it

      Answer: C. An inflectional ending, which, when added to base word, changes its case, gender, or number
      Answer A is incorrect because a bound morpheme cannot stand alone but must be attached to something. Answer B is the definition of a phoneme. Answer D is incorrect because a bound morpheme is the opposite of a root word.

10.   **Using children's literature trade books plus reader's and writers' workshops best demonstrates the_____theory of reading.**
      (Average, Competency 1.0, 18.0)

      A) Top-down

      B) Bottom-up

      C) Transactional

      D) Decoding or phonics

      Answer: A. Top-down
      Top-down theories start with the reader's understanding, construction, and interpretation of print, not with small, decodable segments of text to analyze using phonics first. Transactional theory is a broad way of looking at how different purposes of reading significantly how readers approach the text.

11.	A veteran teacher waited for her adult daughter outside of her daughter's first class in the Teaching of Reading. As she and her daughter talked about the first session of the course, the teacher never heard an explicit mention of the teaching of reading. All she heard about was: *(Easy, Competency 1.0)*

A)	Learning about narratives

B)	Dealing with text structures

C)	Constructing meaning

D)	All of the above.

Answer: C. Constructing meaning
The true purpose of reading is to construct meaning from text . Therefore, reading and constructing meaning can be used interchangeably.

12.	When teaching children to read nonfiction, the knowledge of different text structures will provide them with:
(Easy, Competency 1.0, 11.0, 12.0)

A)	Predictable questions for self-correction

B)	The fluency to promote reading speed

C)	Skills to navigate different parts of the text

D)	Schemata that promotes comprehension

Answer: D. Schemata that promotes comprehension
Once a student recognizes that a paragraph or whole piece is written as a comparison/contrast, this provides a mental "map," or schemata to aid the student's comprehension as she/he reads.

13. **The interrelated skills of reading, writing, listening, and speaking are called:** *(Rigorous, Competency 1.0, 11.0, 12.0)*

   A) Receptive communication arts

   B) Expressive communication arts

   C) Language arts

   D) Communication arts

   Answer: C. Language arts
   We now see reading and even listening as involving active processing and involvement on the part of the child. Reading, writing, speaking, and listening are all important elements of the language arts block.

14. **The teacher is watching the children go from oral speech into writing. The teacher says, "Great job:"** *(Easy, Competency 2.0)*

   A) A good decoding

   B) A good recoding

   C) A good encoding

   D) All of the above

   Answer: B. A good recoding
   The definition of recoding is to change information from one code into another, such as recoding writing into oral speech.

15. **As the child is reading and has made an incorrect attempt, the teacher prompts:** *(Rigorous, Competency 2.0, 11.0, 14.0)*

   A) I know you can get it right

   B) Try again, Lila

   C) Does that make sense to you?

   D) That word's a tough one

   Answer: C. Does that make sense to you?
   This prompts the child to rely on his/her semantic knowledge of English. Answers A and B are encouraging comments, while D is an empathetic one, but C is the best <u>teaching</u> answer to help a child focus on meaning.

16. **As far as the balanced literacy movement is concerned the "whole" when referring to a lesson indicates:** *(Average, Competency 2.0)*

A) All the reading themes will be covered that day

B) The whole class meets for the mini-lesson

C) The complete unit will be covered over the month

D) All of the reading and writing work to be done in connection with one book

Answer: B. The whole class meeting for the mini-lesson.
Normally during a mini-lesson, the whole class is taught one objective in a short period of time, normally within a 5 – 10 minute period. Mini-lessons are part of the balanced literacy movement.

17. **If children are engaged in creating a museum within classroom project to exhibit their work, they are** *(Average, Competency 2.0, 18.0)*

A) Not doing any reading or writing

B) Doing many authentic reading, writing, and researching tasks

C) Not likely to visit a real museum

D) All of the above

Answer: B. Doing many authentic reading, writing, and researching tasks.
In order for students to create a museum within the classroom, they must participate in all of the tasks of research which would include reading, writing, and researching. These would also be considered "authentic" tasks.

18. **The teacher is very concerned about identifying a book that is "just right" for Jay to read independently. This means that Jay should be able to read this book with:**
(Easy, Competency 2.0, 4.0, 5.0)

A) Below 92% accuracy

B) 100% accuracy

C) 95–100% accuracy

D) 92–97% accuracy

Answer: D. 92–97% accuracy
When a student reads independently, they should not know all of the words in a text; 100%. They should have to think and problem solve and apply decoding and comprehension strategies they have learned in guided reading. Therefore, a 92 – 97% accuracy level would be a "just right" book for a student. A lower percentage, such as 92%, is frustrating for the student and does not facilitate independent learning.

19. **All of the following statements are true about the relationship between reading and writing EXCEPT** *(Average, Competency 2.0)*

A) Both reading and writing must be taught

B) When taught together, reading and writing improve achievement

C) Combining reading and writing develops critical thinking

D) Most children can learn to read and write without any instruction

Answer: D. Most children can learn to read and write without any instruction
Though a few children seem to learn to read and write effortlessly and without instruction, even they have been coached and have learned to imitate their parents' modeling. All children need to learn the alphabet, graphophonic relationships, and special phonics conventions (such as the pronunciation of digraphs). The vast majority of these elements must be taught.

20. **Children's oral language background contributes to their understanding of which of the following aspects of written language?** *(Rigorous, Competency 2.0, 14.0)*

A) Syntax: the order in which sentences are expressed

B) Semantics: the meaning of words

C) Phonology: the sounds of language

D) All of the above

Answer: D. All of the above
Native speakers of a language bring syntactic, semantic, and phonological knowledge to their experience of learning to read. Teachers capitalize on this by the questions they ask readers: Does that sound right? Does that word make sense here? Can you hear the difference?

21. **Taking responsibility for a child's own learning will usually involve the child in:** *(Average, Competency 2.0, 3.0, 18.0)*

A) Reading and writing on his/her own

B) Developing a personal literacy project that will later be shared with the teacher and peers and family

C) Putting away books and materials when directed

D) both A and B

Answer: D. both A and B.
Self-directed learners take responsibility for their own learning and extend themselves beyond the immediate requirements of the classroom.

22. **Arrange these phenomena in the order in which children master them in reading:** *(Rigorous, Competency 3.0, 8.0)*

    A) Environmental print, alphabetic principle, phonological awareness, decoding

    B) Environmental print, phonological awareness, alphabetic principle, decoding

    C) Environmental print, decoding, alphabetic principle, phonological awareness

    D) Environmental print, phonological awareness, decoding, alphabetic principle

    Answer: B. Environmental print, phonological awareness, alphabetic principle, decoding
    First, children notice print on signs, billboards, restaurants, and the like. Next they become aware of the sounds of language and are able to manipulate them, as in rhymes. Third, they realize that particular sounds match certain letters and letter combinations, and finally, they crack the code and "unlock" words through correct letter-sound correspondences.

23. **Mark Garner has been told that he will have to support some special needs readers in his classroom in addition to the rest of the students. He can expect to have:** *(Easy, Competency 3.0, 15.0)*

    A) Gifted children who are accelerated in reading skills for their grade and age

    B) Children who have disabilities and will need special support in accessing the content and methods he uses with the rest of the class

    C) Children who come from native language backgrounds other than English

    D) Children who display the capacities and needs detailed in A and B

    Answer D: Children who display the capacities and needs detailed in A and B
    Ability levels of readers in any given classroom will vary from gifted readers to students with special needs. The classroom teacher needs to group students in a way that he or she will be able to reach each of the students on their reading ability level.

24. **Ability grouping means:** *(Easy, Competency 3.0)*

A) Grouping of children according to the results of an IQ test

B) Grouping of children with similar test results for instructional purposes

C) Grouping of children according to their oral reading accuracy rate

D) Grouping of children with similar needs for instructional purposes

Answer: D. Grouping of children with similar needs for instructional purposes.
Sometimes, students must be grouped by ability in order to target the needs of each student and differentiate instruction more easily.

25. **Gracie seems to be struggling with her reading, even in first grade, although her mother works at a publishing firm and her dad is an editor. Her speech is also full of mispronunciations, even though her parents were born in the school neighborhood. Gracie should be checked by:** *(Average, Competency 3.0, 15.0)*

A) A reading specialist

B) A speech therapist or an audiologist

C) A pediatrician

D) A psychologist

Answer: B. A speech therapist or an audiologist
There are no outside influences that would indicate Gracie's mispronunciations stem from background, cultural influences. Therefore, she should be visited by a speech therapist or an audiologist to find the heart of the problem.

26. **Which of the following statements is true concerning individual differences in reading?** *(Rigorous, Competency 3.0)*

   A) Gender differences are highly predictive of reading success

   B) Young children who were read to by adults in the home have an easier time with beginning reading

   C) Socioeconomic class makes no difference in children's early reading efforts

   D) Having a brother or sister who reads is predictive of a children's early success at reading

   Answer: B. Young children who were read to by adults in the home have an easier time with beginning reading
   Being read to is highly predictive of early reading success. While Answer A is not true, some boys do have greater difficulty in learning to read. Answer C is not completely true either. While there are many exceptions, depending on the family, SES does indicate that children from homes in poverty often need more support in early reading than their middle-class peers. Answer D is just plain false.

27. **The concerned parent whose child had a visual impairment wanted as much help for him as the teacher and the school district could give her. She begged: "Please, he didn't attend preschool, he has no prior knowledge." Strictly speaking this is:** *(Average, Competency 3.0)*

   A) Correct, since he didn't get preschool experiences

   B) Incorrect, since prior knowledge covers everyone's experiences

   C) Incorrect, since he did have prior knowledge experiences but these didn't match those of many of his peers, so he would need to enhance his prior knowledge

   D) both B and C

   Answer: D. both B and C
   This is a question that a caring and literate test taker could correctly answer and get D as a response. Everyone has prior knowledge of some sort.

28. **Ms. James is seated with a child by her side. The child is reading aloud from an open book. Ms. James is teaching in a school that has embraced the Balanced Literacy Approach. Therefore, it is most likely that Ms. James is writing and recording:** *(Average, Competency 4.0)*

A) The child's use of expression in reading aloud

B) The child's errors and miscues

C) Her observations of the child's attitude toward reading

D) The child's feelings about the particular passage being read

Answer B: The child's errors and miscues
By recording a child's errors and miscues, a teacher can more accurately instruct a child based on their weaknesses in semantics, syntax, or graphophonics.

29. **The most important reason to keep ongoing assessments of children's phonological awareness is:** *(Rigorous, Competency 4.0, 5.0, 6.0, 17.0)*

A) To be accountable to the principal

B) To compare with teachers of the same grade level

C) To have data for report cards

D) To plan curriculum

Answer: D. To plan curriculum
If your principal is checking on your assessments, as in "A," you're in trouble. Teachers should not be comparing assessments across classes, as in B. If you're teaching phonological awareness, you're probably teaching prekindergarten, kindergarten, or grade 1. Hopefully, you will have narrative report cards. The best place to share this information is with individual parents.

30.	_____ is to the Stanford Achievement Test as_____ is to the Metropolitan Achievement Test. *(Rigorous,4.0, 5.0)*

A) Predictive; diagnostic

B) Individual; group

C) Criterion-referenced; norm-referenced

D) Written; oral

Answer: C. Criterion-referenced; norm-referenced
Both are written group tests, eliminating answers b and d.

31.	**A teacher wants to teach her class how to choose a "just right" book to read independently. What should the teacher teach the class?**
(Easy, Competency 4.0, 5.0)

A) Students should read the summary of the story on the back of the book.

B) Students should read the last page of the story and make predictions about the story.

C) Students should open randomly to the middle of the book and read a page.

D) Students should ask a friend if they had trouble reading the book.

Answer C: Students should open randomly to the middle of the book and read a page
By opening to the middle of a book and reading, students can determine how many words they had trouble decoding. If they are able to read through easily with no errors, the book is too easy for them. If they have a difficult time decoding a lot of the words and the page is difficult to get through, it is a too hard book. If students struggle with a couple of words, but still feel comfortable reading, the book is "just right" for them.

32. **Jay really wants to read a book that he can only read with 94% accuracy. He could be able to read this book as:** *(Easy, Competency 4.0, 5.0)*

   A) An independent reading

   B) A guided reading

   C) A shared reading

   D) All of the above

   Answer: C. A shared reading
   Shared reading will allow Jay to hear the story and understand the plot so he will have more success when reading it on his own.

33. **When taking a child's running record, the kinds of self-corrections the child makes:** *(Average, Competency 4.0)*

   A) Are not important, but the percentage of accuracy is important

   B) May show something about which cueing systems the child relies on

   C) Can be meaningful if analyzed over several records

   D) Both B and C

   Answer: D. Both B and C
   A teacher may notice a pattern in one or several running records. This information is vital to a teacher when planning reading instruction for individual students or small groups of students.

34. **Once a teacher has carefully recorded and documented a running record:** *(Average, Competency 4.0)*

   A) There is nothing further to do as long as the teacher keeps the running record for conferences and documentation of grades

   B) The teacher should review the running record and other subsequent ones taken for growth over time

   C) The teacher should differentiate instruction for that particular student as indicated by growth over time and evidence of other needs

   D) Both B and B

   Answer: D. Both B and C
   Students learn at different rates; therefore, students in any class will be at varying levels of learning. By differentiating instruction and incorporating assessment for learning rather than assessment of learning, teachers can help students succeed. When teachers assess student growth over time and monitor the areas in which they are experiencing difficulty, they can alter the instruction and the activities to match student needs.

35. **The reliability of a standardized test is measured by: (Rigorous, Competency 4.0)**

    A) The percentage of children scoring in a bell-shaped curve

    B) Its lack of bias

    C) Whether it tests what it is supposed to test

    D) Its consistency over time

    Answer: D. Its consistency over time
    A test is reliable if a student would achieve the same or a similar score if she/he took the test at two different times. Answer C is a definition of validity. Answers A and B are simply irrelevant.

36. **A quartile on a test is: (Easy, Competency 4.0)**

    A) A quarter of the grades grouped

    B) The division of the percentiles into four segments each of which is called a quartile

    C) 25% of the tests scored

    D) both B and C

    Answer: C. 25% of the tests scored
    A quartile can be thought of as a quarter. 25% is equal to 0.25 or one quarter.

37. Validity in assessment means: *(Average, Competency 4.0)*

A) The test went off without any previewing of the questions or leaks on its contents

B) The majority of test takers passed

C) The correct time was allowed for the children to complete the test

D) The test assessed what it was supposed to assess and measure

Answer: D. The test assessed what it was supposed to assess and measure.
The validity of a test is measured by how well it assesses the content it is meant to assess. For example, a math test may not be valid because it measures reading comprehension rather than math computation if there are too many word problems.

38. "Bias" in testing occurs when: *(Average, Competency 4.0)*

A) The assessment instrument is not an objective, fair, and impartial one for a given cultural, ethnic, or special needs participant

B) The testing administrator is biased

C) The same test is given with no time considerations or provisions for those in need of more time or those who have handicapping conditions

D) All of the above

Answer: D. All of the above
Biased means that something is more one-sided than it should be. All of the answer choices are one-sided in some respect or another.

39.   **Norm-referenced tests:** *(Rigorous, Competency 4.0)*

A) Give information only about the local samples results

B) Provide information about how the local test takers did compared to a representative sampling of national test takers

C) Make no comparisons to national test takers

D) None of the above

Answer: B. Provide information about how the local test takers did compared to a representative sampling of national test takers.
Norm-referenced test have a "normal" group that the test results are compared to.

40.   **If you get your raw score on a test, you will get** *(Easy, Competency 4.0)*

A) The actual number of points you scored on the test

B) The percentage score of the number of questions you answered correctly

C) A letter grade for your work on the test

D) An aggregated score for your performance on the text

Answer: A. The actual number of points you scored on the test.
Again these are all definitions that the test taker should memorize before the test (see the Glossary in this guide).

41.   **A standardized test will be:** *(Easy, Competency 4.0)*

A) Given out with the same predetermined questions and format to all

B) Not be given to certain children

C) If given out in exactly the same format with the same content, may be taken over a lengthier test period (i.e. four hours instead of three or two)

D) All of the above

Answer: D. All of the above
Standardized tests are just that – standard. Therefore, the content does not change and the presentation is the same too.

42.   **Bill has been called up to the teacher for an individual conference. She asks him to retell one of the books he has listed on his weekly log. He begins and is still talking seven minutes later. Most probably, Bill:** *(Easy, Competency 4.0)*

A) Told the entire story with all its details and minor characters

B) May or may not have really gotten the main points and perspectives of the story

C) May have really liked the story

D) None of the above

Answer: A. Told the entire story with all its details and minor characters
Although young children believe that telling more is better, students must be taught to capture the main ideas and the important story elements.

43, **What does the phrase, "Assessment drives instruction" mean?**

A) After every unit of study there should be a formal assessment

B) A teacher should informally assess students everyday

C) Assessments should be the basis of the following year's curriculum review process

D) Assessment results should be used and analyzed by the teacher to plan the next unit of study

Answer D: Assessment results should be used and analyzed by the teacher to plan the next unit of study
Assessment should not only show what students have mastered on any given topic or subject, but assessments should also serve as road maps for teachers as a way to plan for instruction because it shows what students have not mastered.

44. **All of the following are characteristics of an effective assessment EXCEPT**
(Rigorous, Competency 4.0)

A) It should be an ongoing process by the teacher

B) It should happen every day both informally and formally

C) It should only measure a small portion of what students know

D) It should be reflected on by the teacher as a way to improve instruction

Answer C: It should only measure a small portion of what students know
Choices A, B, and D are all important aspects of good assessments. An assessment should not measure only a small portion of what students know, but should reflect student's actual experiences and the child should be able to explain or react knowledgeably.

45. **The data coordinator of the district who is concerned with federal funding for reading will probably want to start aggregating scores immediately because:** *(Rigorous, Competency 5.0)*

    A) It is interesting to crunch more data

    B) By aggregating, the individual scores can be combined to view performance trends across groups

    C) This will help the district determine which groups need more remedial instruction

    D) both B and C

    Answer: D. both B and C
    Again this is a definition answer and the correct choice is D

46. **The major difference between phonemic and phonological awareness is:** *(Easy, Competency 6.0)*

    A) One deals with a series of discrete sounds and the other with sound-spelling relationships

    B) One is involved with teaching and learning alliteration and rhymes

    C) Phonemic awareness is a specific type of phonological awareness that deals with separate phonemes within a given word

    D) Phonological awareness is associated with printed words

    Answer: C. Phonemic awareness is a specific type of phonological awareness that deals with separate phonemes within a given word.
    This is a sheer memorization question. By definition, phonemic awareness falls under the phonological awareness umbrella. All of the other choices do not deal with the *difference* between the two types of awareness.

47. **Mr. Sanchez is having his students work with one-syllable words, removing the first consonant and substituting another, as in m/ats to h/ats. What reading skill are they working on?** (*Average, Competency 6.0, 9.0*)

A) Morphemic inflections

B) Pronouncing short vowels

C) Invented spelling

D) Phonological awareness

Answer: D. Phonological awareness
While there are inflections ("s") and short vowels ("a") in these words as in answers A and B, neither is the focus of this activity. These words have standard spellings, not invented as in answer C.

48. **All of the following are true about phonological awareness EXCEPT:** (*Easy, Competency 6.0*)

A) It may involve print

B) It is a prerequisite for spelling and phonics

C) Activities can be done by the children with their eyes closed

D) It starts before letter recognition is taught

Answer: A. It may involve print
The key word here is *except*, which will be highlighted in uppercase on the test. All of the options are correct aspects of phonological awareness except the first one, A, because phonological awareness *does not* involve print.

49. **Andrew is just starting school, but it looks like he will be successful in reading because:** *(Rigorous, Competency 6.0, 7.0)*

    A) He comes from a family which cares about his progress

    B) He is phonemically aware and knows his alphabet

    C) He has been in preschool

    D) He is well behaved

    Answer: B. He is phonemically aware and knows his alphabet.
    This *is* a deliberately tricky question. Each of the choices has merit. The best choice is B because that one is confirmed by current research.

50. **Ronald's parents are hearing-impaired. What work will this first grader need *most*?** *(Rigorous, Competency 6.0, 15.0)*

    A) Picture cues to promote visual acuity

    B) Sight word mastery to promote fluency

    C) Rhymes and reads aloud to promote phonological awareness

    D) Letter-sound practice to promote the alphabetic principle

    Answer: C. Rhymes and reads aloud to promote phonological awareness
    Because Ronald's parents either use sign language and/or have compromised articulation, he needs work most on tuning his ear to letter sounds. Answers A and B both deal with visual needs, which are not acute in this child's case. D will become a need once Ronald has mastered phonological awareness.

51. **A stationery store owner in the neighborhood of the school is amused by the fact that the children on a school walk are rushing up to various store signs and street signs. The children are probably exploring:** *(Average, Competency 6.0)*

    A) The alphabetic principle

    B) The principle that print carries meaning

    C) Letter-sound recognition

    D) Phonemic awareness

    Answer: B. The principle that print carries meaning
    From a very early age children learn that symbols and printed words "mean" something. This is one of the very basic, early stages of reading.

52. **The purpose of taking dictation is to:** *(Easy, Competency 6.0, 7.0, 18.0)*

    A) Demonstrate how to copy down speech

    B) Make a connection and promote awareness of the relationship between spoken and written language

    C) Authenticate the children's comments

    D) Raise the children's self-esteem

    Answer: B. Make a connection and promote awareness of the relationship between spoken and written language.
    By watching what the teacher is doing, children learn that what they say can be written down. This insight is a major breakthrough in reading and writing.

53. **Clapping is the best way to learn syllable divisions because:**
(Rigorous, Competency 6.0)

   A) Children enjoy the activity and are motivated to learn

   B) Syllables are rhythmic

   C) The activity is both auditory and kinesthetic

   D) Movement aids memory

   Answer: C. The activity is both auditory and kinesthetic
   Learning supported by two modalities is always stronger than only one. Answer B is incorrect because, well, it's false. While Answer D may be true, it's not as specific as answer C.

54. **The *most important* reason for using children's names in the teaching of concepts of print and the alphabetic principle is:**
(Rigorous, Competency 6.0, 7.0)

   A) It appeals to the children's vanity

   B) These are among the first letters that children learn

   C) These letters are "special" and are highly motivating for the children to use

   D) The children will quickly be able to read every other child's name in the classroom

   Answer: C These letters are "special" and are highly motivating for the children to use.
   Answers B and D are true but not as important as answer C. Answer A is not quite true; the children's names have high interest for them but "vanity" does not accurately characterize this.

55. **The substitute teacher starts reading aloud the Big Book on the easel (which she has never seen before). What do you predict will happen?** *(Rigorous, Competency 6.0, 7.0, 18.0)*

A) The children will enjoy hearing the book read by another voice

B) The teacher's unfamiliarity will lead her to ask excellent prediction questions

C) The teacher will be excited by what she spontaneously discovers in the book

D) The teacher will not read very expressively nor will she have a clear purpose for reading the book

Answer: D. The teacher will not read very expressively nor will she have a clear purpose for reading the book.
Woe is the teacher who reads a book unprepared! Answer A is incorrect because the children will hear her hesitancy and errors. Answer B is incorrect because one can craft the best prediction questions when one knows what's coming. Answer C is probably the last emotion this teacher will feel in the situation.

56. **The value of exposing young children to environmental print is that it** *(Rigorous, Competency 7.0, 9.0, 18.0)*

A) Introduces children to the idea that print carries a message

B) Helps children learn to decode

C) Helps children make sense of their world

D) Introduces children to the world of consumerism

Answer: A. Introduces children to the idea that print carries a message
Environmental print tells children that words around them in signs, in the newspaper, and on buildings give a message. We have no evidence that B is correct; C might help children make some sense of the world, but they sometimes "slip" in their interpretations of environmental print. The business world probably wishes D were correct, but it is not.

57. As visitors from the United Kingdom tour the school, they are pleased to hear a singsong chant, "Don't fall asleep at the page, don't forget the _____." Mr. Adams explains to them that the first graders are learning about pointing at words and moving from the left to the right, this is called: *(Easy, Competency 7.0)*

A) Skimming

B) Return sweep

C) Top to bottom

D) Line for line reading

Answer: B. Return sweep
Younger readers do need to be taught that once they reach the end of a line of reading they need to "sweep" back to the beginning of the next line.

58. Environmental print is available at all of the following EXCEPT: *(Rigorous, Competency 7.0)*

A) Within a newspaper

B) On the page of a library book

C) On a supermarket circular

D) In a commercial flyer

Answer: B. On the page of a library book
The key word here is "except," and environmental print is not defined as print in a library book, so choice B is the right one.

59. **Children learn book handling skills best through:** *(Rigorous, Competency 7.0)*

   A) Teacher modeling during shared reading

   B) Parents reading to their children at home

   C) Imitation of their book buddies or peer tutors from another class

   D) Direct instruction by the teacher

   Answer: A. Teacher modeling during shared reading.
   Children will pick up book handling skills from watching the teacher's handling of Big Books as well as regular-sized books during read-aloud time. Teachers consciously draw children's attention to the book's features, such as orienting the book, the front and back cover, the title page, and the like.

60. **The best way for a primary grade teacher to model directionality and one-to-one word matching would be:** *(Average, Competency 7.0)*

   A) Using a regular library or classroom textbook

   B) Using her own person reading book

   C) Using a Big Book

   D) Using a book dummy

   Answer: C. Using a Big Book
   Key word in this question is "best" and the answer is C because this type of a book is best for teaching and display.

61. An observer enters Julia's first-grade classroom. Children are working with oak tag strips and placing letters on these strips on a sentence strip holder. Then they seem to be involved in some kind of counting. The observer is confused. This activity is taking place during the reading block. Julia explains: *(Average, Competency 8.0, 9.0)*

   A) The children are counting letters

   B) This is word sorting and the children are grouping words by length, common letters, and sound

   C) The children are combining mathematics counting and word study

   D) The children are doing a strategy sheet based on a particular word family

   Answer: B. This is word sorting and the children are grouping words by length, common letters, and sound
   By grouping and sorting words, students notice a commonality between words. This then helps students recognize and spell words.

62. _____is to letter-sound relationships as_____is to word meanings. *(Rigorous, Competency 8.0, 9.0)*

   A) Decoding; syntax

   B) Phonological awareness; phonemic awareness

   C) Syntax; semantics

   D) Graphophonemic awareness; semantics

   Answer: D. Graphophonemic awareness; semantics
   The relationship in this analogy is one of terms to definitions. In answer A, one term is correct (decoding), but the other is incorrect. In answers B and C, neither term is correct.

63. **To decode is to:** *(Easy, Competency 8.0)*

    A) Construct meaning

    B) Sound out a printed sequence of letters

    C) Use a special code to decipher a message

    D) Write out what one hears

    Answer: B. Sound out a printed sequence of letters
    Answer A is incorrect because children, unfortunately, can sometimes decode without grasping meaning. Answer C is appropriate for the CIA but not for reading. Answer D is a definition of encoding.

64. **By November the first graders have a vocabulary of words that they can correctly pronounce and read aloud. These words are their:** *(Rigorous, Competency 8.0, 10.0, 13.0)*

    A) Sight vocabulary

    B) Recognition vocabulary

    C) Personal vocabulary

    D) Working vocabulary

    Answer: B. Recognition vocabulary
    When students can look at a word and say it without sounding It out, they recognize it. Recognition vocabulary are words that the students can look at and say.

65.   A "decodable text" is: *(Easy, Competency 8.0, 18.0)*

   A) A text that a child can read aloud with correct pronunciations

   B) A text that a child can answer comprehension questions about with a high percentage of accuracy

   C) Text written to match the sequence of letter-sound relationships that have been taught

   D) None of the above

   Answer: A. A text that a child can read aloud with correct pronunciations.
   Choice A is the definition of decodable text. Decoding is also known as "word calling" and is different than comprehension.

66.   **What is the optimum order for teaching these phonics skills?** *(Rigorous, Competency 8.0)*

   A) Long vowels, diagraphs and blends, diphthongs, short vowels, and r-controlled words

   B) Short vowels, long vowels, digraphs and blends, diphthongs, and r-controlled words

   C) Digraphs and blends, diphthongs, long vowels, short vowels, and r-controlled words

   D) Short vowels, digraphs and blends, long vowels, diphthongs, and r-controlled words

   Answer: D. Short vowels, digraphs and blends, long vowels, diphthongs, and r-controlled words
   All of the answers above presuppose that children have been taught the consonants first. Next come the short vowels because they appear in so many one-syllable words, followed by digraphs (wh-, sh-, ch, th-, and ph) and blends (bl, cl, tr). Long vowels are followed by the more challenging concepts of diphthongs and r- and l-controlled words.

67. **Mr. Adams has complained to Mr. Mark that there are too many newspapers piled up in his classroom. Mr. Mark has responded that he does not want to throw away these piled-up newspapers because:** *(Average, Competency 8.0, 18.0)*

A) They can be used for letter-sound correspondence

B) They represent environmental print

C) They can be used to create print-meaning signs

D) All of the above

Answer: D. All of the above
This is a question where choice D makes good sense to a teacher who knows the value of having newspapers for class projects.

68. **What is the most important value of allowing children to use invented spelling?** *(Rigorous, Competency 9.0, 14.0)*

A) It frees up the teacher to get around to many children during writing workshop

B) It ultimately contributes to good spelling skills

C) It helps children listen to the sounds of words they are attempting to write

D) It makes children feel proud of their writing

Answer: C. It helps children listen to the sounds of words they are attempting to write
When creating their own temporary invented spellings, children listen carefully and encode sounds sequentially in words. This lays a foundation for later phonics learning.

69.   A word wall is to ____as a story board is to ____. *(Rigorous, Competency 9.0)*

   A) Spelling; characterization

   B) The dictionary; the book

   C) Word families; plot sequence

   D) Sight words; picture cues

   Answer: C. Word families; plot sequence
   This analogy expresses a cause-and-effect relationship. While A is partially right (spelling), a story board is not most helpful regarding characterization. Answer B is partially right as well, for the word wall functions as a classroom-owned dictionary, but the second answer is irrelevant. Answer D is incorrect because the word wall has nothing to do with sight words, just as a story board does not relate to picture cues.

70.   The word "bat" is a ___word for "batter-up":
       (Rigorous, Competency 9.0)

   A) Suffix

   B) Prefix

   C) Root word

   D) Inflectional ending

   Answer: C. Root word
   Root words are the base words from which all other words are created. Prefixes and suffixes are added on to root words to change their meaning.

71. _____ is a compound word, while _____ is a contraction. *(Rigorous, Competency 9.0)*

    A) Trenchcoat; its

    B) Flip chart; whose

    C) Big top; it is

    D) Ballgame, who's

    Answer: D. Ballgame, who's
    This analogy expresses the relationship of "example to term." Answer A is wrong because "its" is a possessive, not a contraction (as in, "its motor died"). Answer B is wrong because "flip chart" is not a compound word; "whose" is a possessive. Answer C is wrong because "it is" is not a contraction.

72. **As Mr. Adams exits his school building, he notices that Mr. Mark, a new teacher, is leading a group of happy-looking fifth graders back into the building. They are carrying all kinds of free pamphlets and circulars from a local coffee house. Mr. Adams immediately asks Mr. Mark why the class went to that coffee house during the lunch break. When he hears Mr. Mark's answer, he is delighted:** *(Average, Competency 9.0, 18.0)*

    A) Mr. Mark says they went looking for environmental print and words with a café and latte root

    B) Mr. Mark says they didn't spend any money and got free hot chocolate

    C) The children will have to summarize a pamphlet as homework

    D) All of the above

    Answer: A. Mr. Mark says they went looking for environmental print and words with a café and latte root.
    Not only can the students find common logos in the materials they bring back, but they can also build their understanding of words like "cafeteria," based on the root word "café."

73. **In the following sentence, identify the underlined words: "The tourniquet was <u>wound</u> around the <u>wound</u>."** *(Average, Competency 9.0)*

A) Homophones

B) Homodicts

C) Homonyms

D) Homographs

Answer: D. Homographs
Homographs are spelled the same but pronounced differently and have different meanings, such as lead and lead. Homophones (answer A) are the same as homonyms (answer C): They sound the same but have different spellings, such as red and read. Homodicts (answer B) do not exist.

74. **To promote word study, children can:** *(Average, Competency 10.0)*

A) Be required to go to the dictionary at least once or twice a day

B) Collect and share words of interest they find in their readings

C) Do vocabulary work sheets from a basal reader or commercial vocabulary book

D) Do all of the above

Answer: D. Do all of the above
All of the answers will promote vocabulary, so the answer is D.

75. **In order to get children to compile specialized vocabulary, they can use:** *(Average, Competency 10.0)*

   A) Newspapers

   B) Internet resources and approved Web sites that focus on the special interest

   C) Experts they can interview

   D) All of the above

   Answer: D. All of the above
   All of the responses are correct.

76. **Teachers should select at least ___words for pre-reading vocabulary discussion:** *(Easy, Competency 10.0)*

   A) 12

   B) 15

   C) 2–3

   D) 8–10

   Answer: C. 2–3 words.
   Teachers should select a small number of words for pre-teaching to allow the students time to comprehend the text and achieve the objectives related to the reading. For example, in a nonfiction text, these words could be key terms related to the main topic. Even students with an extensive oral vocabulary may not be able to recognize words in print because they are not words that they normally encounter in their reading. The activities the teacher plans in relation to the words will help the students internalize the strategies more readily when only a few words are selected each time.

77. Pre-teaching vocabulary is to____as choral reading is to____.
   (Rigorous, Competency 10.0)

   A) Comprehension; letter-sound relationships

   B) Fluency; articulation

   C) Esthetic appreciation; comprehension

   D) Comprehension; fluency

   Answer: D. Comprehension; fluency
   This analogy is one of cause and effect. Answer A is incorrect because the second term, "letter-sound relationships," is false. Answer B is incorrect because the first term, "fluency" is not what pre-taught vocabulary promotes. Answer C is incorrect because neither term applies to the relationship.

78. **Two steps a teacher might take before selecting words for study are:**
   (Easy, Competency 10.0)

   A) Reading the story and story mapping

   B) Asking advice from a veteran teacher and the grade leader

   C) Looking in a teacher's guide and copying out the words listed there

   D) All of the above are correct

   Answer: D. All of the above are correct
   This is one you can reason through and choose D easily. All words that a teacher chooses to use for word study should be grade appropriate and relevant to students' lives.

79.   **In a balanced literacy classroom, new vocabulary would most likely appear on:** *(Average, Competency 10.0)*

A) An experiential chart

B) A class newspaper

C) The word wall

D) Outside the room on a bulletin board

Answer: C. The word wall
Word walls are essential to every classroom to improve vocabulary. They give students a point of reference.

80.   **An effective way to build vocabulary and to make connections with mandated science and mathematics material is to teach Greek and Latin roots using:** *(Average, Competency 10.0, 11.0, 12.0)*

A) Semantic maps

B) Hierarchical arrays

C) Linear arrays

D) Word webs

Answer: D. Word webs
Historically these have been used to teach Greek and Latin roots. It is proven that when children make personal connections with material, they learn it and retain it better.

81. **Cause-and-effect is to ___ as chronological is to ___.**
   (Rigorous, Competency 11.0)

   A) Nonfiction; fiction

   B) Text structure; story

   C) Comprehension; appreciation

   D) Writing; reading

   Answer: B. Text structure; story
   The relationship in this analogy is characteristic-to-thing. Cause and effect is one way a text structure is organized; stories are conventionally organized chronologically. Answer A is incorrect because cause and effect and chronology are both used in fiction and nonfiction. Answer C is incorrect because chronological order has nothing to do with appreciation. Answer D is incorrect for the same reason as is answer A.

82. **Asking a child if what he or she has read makes sense to him or her is prompting the child to use: (Average, Competency 11.0, 14.0)**

   A) Phonics cues

   B) Syntactic cues

   C) Semantic cues

   D) Prior knowledge

   Answer: C. Semantic cues
   Semantic cues are the hints that students can discern from the reading to help them make sense of the text. In some cases, the message of the text depends on the other words around them, so students learn how to determine the meaning from context clues.

83.   When you ask a child if what he or she has just read "sounds right" to him or her, you are trying to get that child to use: *(Average, Competency 11.0, 14.0)*

A) Phonics cues

B) Syntactic cues

C) Semantic cues

D) Prior knowledge

Answer: B. Syntactic cues
This is another one of those answers using the language of linguistics in reading. The answer has to be B, syntactic clues.

84.   As part of study about the agricultural products of their state, children have identified 22 different types of apples produced in the state. They can use a _____ to compare and contrast these different types of apples: *(Rigorous, Competency 11.0, 12.0)*

A) Word web

B) Semantic map

C) Semantic features analysis grid

D) All of the above

Answer: D. All of the above
The answer here is D and all of these graphic organizers would work with the topic of apples.

85.   One of the many ways in which a child can demonstrate comprehension of a story is by: *(Average, Competency 11.0)*

A) Filling in a strategy sheet

B) Retelling the story orally

C) Retelling the story in writing

D) All of the above

Answer: D. All of the above
All the options are good ones.

86.   **The technique SQ3R is an aid to students' comprehension when used with non-fiction texts. The steps are as follows:** *(Average, Competency 11.0, 13.0)*

A) Start Questioning, then Read, Remember, and Report

B) Survey, Question, Read, Recite, and Review

C) Stay Quiet, Read for 3 minutes, and then Remember main points

D) Start with a Question, find 3 Answers, and then Read on

Answer: B. Survey, Question, Read, Recite, and Review.
Students first survey the text to activate their background knowledge. From here, students form questions. This becomes their purpose for reading – to try and find the answers to the questions they formed. Next, to find the answers to the questions, students must read the material. Recite, is like stating the answer to the questions asked. Review is when the reader makes sure that their answers make sense. This is a particularly helpful strategy when reading non-fiction texts because it will aid in the comprehension of the more difficult material.

87. **The Stop and Think Strategy means that the child reader will:** *(Average, Competency 11.0)*

   A) Read through until the end of the story or text

   B) Ask himself or herself if what he or she has read makes sense to him or her

   C) Stop after reading some text and write down his/her concerns

   D) All of the above

   Answer: B. Ask himself or herself if what he or she has read makes sense to him or her.
   This is a tricky question and requires that the test taker know the very specific definition of the Stop and Think strategy to know that the only correct answer is B.

88. **An excellent research project that can combine dictionary study with science research would be:** *(Average, Competency 11.0, 12.0, 18.)*

   A) A student-authored dictionary terms and phrases about earthworms

   B) A teacher developed specialized dictionary of words and phrases about earthworms

   C) A collection of articles on earthworms put together by the school librarian

   D) both B and C

   Answer: A. A student-authored dictionary terms and phrases about earthworms
   This question is tricky in that only choice A, which deals with a student product, is correct. The others are all adult-centered.

89. **Mr. Mark is a brand new teacher who is not from the neighborhood where his school is located. He is a bit nervous as this is his first teaching assignment. He does not yet know how to relax enough to get his students to activate prior experience. He should:** *(Rigorous, Competency 11.0)*

    A) Try a free recall question: Tell us what you know about . . .

    B) Try an unstructured Question: Let's talk about . . .

    C) Use word association: What do you associate X with?

    D) All of the above

    Answer: D. all of the above
    Again this is a common sense question and D is the correct choice.

90. **Among the literary strategies that teachers can use to activate prior knowledge are:** *(Average, Competency 11.0)*

    A) Predicting and previewing a story

    B) Story mapping

    C) Venn diagramming

    D) Linear arrays

    Answer: A. Predicting and previewing a story
    This is a question that a literate test taker could answer, and the best choice is A because in their predictions, children evidence prior knowledge.

91. Ms. Ancess used to take time to have her children memorize major poems and even had an assembly for parents and school staff where the children dramatically recited various poems. Now that she is worried about the children's reading scores, she doesn't want to waste time with this memorization. Actually if she still includes this high interest, child-centered experience: *(Rigorous, Competency 11.0)*

    A) The children can use their oral fluency and her modeling as a bridge for enhanced comprehension

    B) The children can get a sense of "ownership" of the words

    C) Children and parents will have a "break" from worrying about the test

    D) None of the above

    Answer: A. The children can use their oral fluency and her modeling as a bridge for enhanced comprehension.
    Fluency is an important skill that will improve comprehension. If a student reads fluently, he or she will understand the material better because it will sound more like talking and make more sense to the reader. Therefore, comprehension will improve.

92. **To help children with "main idea" questions, the teacher should:** *(Average, Competency 11.0)*

    A) Give out a strategy sheet on the main idea for children to place in their reader's notebooks

    B) Model responding to such a question as part of guided reading

    C) Have children create "main idea questions" to go with their writings

    D) All of the above

    Answer: D. All of the above
    The more practice students have with identifying and finding the main idea, the easier it will be for them to find it various reading passages.

93. The teacher is working on a life science unit in grade 5 and using many print and electronic sources for information. Some of the words in the unit have a serial and others a categorical relationship to one another. To help the children's comprehension, the teacher could now: *(Rigorous, Competency 11.0, 12.0, 18.0)*

A) Use a root family diagram or tree

B) Work with base words

C) Use hierarchical and linear arrays

D) Create separate semantic maps of each word

Answer: C. Use hierarchical and linear arrays
It is the best answer because of the relationships—serial and categorical—among the words the teacher wants the children to tackle. Neither answer A nor B would help children see relationships among words. Answer D might do so if a large, interrelated semantic map were created.

94. When teaching children how to comprehend different text structures, two techniques that work well are: *(Average, Competency 11.0, 12.0, 13.0)*

A) Small group work and story maps

B) Semantic features analysis and Venn diagrams

C) Word webs and "clue words"

D) Cloze procedure and Kid Pix

Answer: C. Word webs and "clue words."
Word webs help students see the different relationships of text structures, such as cause and effect or comparison/contrast, and "clue words," such as "first, second, third," or "if . . . then," which are like little signposts to look for when cruising through the text.

95. As part of a study for a unit on the history of Massachusetts, Mr. Gentry is using the early childhood book *26 Letters and 99 Cents* by Tina Hoban. He wants his readers to study it and create a more detailed guide to their state using its concept. This is a technique frequently used in: *(Average, Competency 12.0, 18.0)*

A) Reading and writing workshop.

B) Writing process instruction

C) Readers workshop

D) Technical writing

Answer: A. Reading and writing workshop
The fact that Mr. Gentry wants his class to use this for both reading and writing should help you pick the right choice even if you don't know the answer.

96. The science fair is coming up and Ms. Gardner is trying to find time in her busy schedule to work on her class's earth worm diary project. With all of the mandated tests and assemblies, she has not found time to start her students on their earth worm research. Within the context of reading instruction, she can: *(Average, Competency 12.0, 18.0)*

A) Begin a thematic study unit

B) Start with read-aloud time of the *Diary of an Earth Worm* by Doreen Cronin

C) Scaffold the research process by going online with her children using an approved search engine to find matches for earthworm sites

D) All of the above

Answer: D. All of the above
This is a question someone who has taught or gone through course work should ace to get D. Remember, going online with children and using approved search engines is fine.

97.   **Study guides can often help students navigate nonfiction or expository text. Find the false statement about study guides in this group:** *(Rigorous, Competency 13.0)*

A) They may be successfully used at any grade level

B) The more structured and directive they are, the most support study guides provide

C) They help students construct meaning

D) They are most effective in grades 4 and up

Answer: A. They may be successfully used at any grade level.
Study guides are not useful for emergent or even beginning readers. Though they can be simplified for use in grades 2 and 3, their best use is in grades 4 and up.

98.   **One of the most important features in nonfiction books that children should learn to read includes:** *(Rigorous, Competency 13.0)*

A) Page numbers

B) Picture cues

C) Characterization

D) Captions

Answer: D. Captions
Children should know page numbers as soon as they begin to read. Answer B, picture cues, is a strategy used early on with fiction books. Answer C, characterization, does not typically appear in nonfiction.

99. **When they are in sixth grade, children should be able to independently go through an unfamiliar collection and:** *(Average, Competency 13.0)*

   A) Use only the table of contents

   B) Use the first line indices and find a poem by author and subject

   C) Use only the glossary

   D) None of the above

   Answer: B. Use the first line indices and find a poem by author and subject.
   This is a question you can reason out. The most complex task described here is B.

100. **In Ms. Francine's class, dictionary use is a punishment. Mr. Adams is:** *(Average, Competency 13.0)*

   A) Pleased with the way that Ms. Francine approaches dictionary use

   B) Unconcerned with this approach to the use of the dictionary

   C) Convinced that the teacher should model her own fascination and pleasure in using the dictionary for the children

   D) Delighted by the fact that children are being forced to use the dictionary

   Answer: C. Convinced that the teacher should model her own fascination and pleasure in using the dictionary for the children
   The word "punishment" in the question should alert the test taker to the answer that the only choice C can be right.

101. **Dictionary study:** *(Average, Competency 13.0)*

    A) Can begin in grades 1 or 2

    B) Can begin in pre-kindergarten using the lush picture dictionaries

    C) Should start on grade 3 level

    D) both A and B

    Answer: D. both A and B
    This is a question that any literate test taker who has been in a children's book section recently can answer. Choice D is correct.

102. **"Beautiful Beth is the Best Girl in the Bradley Bay area." This sentence could be used to help children learn about:** *(Average, Competency 14.0)*

    A) Assonance

    B) Alliteration

    C) Rhyming pairs

    D) None of the above

    Answer: B. Alliteration
    When the first consonant sound of a word is repeated, it is called alliteration.

103. **Is it easier for ELL students who read in their first language to learn to read in English?** *(Rigorous, Competency 14.0, 15.0)*

A) No, because the letter-sound relationships in English are unique

B) Yes, because this will give the children confidence

C) No, because there is often interference from one language to the next

D) Yes, because the process is the same regardless of the language

Answer: D. Yes, because the process is the same regardless of the language
Answer A is incorrect because literate ELL students master the letter-sounds in English as well as native speakers do. Answer B does not hold true for all students. Answer C is incorrect because while there may be some interference in oral language, this does not usually happen in reading.

104. **A very bright child in a grade 1 class came from a family that did not a have a strong oral story telling or story reading tradition in its native language. This child would need support in developing:** *(Rigorous, Competency 14.0)*

A) Letter-sound correspondence skills

B) Schemata for generic concepts most children have in their memories and experiences based on family oral traditions and reading aloud

C) Oral expressiveness

D) both B and c

Answer: B. Schemata for generic concepts most children have in their memories and experiences based on family oral traditions and reading aloud
Although the question appears to be a very technical one, it actually can be easily and correctly answered by seeing how choice B echoes the fact that most children would have schemata based on family oral traditions.

105. **By definition, which children in a classroom will have trouble with syntactic cues?** *(Rigorous, Competency 14.0, 15.0)*

    A) Those from families who do not have household libraries

    B) Those not in a top reading group

    C) Those from ELL backgrounds

    D) All of the above

    Answer: C. Those from ELL backgrounds
    Choice A is not correct. All children are capable of becoming good readers and the other choices, given Ms. James's dedication, are not the most likely reason these three children (a minority of the class) are struggling. They are probably struggling to discriminate sounds because they are ELL students. Thus answer C is correct.

106. **The clearest predictor of a child's early reading achievement is:** *(Rigorous, Competency 14.0, 19.0)*

    A) Parents who read to their children at home

    B) Number of books and magazines a family owns

    C) The child's attendance at a good preschool

    D) Parents' educational levels

    Answer: A. Parents who read to their children at home
    Though all of these answers might seem persuasive, A is the correct answer, which supported by research. Reading to their children is the single greatest gift parents can give to their children's literacy development.

107. **Most of the children in first-year teacher Ms. James's class are really doing well in their phonemic awareness assessments. However, Ms. James is very concerned about three children who do not seem to be able to distinguish between spoken words that "sound alike" but are different. Since she is a first-year teacher, she feels her inexperience may be to blame. In truth, the reason these three children have not yet demonstrated phonemic awareness is most likely that:** *(Rigorous, Competency 14.0, 15.0)*

A) They are not capable of becoming good readers

B) They are bored in class

C) They may be from an ELL background

D) Ms. James does not pronounce the different phonemes clearly enough

Answer: C. They may be from an ELL background
Children who speak a first language other than English may have a harder time discriminating initial sounds in words.

108. **Chard and Osborn (1999) found that children with reading disabilities need to learn the alphabetic principle because:** *(Rigorous, Competency 15.0)*

A) The alphabet has predictable letter-sound relationships

B) Learning sight words is harder for the disabled reader

C) Knowing the alphabet will give these readers confidence

D) The relationship between letters and sounds is central to early reading

Answer: D. The relationship between letters and sounds is central to early reading
A is incorrect because the alphabet has some unpredictable letter-sound relationships. B is not a good choice because learning sight words is not more difficult for disabled readers. C is a good distracter but is not as important for learning as are letter-sound relationships.

109. **While the supervisor is pleased overall with Barbara's first year of teaching, he feels that given the fact that two of her students are transfers from Mexico and one student has a hearing impairment, she has to plan for:** *(Rigorous, Competency 15.0, 17.0)*

A) Extra homework for all of them

B) Extra time for the hearing impaired child

C) A buddy to work with the two students from Mexico

D) Differentiated instruction to meet these students' varied special needs

Answer: D. Differentiated instruction to meet these students' varied special needs.
This is a tricky question because all of the choices have an element of truth in them. But the best choice is D because it includes the special approaches Barbara will have to take with her ELL and special needs students.

110. **Advantages of the basal reading series include all of the following except:** *(Rigorous, Competency 16.0, 17.0, 18.0)*

A) A clearly sequenced set of skills to teach

B) Highly interesting stories that appeal to children

C) A continuum of scope and sequence across grade levels

D) Daily lesson plans available for the teacher

Answer: B. Highly interesting stories that appeal to children
Using individual trade books of children's literature is the best way to accomplish B, not through a basal reading series. The strengths of a basal series lie in the sequence of skills within and across grades plus the availability of lesson plans to demonstrate how one might teach specific skills.

111. **In terms of a balanced literacy classroom, a "leveled bin" indicates: (Easy, Competency 16.0, 18.0)**

    A) A bin of paperback books set at the child's eye level for reading choices

    B) A bin with books the child has selected for him or herself

    C) A bin with books leveled by the teacher

    D) A bin with different reading materials, including magazines at a child's level

    Answer: C. A bin with books leveled by the teacher
    Baskets or bins can be used to hold books of the same guided reading level. This allows students to easily find "just right" books that will interest them quickly and easily.

112. **A natural role for a highly proficient reader would be: (Average, Competency 16.0, 17.0)**

    A) To assist the teacher with cleaning the classroom and organizing the student folders

    B) To develop charts for the teacher by copying needed poems for full class study

    C) Tutor and support struggling readers

    D) Work on his/her own interests while the teacher works with the rest of the class

    Answer: C. Tutor and support struggling readers
    While all of the choices are possibilities, the concept of the highly proficient reader tutoring leads to answer C.

113. **When displaying children's books in the classroom, the best way to display them for younger readers is:** *(Rigorous, Competency 16.0, 18.0)*

    A) In a reading center called the "library," with the books shelved alphabetically

    B) In crates that display various reading levels

    C) Face-up in order to see the title and cover page

    D) Placed strategically throughout the room in various learning centers

    Answer: C. Face-up in order to see the title and cover page.
    The best answer for the younger reader is C. Depending on their reading progress, kindergartners and some first graders may not yet be reading titles, so seeing the title coupled with the picture on the front cover assists younger readers is making a choice of an appealing book to read.

114. **The virtue of teaching integrated units of study (rather than separate subjects) is:** *(Rigorous, Competency 17.0)*

    A) It is easier for a teacher to organize

    B) It results in more purposeful learning

    C) It allows more children's literature to be used in the curriculum

    D) Embedding skills in integrated curriculum aids transfer of knowledge, and content is more interesting and motivating to study

    Answer: D. Embedding skills in integrated curriculum aids transfer of knowledge, and content is more interesting and motivating to study.
    Integrated units typically take time for a teacher to organize. We cannot guarantee that B is more true when teaching integrated rather than separate subjects. Good teachers of reading are doing C no matter what kind of curriculum they are teaching.

115. **A teacher discovers after considering his class's prior knowledge of the story material that he would need to teach 12 words at least before he starts teaching the story to the whole group. This indicates:** *(Average, Competency 17.0)*

    A) The children will need read -aloud time

    B) The children will need independent reading

    C) The children will need guided reading

    D) The children will need shared reading

    Answer: C. The children will need guided reading
    This is one you can reason through, if you know that generally during read-aloud time you do not stop to explain many words. You would not want to give material for independent or shared reading where so many words had to be explained. Hence the correct choice is C, guided reading.

116. **A district observer notes that fifth graders are showing younger peers in the first grade how to hold a book and walk around with it, they assume:** *(Average, Competency 17.0)*

    A) That the fifth graders are particularly theatrical

    B) That the fifth graders are proud of how they read stories aloud

    C) That the fifth graders are training the younger children in book holding

    D) That this has nothing to do with instruction

    Answer: C. That the fifth graders are training the younger children in book holding.
    Older students are often used as peer instructors or book buddies. One of the reasons teachers set-up this arrangement is so younger students can learn from older students.

117. **It is 4:00 p.m., yet Francine is still in her classroom. The seats in her classroom are filled with adults of various ages who are holding books. They are seated two by two with both holding copies of the same book. Francine probably is:** *(Average, 17.0, 19.0)*

A) Explaining to parents how she will teach a particular story

B) Demonstrating shared reading with a buddy for volunteer parents

C) Hosting a parent's organization meeting for her grade level

D) Distributing old books from the class library to parents

Answer: B. Demonstrating shared reading with a buddy for volunteer parents.
Because the question details that the adults are seated two-by-two holding copies of the same book, this is the buddy reading style.

118. **SSR and DEAR have one thing in common. It is:** *(Easy, Competency 17.0, 18.0)*

A) Both are r-controlled words

B) Both refer to everyone in the school reading at the same time

C) Both are bottom-up approaches to reading

D) Both could be located on a map 20 years ago

Answer: B. Both refer to everyone in the school reading at the same time.
SSR stands for "sustained silent reading," and DEAR is "drop everything and read." Everyone from the classroom teacher to the children to the janitor is supposed to read during this period of time.

119. **Randy is proud of how many new vocabulary words he has learned. He enjoys playing with a device his teacher has, since it helps him to show all the words he can create from various letters. The device is a: (Average, Competency 18.0)**

    A) Word strip

    B) Letter holder for making words

    C) Word mask

    D) None of the above

    Answer: B. Letter holder for making words
    This is a familiar device in today's reading classroom.

120. **It is likely one could use the newspaper to teach all of the following except: (Easy, Competency 18.0)**

    A) Functional reading

    B) Lifelong reading

    C) Reading charts and graphs

    D) Literary criticism

    Answer: D. Literary criticism
    Rationale: There are few literary pieces printed in most daily newspapers.

121. **Mr. Adams was pleased with Ms. Ramirez's reading lesson, but he realized that she would have visually represented the comparisons she was trying to get the children to make better, if she had used:** *(Average, Competency 18.0)*

A) A Big Book

B) More expressive language

C) A better literary example

D) A graphic organizer

Answer: D. A graphic organizer
The best organizer to use when comparing two things is a Venn Diagram. A Big Book is great to use in a shared reading experience and will offer visuals, but is not the best way to compare.

122. **The most effective way to communicate with parents about current thinking about literacy development is:** *(Easy, Competency 19.0)*

A) A monthly classroom newsletter

B) A Power Point presentation on the teacher's Web site

C) Parent-teacher conferences

D) Face-to-face parent-teacher meetings

Answer: D. Face-to-face parent-teacher meetings.
Of the answers above, only two are interactive: For answers C and D, parents need an opportunity to ask questions and create a dialogue about the teacher's approach to literacy, the meaning of various assessments, and their role in the process. The best choice is D, with meetings clearly labeled in advance so parents know what they will be learning and talking about with the teacher.

123. **When teaching adults (whether parents or colleagues), what will appeal *most* to them? (Average, Competency 19.0)**

    A) Anecdotes that demonstrate theories and practical information

    B) Theoretical background that demonstrates the why of what we do in teaching reading

    C) Facts displayed through charts, pictures, and other graphic displays

    D) Humor and light-hearted banter to help them relax

    Answer: A. Anecdotes that demonstrate theories and practical information.
    Adults, including teachers, are impatient with too much theoretical or factual information without specific practical applications. Humor by itself does not insure a successful teaching encounter with adults.

124. **The most important reason to attend professional conferences is: (Rigorous, Competency 20.0)**

    A) To meet new colleagues from other communities and share one's teaching stories

    B) To keep up-to-date with new theories and strategies about teaching reading

    C) To stimulate and re-inspire oneself about teaching

    D) To relax and reflect about one's professional direction in life in a new environment

    Answer: B. To keep up-to-date with new theories and strategies about teaching reading.
    Though all of these answers might be reasons for attending a professional conference, after one has finished his or her college or university education, professional conferences are the best way to seek out educational opportunities for oneself.

125. **The reading specialist should be familiar with which of the following professional organizations on reading?** *(Average, Competency 20.0)*

A) International Reading Association and National Council of Teachers of English

B) National Council of Teachers of Mathematics and the National Science Association

C) National Council of Reading Professionals and National Council of Teachers of English

D) International Reading Association and the National Reading Association

Answer: A. International Reading Association and National Council of Teachers of English

These organizations are often referred to by their initials: IRA and NCTE. Both are targeted toward reading professionals and publish multiple, wonderful journals for the reading professional. In the answers above, the National Council of Reading Professionals (answer C) and the National Reading Association (answer D) do not exist.

ADDITIONAL CITATIONS

Block, Cathy Collins. 2002. *Comprehension Instruction: Research Based Practices.* New York: The Guilford Press.

Calkins, Lucy McCormick. 2001. *The Art of Teaching Reading.* New York: Longman.

Cambourne, Briane. 2002. "Conditions for Literacy Learning." *The Reading Teacher* 55 (8): 758–62.

Cambourne, Briane. 1993. *The Whole Story: Natural Learning and the Acquisition of Literacy in the Classroom.* Auckland, NZ: Ashton, Scholastic.

Cunningham, Patricia M. 2000. *Phonics They Use: Words for Reading and Writing.* 3rd Edition. New York: Addison Wesley Longman.

Evidence Based Reading Instruction. 2002. Articles from International Reading Association. Newark, DE: International Reading Association.

Hoyt, Linda. 2002. *Make it Real-Strategies for Success with Informational Texts.* Portsmouth, NH: Heinemann.

Kimball-Lopez, Kimberley. 1999. *Connecting with Traditional Literature.* Boston: Allyn and Bacon.

Moustafa, Margaret. 1997. *Beyond Traditional Phonics.* Portsmouth, NH: Heinemann.

Owocki, Gretchen. 2003. *Strategic Instructions for K-3 Students.* Portsmouth, NH: Heinemann.

Owacki, G, and Y. Goodman. 2002. *Kidwatching-Documenting Children's Literacy Development.* Portsmouth, NH: Heinemann.

Quindlen, Anna. 1998. *How Reading Changed My Life.* New York: Ballantine Books.

Routman, Regie. 2000. *Conversations.* Portsmouth, NH: Heinemann.

Schultz, C. 2000. *How Partner Reading Fosters Literacy Development in First Grade Students.* Action Research Project. University Center, MI: Saginaw Valley State University.

Short, K., J. Harste, and C. Burke. 1996. *Creating Classrooms for Authors and Inquirers.* Portsmouth, NH: Heinemann.

Trelease, Jim. 2001. *The Read-Aloud Handbook*. 4th Ed. New York: Penguin.

Wilde, Sandra. 2000. *Miscue Analysis Made Easy: Building on Student Strengths.* Portsmouth, NH: Heinemann.

Wilde, Sandra. 2000. *Reading Made Easy*. Portsmouth, NH: Heinemann.

XAMonline.com

XAMonline, Inc.
25 First Street, Suite 106
Cambridge, MA 02141
P. 1-800-509-4128
F. 617-583-5552
www.XAMonline.com

2010

New York State Teacher Certification Examinations (NYST(

PO#:		Store/School:	
Address 1:			
Address 2:			
City, State, Zip:			
Credit Card #:		Exp:	
Phone:		Fax:	
Email			

Titles	Paperback Information								
Titles	Paperback ISBN	Retail	Qty.	Paperback Subtotal	eISBN	Retail	Qty.	eBook Subtotal	Title Subtotal
ATS-W Assessment of Teaching Skills - Written 091	978-1-60787-155-2	$34.95			978-1-60787-665-6	$31.95			
CQST Communication and Quantitative Skills Test 080	978-1-58197-865-0	$17.95			978-1-60787-884-1	$14.95			
CST ATAS Assessment of Teaching Assistant Skills 095	978-1-58197-260-3	$59.95			978-1-60787-881-0	$56.95			
CST Biology 006	978-1-58197-289-4	$59.95			978-1-60787-882-7	$56.95			
CST Chemistry 007	978-1-58197-855-1	$59.95			978-1-60787-883-4	$56.95			
CST Earth Science 008	978-1-58197-632-8	$59.95			978-1-60787-885-8	$56.95			
CST English 003	978-1-58197-267-2	$59.95			978-1-60787-886-5	$56.95			
CST French Sample Test 012	978-1-58197-858-2	$15.00			978-1-60787-887-2	$12.00			
CST Library Media Specialist 074	978-1-58197-863-6	$59.95			978-1-60787-889-6	$56.95			
CST Math 004	978-1-58197-296-2	$34.95			978-1-60787-891-9	$31.95			
CST Physical Education 076	978-1-58197-579-6	$59.95			978-1-60787-893-3	$56.95			
CST Physics 009	978-1-58197-042-5	$59.95			978-1-60787-894-0	$56.95			
CST Social Studies 005	978-1-58197-265-8	$59.95			978-1-60787-895-7	$56.95			
CST Spanish 020	978-1-58197-396-9	$59.95			978-1-60787-896-4	$56.95			
CST Students with Disabilities 060	978-1-58197-258-0	$73.50			978-1-60787-897-1	$70.50			
LAST Liberal Arts and Science Test 001	978-1-60787-019-7	$24.95			978-1-60787-666-3	$21.95			
NYSTCE CST English to Speakers of Other Languages (ESOL) 022	978-1-60787-153-8	$59.95			978-1-60787-694-6	$56.95			
NYSTCE CST Multi-Subjects 002	978-1-58197-290-0	$39.95			978-1-60787-892-6	$36.95			
				SUBTOTAL					
1 book $8.70, 2 books $11.00. 3+ books $15.00				Ship					
				TOTAL					

LaVergne, TN USA
12 April 2011
223825LV00001B/51/P